T0319936

Measuring and Improving Productivity in Services

SERVICES, ECONOMY AND INNOVATION

Series Editor: John R. Bryson, *Professor of Enterprise and Economic Geography, School of Geography, Earth and Environmental Sciences, The University of Birmingham, UK and Distinguished Research Fellow, Foundation for Research in Economics and Business Administration (SNF), Bergen, Norway*

An ever-increasing proportion of the world's business involves some type of service function and employment. Manufacturing is being transformed into hybrid production systems that combine production and service functions both within manufacturing processes as well as in final products. Manufacturing employment continues to decline while employment in a range of services activities continues to grow. The shift towards service dominated economies presents a series of challenges for academics as well as policy makers. The focus of much academic work has been on manufacturing and until recently services have been relatively neglected. This is the first book series to bring together a range of different perspectives that explore different aspects of services, economy and innovation. The series will include titles that explore:

- The economics of services
- Service-led economies or enterprises
- Service work and employment
- Innovation and services
- Services and the wider process of production
- Services and globalization.

This series is essential reading for academics and researchers in economics, economic geography and business.

Titles in the series include:

The New Service Economy
Challenges and Policy Implications for Europe
Luis Rubalcaba

Creating Experiences in the Experience Economy
Edited by Jon Sundbo and Per Darmer

Measuring and Improving Productivity in Services
Issues, Strategies and Challenges
Faridah Djellal and Faïz Gallouj

Measuring and Improving Productivity in Services

Issues, Strategies and Challenges

Faridah Djellal

Professor of Economics, University of Tours, France

Faïz Gallouj

Professor of Economics, University of Lille 1, France

SERVICES, ECONOMY AND INNOVATION

Edward Elgar
Cheltenham, UK • Northampton, MA, USA

Published by
Edward Elgar Publishing Limited
The Lypiatts
15 Lansdown Road
Cheltenham
Glos GL50 2JA
UK

Edward Elgar Publishing, Inc.
William Pratt House
9 Dewey Court
Northampton
Massachusetts 01060
USA

A catalogue record for this book
is available from the British Library

Library of Congress Control Number: 2008937104

Mixed Sources
Product group from well-managed
forests and other controlled sources
www.fsc.org Cert no. SA-COC-1565
© 1996 Forest Stewardship Council

FSC

ISBN 978 1 84720 269 7

Printed and bound in Great Britain by MPG Books Ltd, Bodmin, Cornwall

Contents

Figures

Tables

Boxes

Acknowledgements

The basis for this book was laid in a research project funded by the French Ministry of Health and Social Affairs. We would like to express our gratitude to Etienne Marie (Director of DAGPB: Directorate for General Administration, Personnel and Budget) and to Fabienne Grizeau-Hoarau for their support. We also warmly thank Jean Gadrey (Emeritus Professor at Lille University) who has in various ways inspired our work and Andrew Wilson who provided the translation of the French version of this book. Thanks also to Laurence Converset, Carole Picault and Véronique Testelin. Their professionalism provides the clear evidence that productivity and performance in public services are not just theoretical problems.

Faridah Djellal and Faïz Gallouj

General introduction

The productivity of a firm, organization or nation is a gauge of the relationship between its production of goods and services and the factors of production used (labour, machinery, raw materials and so on). Thus it measures the ratio of outputs to inputs or a firm's productive efficiency. It is a basic analytical tool used in economics and management, since any increase in its value indicates that scarce and expensive human and material resources are being used more efficiently.

In 'The Great Hope of the 20th Century', Jean Fourastié (1949), drawing in particular on the work of Clark (1940), established this concept as the intrinsic technical criterion that made it possible to distinguish between the primary, secondary and tertiary sectors. Thus Fourastié argued that services were, by their very nature, characterized by a rate of productivity growth that was low in comparison with agriculture and, particularly, manufacturing industry.

Although it does not altogether call into question the hypothesis that productivity in services is low, the development of modern service economies does cast some doubt on the 'naturalness' or 'technical nature' of this low productivity. Other interpretations have also been put forward; in particular, some question the validity and relevance of the traditional methods of measuring productivity, which are regarded as too 'industrialist' and unsuited to the distinctive nature of services. Thus, it is argued, productivity in services is not necessarily always low but tends in many cases to be poorly measured, sometimes even in ways that are conceptually inappropriate.

This questioning of the supposedly inherent low productivity in services does of course raise the question, for both organizations and public authorities, of how it might be improved. If services are not characterized by a naturally low level of productivity, then their backwardness in this area may suggest the existence of enormous reservoirs of productivity waiting to be discovered and tapped.

This question very quickly became a fundamental element in the strategic thinking of market service providers operating in competitive environments. And it was not long before it infiltrated public services as well. As a result, the question of how to measure and improve productivity in public services has been a recurrent topic in political debates and in academic

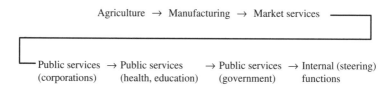

Figure I.1   The all-pervasiveness of productivity improvement strategies

studies for several decades[1] (Le Pen, 1986; Castagnos, 1987). This preoccupation became all-pervasive and eventually infiltrated the public sphere, starting with public service corporations before going on to affect government and other public services as well. It subsequently spread within these services to the eminently intellectual design, planning and steering functions which, rightly or wrongly, had hitherto been protected. The trajectory taken by this preoccupation, depicted in Figure I.1, became increasingly full of pitfalls as it progressed. As will become clear in the course of this book, the further this concept progressed along its trajectory, the more difficult it became to define, measure and legitimate it.

Thus the question of productivity in public services (and particularly in government services) is not in itself new. For some years now, however, it has undeniably been attracting renewed interest from academics, national and international statistical institutes and governments. The following reasons – some old, some more recent – are generally adduced to explain this interest or revival of interest.

1.   In all developed countries, public services account for a considerable share of national wealth and employment. Thus any change in productivity in this sector automatically gives rise to a significant change in productivity in the national economy as a whole.
2.   Public services contribute to the development of other economic activities. In other words, the performance (productivity) of public services influences that of the rest of the economy. This is particularly the case with education, publicly funded research, health, transport infrastructure and so on. However, it is equally true of the police, justice system and so on. Thus productivity in public services is both an object of concern in its own right (previous argument) and an essential factor in or determinant of productivity in other sectors. As we shall see, public services are at the heart of what, in Chapter 5, we will call the political and institutional factor.
3.   Public services funded out of taxation have to be accountable to taxpayers, who are increasingly concerned with rigorous management of resources and increasingly likely to see themselves as customers of

government agencies and other public bodies that are nothing more than service providers. Thus the underlying hypothesis is that, unlike their counterparts in market services, public service managers have tended to disregard productivity targets. These new preoccupations have emerged in a context in which certain socio-economic variables are exerting pressure for increased public expenditure; these include an ageing population and Baumol's cost disease (Baumol, 1967), for which a cure does not seem to have been found. Nor are they wholly unconnected with the development of certain socio-political variables that are forcing public services, long protected by (natural) monopolies, to confront market principles in one way or another, whether directly or indirectly. Thus high productivity levels are regarded as an indication of sound resource management.

4. The issues at stake in the measurement of productivity in public services (and in particular the choice of the type of indicator to be used) are crucial to service providers as organizations or basic units in the economic decision-making process. After all, these indicators replace price and market-based judgements in assessments of organizations and their managers.

5. Public services, and indeed all services, continue to pose difficult problems not only for researchers but also for national and international statistical agencies. These problems have not yet been resolved, despite the considerable progress the pioneering studies on the subject made in formulating these difficulties and putting forward certain answers (Fuchs, 1969; Griliches, 1984; Jorgensen, 1995). The problems involved are not just the technical ones of definition and measurement (particularly of output) but also, in some cases, problems with the conceptual validity of the notion of productivity itself and the difficulties of making trade-offs at the operational level between often contradictory objectives (for example the deterioration in 'product' quality and employee demotivation caused by an excessively intensive productivity strategy).

The aim of this book is to take stock of the question of productivity in services on the theoretical, methodological and operational levels (this last being the level at which the factors that determine productivity are put to use).

The book is divided into two parts. The first part is given over to a survey of the (recent) conceptual and methodological debates on the notion of productivity. Thus we will be examining the various definitions of productivity and the main methods of measuring it. This part comprises four chapters. Chapter 1 provides a general survey of the notion of productivity. We

examine the main definitions and methods of measurement, the main theoretical and operational issues and the theoretical controversies to which the
notion has given rise. In the following three chapters, we analyse in greater
detail the way in which the notion of productivity is applied to market services, then to public services and finally to internal steering services. In each
of these chapters, we begin by examining analytically the theoretical consequences for the notion of productivity of certain characteristics regarded as
representative of the service category before going on to examine attempts
that have been made to measure them.

In the second part, we adopt a more operational and strategic perspective in order to identify and analyse the main levers (factors or determinants) for improving productivity and, more generally, the actual strategies
adopted for this purpose in firms and organizations. Chapter 5 offers a
general survey of the main determinants of productivity examined in the
literature. In the following chapters, we attempt to analyse, in terms of both
theory and the strategies actually adopted, the particular specificities of
market services, public services (particularly government services) and their
internal services (particularly steering services) in order to identify the
levers or factors likely to improve productivity. We will be referring to a
number of case studies with a view to engaging in an organizational, sectoral and/or international benchmarking exercise.

In each of these two parts, whether we are dealing with definitions,
methods, determinants or strategies, we will start with a general set of questions and then gradually narrow the focus in order to examine, first, services in general, and then public services at the organizational and
intra-organizational level.

NOTE

1. There are even academic journals dedicated exclusively to this question, for example the
    Public Productivity and Management Review, which was founded in 1975 in the USA and
    has now become the *Public Performance and Management Review*. There are also special-
    ist journals devoted to the question of productivity in general, for example the *Journal
    of Productivity Analysis*, the *International Journal of Productivity and Performance
    Management*, the *International Journal of Productivity and Quality Management* and the
    National Productivity Review.

PART I

Productivity: definitions and methods of measurement

1. A key notion in economic analysis: definitions, measurements, issues and controversies

INTRODUCTION

Productivity is a notion that is apparently easy to define but difficult to measure. The issues surrounding it are regarded as extremely important, not only for the models used by economists and managers but also, and above all, in the day-to-day management of firms and other organizations. Thus it lies at the heart of all economic theories. Corporate managers seldom make a statement without exhorting their workforces to be more productive and the distribution of productivity gains continues to be the focus of tough negotiations between trade union representatives and company managers. For all its centrality, however, its validity under certain circumstances has been called into question and it has given rise to a certain number of theoretical and methodological controversies.

This general introductory chapter, which does not put services at the heart of the analysis, is divided into three sections. The first section is given over to a general definition of the notion of productivity, in which we indicate the various levels of analysis that can be envisaged and note the confusions to be avoided. In the second section, we survey the main methods used to measure productivity, whether they be index-based methods or (parametric or non-parametric) frontier techniques. The third section is devoted to a theoretical consideration of the place of the concept of productivity in economic theory. By way of conclusion, we outline a number of current controversies that call into question what is regarded as the hegemony of a concept that is not relevant in all cases and at all times.

GENERAL DEFINITION, LEVEL OF ANALYSIS AND RELATED CONCEPTS

Productivity (p) is nothing other than the relationship between the production (P) of a good or service and the factors of production used

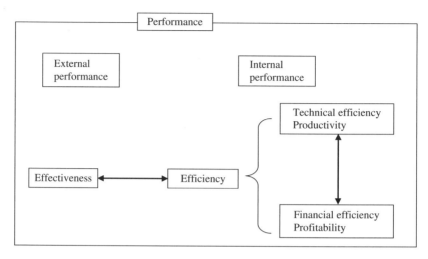

Figure 1.1   Productivity, efficiency, effectiveness, performance

(F): $p = P/F$. It is an indication of the productive efficiency of a given production unit for a given period. It is not to be confused with other concepts, such as (undifferentiated) efficiency, effectiveness or performance (see below). It can be defined and measured at different levels: country, industry, firm, production unit or individual (p. 6).

Confusion with Other, Related Notions

The notion of productivity has links with other notions, from which it is important to distinguish it. These other notions are performance, effectiveness and efficiency (see Figure 1.1). These three notions are not independent of each other. The aim of this section is to briefly clarify the differences between them.

Performance is the broadest of these concepts. It denotes the ability of an organization (or of any other analytical unit) to achieve a certain number of general, pre-defined objectives relating to various aspects of its development. It encompasses (or may encompass) a multiplicity of objectives, not just economic goals, but social, ethical and ecological ones as well. It also includes the two other concepts, namely effectiveness and efficiency, which are sometimes also denoted by the terms 'external performance' and 'internal performance' respectively.

Effectiveness denotes the extent to which the objectives, whatever they may be (economic, social, ethical, ecological, and so on), are achieved, without any account being taken at this level of the costs (of production factors) incurred or the volume of outputs produced. Thus an organization is effective when it attains the targets set for it (targets for sales, improvements to customer service, social integration, reduction in pollution, and so on). As we shall see, effectiveness (or external performance) thus defined is closely related, as far as the product is concerned, to the notion of indirect output or outcome.

Efficiency, finally, denotes the extent to which the objectives (here usually economic in nature) have been achieved while at the same time minimizing the use of resources. Efficiency can be considered from two different, but complementary points of view, one financial, the other technical. The financial perspective can be expressed in terms of profitability ratios, for example. The technical perspective equates to what is generally referred to as productivity. Thus productivity, which measures a technical performance (ratio of a volume of output to a volume of input), is a measure of technical efficiency.

To some extent, it can be said that technical or operational efficiency (that is productivity) is an engineer's concept that is not directly concerned with costs or customer satisfaction but with physical or real outputs, that monetary efficiency is an economist's concept that is concerned primarily with minimizing costs and maximizing profits and, finally, that effectiveness is a politician's concept that reflects a concern with users' well-being and satisfaction (which in turn are guarantees of his or her re-election). To say that technical efficiency (productivity) is an engineer's concept does not of course mean that economists should stop using it (or at least not for that reason), but rather that they should remember to regard it as such and not confuse it with other, related concepts. Similarly, describing effectiveness as a political notion is in no way intended to suggest that politicians are not also concerned with efficiency.

Thus productivity is one of the aspects of efficiency, the other being profitability. The links between the two can be revealed very simply if it is assumed that a firm's strategies for improving productivity are intended to increase profits π, that is the difference between the firm's revenues and its production costs.

$$\pi = pq - (p_l L + p_k K + p_c C) \qquad (1.1)$$

After all, all other things being equal, the effects of productivity on profits can be identified at two levels: first the increase in the level of output (q) alone; or second the reduction in the use of one or more factors of production: capital (K), labour (L) or intermediate consumption (C).

It would be reasonable to suppose that there is a simple, mechanical and consistent link between the concepts of effectiveness and efficiency, through which they mutually reinforce each other. After all, it might be argued, the strategies and ratios developed to improve and measure effectiveness set the targets that the strategies and ratios designed to increase and measure efficiency seek to attain in the best possible economic conditions. In reality, however, the relationship between the two is much more complex and problematic (Schwartz, 1992; Du Tertre and Blandin, 1998). First, both concepts come up against the problem of 'scaling'. It is necessary but always difficult, since there are various possible scaling methods and consequently scope for debate and power struggles, to move from general principles (for example improvements in health, justice and levels of education, reduction in crime, and so on) to concrete and operational ratios. This is particularly obvious in the case of effectiveness but also applies to efficiency. Furthermore, it is not uncommon in reality for efficiency strategies and ratios to be decoupled from effectiveness targets and to be defined independently of them.

Different Levels of Analysis

The problem of measuring productivity can be considered at four different levels: meso and macroeconomic, microeconomic, intra-organizational and individual.

1. The meso and macroeconomic level is that of national accounts, which record the contribution of service activities to the major aggregates (GNP, GDP). As we shall see, it is difficult to measure value added in some market services (banking and insurance, for example) and in most non-market services.
2. The microeconomic level is that at which a given firm or government department operates. The question of measuring productivity in this case differs little from the previous level, since national accounting bodies use the accounts of companies and organizations to construct their sectoral or national aggregates. Thus the problems at the microeconomic level are the same as those posed at the macroeconomic level with regard to the definition of output and inputs. However, it does pose an additional difficulty, namely how to aggregate the microeconomic data in order to reach the meso or macroeconomic level.
3. On the other hand, major difficulties arise, particularly in the case of service activities, as soon as one enters the 'black box' of the organization, that is when researchers (or the managers of a company or organization or the supervisory public authority) start to investigate the performance of individual units within an organization (an establishment, department, workshop or functional service); in other words

when the attention switches away from final products to intermediate products. This is particularly the case when the aim is to compare individual units, to force them to compete with each other or to distribute resources among them. Here too, there are many possible ways of defining products (outputs) and results. Furthermore, the links between factors of production and output are more difficult to determine within an organization than elsewhere. Differential environmental variables come into play that are difficult to 'neutralize' (particularly for the purposes of comparison). In Chapter 4 and in the last part of Chapter 7, it is this intermediate, intra-organizational level that will be the focus of our investigation, and in particular steering functions in public administration.

4. Evaluations can also focus on the performance (productivity) of individuals or small groups. Management science has produced a number of sophisticated tools for evaluating individuals or small groups of individuals, particularly with a view to encouraging them to improve their performance (Le Maître, 1993; Bernatchez, 2003). In all organizations, *individuals* are entrusted with a given set of tasks that constitute their 'output'. If a given individual timed on two successive occasions carries out the same tasks more quickly, then labour productivity gains can be said to have been achieved in the performance of the tasks in question. There are three difficulties with this type of measurement of output and productivity: first the tasks in question are not always easily codifiable and in some cases have a significant tacit and discretionary dimension; second they are seldom stable over time, which dashes any hope of seriously measuring the evolution of productivity; and third individuals are never isolated: they belong to groups and are always embedded in social structures characterized by cooperation and solidarity, which blur individual measurements. To parody national accounting terminology, we could call these basic groups of individuals 'homogeneous production units', since they are work groups dedicated to a given 'output' or 'task' or to a given basket of 'outputs' or set of tasks that form a credible whole. It is undoubtedly at this level that the feeling of belonging to a group finds its strongest expression and the 'strong ties' (solidarity at work) that help to blur the individual level of analysis are most evident.

THE MEASUREMENT OF PRODUCTIVITY

The apparent simplicity of the general definition of productivity conceals some formidable measurement problems and a multiplicity of indicators and techniques that cannot be exhaustively investigated here. The sources of difficulty are indeed many and various (for a survey see OECD, 2001; Schreyer and Pilat, 2001; Gamache, 2005). We shall confine ourselves, therefore, to listing a number of general problems (without at this stage indicating the activity or sector in question), some aspects of which we will explore in greater depth in the following chapters given over to services.

We will concentrate here essentially on index-based methods (the commonest ones, and those used by experts in national and international statistical bodies). However, we will also mention, more briefly, other methods of measuring productivity, which are based for the most part on so-called frontier techniques (parametric or non-parametric): data envelopment analysis methods (DEA) and econometric methods. These are techniques used mainly in academic studies, but they are occasionally used by some statistical institutions and even by some firms and organizations.

Index-based Methods

Using indices to measure productivity is the simplest method in formal terms, and the most commonly used. However, since the numerator and denominator can both vary (whether in terms of the magnitude adopted or the method used to estimate it), there is a great diversity of indices, each of which is problematic to a greater or lesser extent.

Monofactorial and multifactorial indicators

Productivity indicators always include production (P) in the numerator, although, as we shall see, the production can be measured in a number of different ways (in terms of gross output or value added). On the other hand, factors of production are heterogeneous, since they include labour, capital and a considerable number of different types of intermediate consumption. It is possible, in theory, to calculate productivity for each type of factor of production separately (monofactor indices: for example, labour productivity, capital productivity or the productivity of intermediate consumption) or for some or all of these factors (multifactor indices).

Labour productivity is generally regarded as the most important indicator (and particularly so in services). It measures the productive efficiency of the workforce in a firm, an economy or any other production unit. However, the productive efficiency of labour is not independent of the other factors of production. In particular, gains in labour productivity may stem from the use by labour of different units of capital (incorporating various degrees of technical progress), which make their work easier. The quantity and quality (technological level) of capital made available to workers generally have a much more significant effect on productivity than the intensity of the effort made by the workforce. Thus organizations may prefer a global (or multifactor) productivity indicator to this partial indicator based on a single factor.

Physical productivity, in value and volume terms
Physical productivity, which can be used for an output of homogeneous goods (and indeed services), compares an output measured in physical units (quantity) with a factor of production that is itself measured in physical units. This may be, for example, the number of tonnes of minerals extracted per worker, the number of vehicles produced per individual or the number of technical operations (account openings and closures in a bank, for example) performed per individual.

However, when the output is heterogeneous, it has to be homogenized by being expressed in monetary units, that is in value terms. In order to eliminate the influence of price variations (inflation), that is in order to prevent changes in productivity merely reflecting changes in prices, particularly when the aim is to make comparisons over time, it is essential to express output (and productivity) in volume terms, that is in constant prices. This is generally done by deflating the value of the output by the appropriate price index.

The headache of measuring the indicators
Although productivity is merely a comparison of output and the resources used to produce it, the answers to the following questions are far from simple: First, how is output to be defined and measured? Second, what resources should be taken into account and how are they to be measured? Third, how is productivity at intermediate levels to be aggregated in order to get to the higher levels (whether it is a question of moving from the intraorganizational to the organizational level or from the organizational to the sectoral or national level)?

These questions are hardly new, but they arise with renewed acuteness in post-industrial, post-Fordist economies, in quality (Karpik, 1989) or knowledge-based economies or in economies characterized by permanent innovation. In such economies (whatever the term used to describe them), outcomes are becoming increasingly important in relation to outputs. Quality and innovation life cycles are becoming shorter and shorter, which increases the risk of comparing, whether in space or in time, products and factors of production that are no longer the same.

We will confine ourselves here to investigating the first question, which concerns the definition and measurement of output, since it is here that most of the difficulties lie, particularly the conceptual ones. The two other questions raise fewer difficulties (and in any case, with those they do raise there is little difference between goods and services). They are essentially methodological problems, for which technical solutions of varying degrees of sophistication can be found. We will, therefore, investigate the second question very briefly; as far as the third question is concerned, readers are referred to the technical literature (see OECD, 2001).

Defining and measuring output   The output that appears in the numerator of productivity indicators can be represented by gross output or by value added, that is by output minus intermediate consumption ($VA = P - IC$). The justification for this second alternative is simple. The productivity gains recorded may owe nothing (or very little) to more efficient utilization of the factors of production. They may simply be a consequence of better-quality intermediate goods (raw materials, semi-finished products and so on). In other words, the increased productivity of a given production unit may essentially be the result of increased productivity in another entity situated upstream. Thus using gross output to measure productivity particularly penalizes those units that are most strongly vertically integrated. Thus since all production units transform inputs from other units into outputs using their own factors of production, the idea is that what it really produces is the difference, that is what it adds to the inputs it consumes. However, it is not always easy to determine the quantity added, since it is never 'a concrete additional quantity'.

This choice between gross output and value added helps us to identify several types of productivity. First, it enables us to introduce a distinction between gross productivity and net productivity. After all, the notion of gross productivity uses gross output as an indicator, whereas net productivity is based on value added. This distinction between gross and net productivity is all the more important since there is a significant difference between gross output and value added. For example, this applies in general to services, such as distribution, whose purpose is to process tangible goods. On the other hand, the distinction between these two types of productivity is less important when the intermediate consumption is insignificant relative to the value added. Second, when combined with the diversity of types of production factors, this choice between two measures of productivity enables us to bring to the fore the main indicators of productivity generally used (Table 1.1).

As has already been noted, output generally has to be expressed in terms of volume or constant prices in order to 'neutralize' the effects of variations in prices. Statistically at least, it is easy to deflate gross output. The output index expressed in value terms is simply divided by an output price index. The deflation procedure is no more complicated statistically when the aim is to measure value added. In this case, the procedure is carried out in two

Table 1.1   Overview of the main measures of productivity (OECD, 2001)

Types of output measure	Type of input measure			
	Labour	Capital	Capital and labour	Capital, labour and intermediate inputs (energy, materials and services)
Gross output	Labour productivity (based on gross output)	Labour productivity (based on gross output)	Capital–labour multifactor productivity (based on gross output)	KLEMS multifactor productivity
Value added	Labour productivity (based on value added)	Capital productivity (based on value added)	Capital–labour multifactor productivity (based on value added)	
	Single-factor productivity measures		Multifactor productivity (MFP) measures	

stages (double deflation). Gross output is first deflated by a production price index and then the intermediate consumption is deflated by an inter-mediate consumption price index. Value added in volume terms is obtained by the following subtraction procedure: (*value of gross output in constant prices*) − (*value of intermediate factors in constant prices*). Nevertheless, this optimism has to be tempered by pointing out that it is difficult in some industries (particularly in service sectors such as health, education and financial services) to calculate price indices.

However, attempts to value output (whether they are based on gross output or value added) come up against a major difficulty (long recognized but becoming increasingly prominent), namely how to take account of vari-ations in quality and of new products. When quality is varied, products improved or new products introduced at a relatively slow pace, these 'outputs' can be added at regular intervals to the representative sample used to construct the prices index. This does not apply, however, to informa-tion and communication technologies, which are characterized by an extremely rapid rate of change and very fast and often spectacular falls in prices that make it difficult for them to be included in the price indices (at least at the right time). In these cases, it is not unusual for the improvement in quality to be greater than the difference in price. Consequently, variations in quality will tend to be undervalued and variations in price overvalued, which is why increases in output and productivity are frequently underestimated.

It should be mentioned that investigations are sometimes conducted into techniques that can be used to estimate so-called reservation prices for new products, that is to impute to them hypothetical prices for the period before the products in question were available in the market. One such technique is the so-called hedonic pricing method.

Defining and measuring labour and capital Measurements of labour and capital are often regarded similarly, as two forms of capital, one human, the other technical. This approach provides the basis for a certain number of analogies. For example, both labour and capital are valued in terms of the 'volume of services produced'.

The number of hours worked is the usual basis for measuring labour productivity, since the alternative basis – the size of workforce – may well conceal very different situations, such as part-time working, variations in overtime worked and absences and multiple jobs. Nor does this alternative take account of self-employed workers, and so on.

Since the volume of 'hours worked' is a measure of the 'volume of services produced' by labour (labour services), average hourly pay (that is, the wage rate from the employer's point of view) is generally regarded as the price of that labour.

The volume of 'hours worked' provides no information about workers' skills or effort, whereas in fact, as we saw with 'output', underestimating the quality of labour (or that of capital or of any other resource) may cause productivity to be underestimated. However, labour is heterogeneous in terms of quality, and this fact has to be taken into account. This can be done by using workforce typologies that combine a varying number of qualitative characteristics (age, sex, education, health and so on). However, the difficult problem of weighting these various categories then needs to be resolved.

The measurement of capital is similar to that of labour in a number of ways. In particular, the volume of capital is measured not in terms of the amount of equipment used but rather in terms of the 'services' provided by the capital employed (capital services), that is total machine hours (which is generally regarded as a fixed share of the capital stock). The price of capital is defined as the 'cost of capital utilization per unit of capital services'. As with labour, it is necessary (but difficult) to take account of variations in the quality of capital in order not to underestimate productivity.

Table 1.2   Methods for measuring efficiency and productivity

	Parametric	Non-parametric
Deterministic	• Parametric mathematical programming • Deterministic (econometric) frontier analysis	• Data envelopment analysis (DEA)
Stochastic	• Stochastic (econometric) frontier analysis	• Stochastic data envelopment analysis

Source: Hollingsworth *et al.*, 1999.

Frontier Techniques

Index-based methods of measuring productivity are favoured by both national and international statistical bodies and professional actors (firms and other organizations, trade unions and employers' associations and so on). However, other methods also exist. So-called frontier techniques have been used very successfully in academic studies, particularly when the aim has been to assess the productivity or technical efficiency of market and non-market services.

Farrell (1957) is generally regarded as the father of frontier techniques, although their roots are to be found in Koopmans (1951) and Debreu (1951). The basic aim of frontier techniques is to model the production process in order to explain the relative efficiency of different production units. Thus the production frontier is made up of the most efficient production units in a given sample (whether they be firms, other organizations or any other decision-making level). The efficiency of the other units is assessed relative to this empirical frontier.

Since Farrell's path-breaking article, frontier techniques have been considerably improved and refined (for a survey, see Bauer, 1990; Chaffai, 1997; Murillo-Zamorano, 2004). However, a rudimentary typology can be drawn up on the basis of two characteristics: is the technique in question parametric or non-parametric and is it deterministic or stochastic (cf. Table 1.2)? Unlike non-parametric methods, parametric methods are based on a specific functional form of the production frontier. In stochastic methods, it is assumed that part of the distance between a given production unit and its frontier can be explained by a random error, whereas in deterministic methods this distance is attributed solely to inefficiency.

It is not our intention here to examine each of these methods in detail. Rather we will first re-examine (briefly) the notion of efficiency,

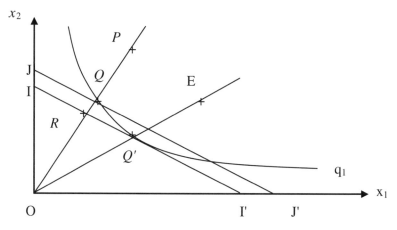

*Figure 1.2   Technical efficiency, allocative efficiency and overall efficiency
(Farrell, 1957)*

particularly as it emerges from Farrell's pioneering work, and then (again briefly) survey the general principles underlying parametric and non-parametric techniques.

The notions of technical or productive efficiency and production frontier
This notion of efficiency has already been mentioned on pp. 3–7. We briefly outline here its basic concepts in microeconomic terms. Figure 1.2 constitutes a rudimentary representation of efficiency in the simple case of a production function reduced to two production factors x_1 and x_2. The isoquant q_1 constitutes the production frontier, that is the maximum volume of output that can be obtained with variable quantities of inputs: $q_1 = f(x_1, x_2)$.
    Farrell (1957) identifies three types of efficiency:

1. Technical (or productive) efficiency denotes the production of the maximum output with a given quantity of inputs or the production of a given quantity of output with a minimal quantity of inputs.
2. Allocative efficiency takes into account the relative prices of the inputs. It denotes the maximization of output under input cost constraints or the minimization of costs subject to a given level of output.
3. Economic efficiency (overall efficiency in Farrell's terminology) is the combination of the two.

Thus a firm is technically efficient when it operates on its production frontier (q_1). Technical inefficiency is measured by the distance from this frontier (either production is inadequate in view of the volume of inputs used or excessive inputs are used for a given level of output). An economically efficient firm, for its part, operates on its cost or revenue frontier.

The technically possible (feasible) combinations of inputs are necessarily located to the right of the isoquant q_1.

- If, in order to produce q_1, an organization is located at point P, it is, nevertheless, technically inefficient, since it could obtain the same result by positioning itself at point Q (more economical use of factors of production). Thus technical efficiency TE at point P can be measured by:

$$TE = \frac{OQ}{OP} \quad (0 < TE \leq 1) \qquad (1.2)$$

When $TE = 1$, the firm is technically efficient (it is located on its production frontier). The closer TE is to 0, the more technically inefficient the firm is (it uses too many inputs and is moving away from its production frontier).

- If the relative prices of the production factors are introduced (that is, the isocosts line II'), then the optimum (that is, the situation in which output is maximized and production costs minimized) is reached at point Q'. If a firm operating at P is to be *technically efficient*, it will have to operate at Q, as we have already noted. It is at this point that it can generate an output at minimum cost. However, if it operates in this way, it is *allocatively inefficient*, since it is positioned on a line of isocost JJ' that is located below II' (the allocative inefficiency is the consequence of an inadequate combination of inputs). As a result, the allocative efficiency can be measured by:

$$AE = \frac{OR}{OQ} \quad (0 < AE \leq 1) \qquad (1.3)$$

- Economic efficiency (the term in current use – Farrell uses the term overall efficiency) is the combination (product) of technical and allocative efficiency. It is located at point Q'. It can be measured as follows:

$$EE = TE.AE = \frac{OQ}{OP}\frac{OR}{OQ} = \frac{OR}{OP} \quad (0 < EE \leq 1) \qquad (1.4)$$

When $EE = 1$, the firm is located at point Q'. The closer it gets to 0, the less economically efficient the firm is. It should be noted that, at point E, a firm is allocatively efficient but technically inefficient, while at point Q, it is technically (but not allocatively) efficient.

Non-parametric methods of measuring productivity

Non-parametric (frontier[1]) techniques are frequently used to compare the efficiency and productivity of different organizations or, in the words of Charnes *et al.* (1978), of different 'decision-making units' or DMUs. They are used mainly in academic studies, but national statistical bodies and, on occasions, firms also use them. More rarely, they may also be used to conduct international comparisons at an aggregated level. We shall confine ourselves here to outlining briefly the general principles of the most frequently used of these non-parametric methods.

By far the most commonly used non-parametric method is so-called data envelopment analysis (DEA). Based on linear programming techniques, the DEA method involves the construction of a production frontier equating to best practices in matters of technical efficiency. The efficiency level of the other organizations is valued by comparison with this empirically established 'frontier benchmark'.

The DEA method has a number of advantages (some of which are useful for investigations of productivity in services in general and in public services in particular):

1. It is particularly well suited to analysis of organizations using many inputs to produce many outputs.
2. Its use does not require a form of the production function to be expressed a priori.
3. It does not require information on prices either (which is obviously an advantage in public services, where such prices do not exist or are not significant).
4. Efficiency is not assessed relative to an average performance (as is often the case in econometric techniques) but rather relative to the best performances observed.

DEA methods can be divided into two categories: deterministic DEA and stochastic DEA. Because of its deterministic nature, the former is particularly sensitive to extreme values. However that may be, it is by far the most commonly used. To date, very little use has been made of stochastic DEA methods in studies of services, which is why we will disregard them here.

Thus the DEA method concerns only one of the forms of efficiency identified by Farrell, namely technical efficiency (Charnes *et al.*, 1978). In the case of a multi-product, multi-input organization, technical efficiency is written as follows:

$$TE = \frac{\sum_{r=1}^{p} u_r.y_r}{\sum_{i=1}^{m} v_i.x_i} \quad (0 < TE \le 1) \tag{1.5}$$

This represents the relationship between the weighted sum of the outputs (y_r, the output r is weighted by u_r) and the weighted sum of the inputs (x_i, the input i is weighted by v_i).

The DEA method quite simply involves calculating this ratio for each organization or *decision-making unit* DMU included in the analysis (a group of hospitals, bank branches, the various bodies of a public administration, and so on), in the knowledge that each organization will seek to maximize this ratio which, if they succeed, will be equal to 1 (and <1 if they do not succeed). If the analysis includes n organizations ($j = 1, \ldots, n$), then the programming model to be solved is as follows:

$$\text{Maximize: } TE_0 = \frac{\sum_{r=1}^{p} u_r.y_{r0}}{\sum_{i=1}^{m} v_i.x_{y0}}$$

$$\text{Subject to: } \frac{\sum_{r=1}^{p} u_r.y_{rj}}{\sum_{i=1}^{m} v_i.x_{ij}} \le 1, \quad j = 1,\ldots,n \ \ \textit{organizations}$$

$$u_r > 0, \quad r = 1,\ldots,p$$
$$v_i > 0, \quad i = 1,\ldots,m \tag{1.6}$$

TE_0 is the efficiency of organization 0 among the n organizations included in the analysis. Thus the aim is to maximize technical efficiency, subject to the constraint that, for all the other organizations, this efficiency is less than or equal to 1. This problem can be easily resolved by linear programming techniques.

From technical efficiency and DEA to the Malmquist productivity index
The shift from efficiency measured by the DEA method to the measurement of productivity in the strict sense of the term is often effected by means of the Malmquist productivity index. Indeed, the Malmquist index can be derived from the DEA method.

This Malmquist index is a product of consumer theory (Malmquist, 1953). It is defined in terms of 'distance functions'. It was Caves *et al.* (1982) and then Färe *et al.* (1985, 1994) who introduced it into the field of

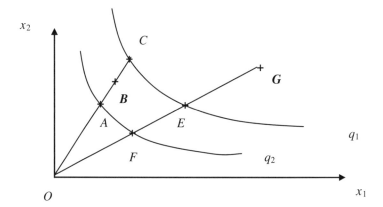

*Figure 1.3   Efficiency, productivity and the Malmquist index
(Hollingsworth et al., 1999)*

production theory and productivity measurement. In fact, the distance
functions that define the Malmquist index turn out to be nothing other
than the converse of technical efficiency as defined by Farrell (and the DEA
model). Thus it is possible to calculate the Malmquist productivity index
by using data derived from the DEA techniques (Charnes *et al.*, 1995).

The link between Farrell's notion of efficiency (and that on which DEA
is based) and the Malmquist productivity index is established in Figure 1.3,
which represents a production function in a dynamic context. Thus in
contrast to Farrell's analysis, which is static, Figure 1.3 shows a shift in the
production frontier from q_1 to q_2 as a result of technological change.

Let us assume that a firm that used to operate in G at time t_1 now operates in B. Its technical efficiency at t_1 is $TE_1 = OE/OG$. At t_2 it is $TE_2 = OA/OB$.

If the technology of t_2 is taken as a reference point, technological change
is $TC_1 = OF/OE$ when expressed in the terms (combination of inputs) of the
technique of period t_1. This technological change is $TC_2 = OA/OC$ when
expressed relative to the technique (combination of inputs) of period t_2.

As has already been noted, the Malmquist productivity index is formulated in terms of distance functions, which are the converse of measures of
technical efficiency. Thus there is no difficulty in expressing this index in
terms of measures of technical efficiency. In our diagram, it takes the
following form:

$$I = \left[\frac{OE/OG}{OC/OB} \times \frac{OF/OG}{OA/OB} \right]^{0.5} \tag{1.7}$$

This is an 'input-oriented' index, which means that the emphasis is on the reduction of the inputs required to produce a given level of output (in the converse case, we would be dealing with an 'output-oriented' Malmquist index).

It equates to the geometric average of two indices, the first of which takes as its reference point the production frontier in period 1, while the second one takes the production frontier in period 2. In each case, the index measures the distance between two production points (*G* and *B*) and the given frontier. An index smaller than 1 means that the firm's productivity rises as it moves from *G* to *B*.

The Malmquist productivity index can be very simply decomposed into two other indices: an index of efficiency change and an index of technological change:

$$I = \frac{OE/OG}{OA/OB}\left[\frac{OA}{OC} \times \frac{OF}{OE}\right]^{0.5} \tag{1.8}$$

$$I = \frac{TE_1}{TE_2}[TC_2.TC_1]^{0.5} \tag{1.9}$$

Parametric (frontier) methods of productivity measurement
The major national and international statistical bodies (OECD, Eurostat) favour index-based methods. A small number of countries (Sweden, for example) use DEA methods. Econometric methods are favoured in academic analyses, although they are also used occasionally in some companies. These methods use econometric techniques to estimate the parameters of a production function in order to derive direct measures of growth and productivity. Parametric techniques can also be used to estimate either a deterministic or a stochastic frontier function.

Deterministic frontier techniques　If a technical efficiency parameter is incorporated into it, the production function can be written:

$$y_i = f(\mathbf{x_i}, \boldsymbol{\beta}).TE_i \tag{1.10}$$

y_i is the output of firm i ($i = 1, 2, \ldots, I$). f is the production function. It depends on vector $\mathbf{x_i}$ of the N inputs and on vector $\boldsymbol{\beta}$ of the technological parameters. TE_i is the technical efficiency of firm i. It can be written $TE_i = y_i/f(x_i, \boldsymbol{\beta})$, which is the ratio of the observed output to the maximum possible output.

In the case of a Cobb–Douglas technology, Aigner and Chu (1968) first modelled technical inefficiency by an asymmetric error variable:

$$\ln y_i = \beta_0 + \sum_{n=1}^{N} \beta_n \ln x_{ni} - u_i \text{ in which } u_i \geq 0 \qquad (1.11)$$

Technical efficiency is then $TE_i = \exp(-u_i)$.

One of the weaknesses of these deterministic frontiers is that they take no account of random measurement errors. Rather, the whole of the distance from the frontier is regarded as technical inefficiency.

Stochastic frontier analysis (SFA)   Stochastic frontier models (SFA) were first proposed in papers by Aigner *et al.* (1977), Battese and Cora (1977) and Meeusen and van den Broeck (1977). Like the preceding models, these models comprise a positive efficiency term, but they have the advantage of taking account of errors in the measurement of output. Thus the error term comprises technical inefficiency component u_i and a random error term (noise) v_i.

Then the stochastic production frontier is as follows: $y_i = f(x_i, \beta).TE_i.\exp(v_i)$.

The Cobb–Douglas function to be estimated can be written thus:

$$\ln y_i = \beta_0 + \sum_{n=1}^{N} \beta_n \ln x_{ni} + v_i - u_i \qquad (1.12)$$

The econometric approach to productivity has certain advantages (OECD, 2001). In particular, econometric techniques can be used to take account of the adjustments costs and of the variations in capacity utilization. This is advantageous, since the cost of these variations depends on the speed with which resources are deployed. Furthermore, the econometric approach can be adapted to any hypothesis concerning the form of technical changes, whereas index-based methods depend on the hypothesis that technical progress is neutral, as in Hicks' definition of the term (in which the factors of production are each reduced to the same extent). However, this econometric approach also has certain disadvantages (OECD, 2001). First, the refinement of the solutions provided for complex technical problems casts doubt on the validity of some of the results. For statistical institutes, furthermore, these econometric methods require the deployment of significant resources in terms of data, updating of equation systems and training for users of statistics.

THE NOTION OF PRODUCTIVITY: AT THE HEART OF ECONOMIC THEORY, NOW AS IN THE PAST

Whether at the macro, meso or microeconomic level, the concept of productivity, now as in the past, occupies a central place in economic theory, regardless of approach (classical, neo-classical, Marxist and so on). As Gadrey notes (Gadrey, 2002a: 1099), 'orthodox and heterodox economists may be divided on the method of analysing growth, on the determinants of productivity and growth and on whether institutions and rules should be regarded as endogenous or exogenous. With a few exceptions, however, they are not divided on this shared paradigm (a certain notion of economic wealth and the technical origin of increases in that wealth)'. Before concluding this chapter by investigating a recent challenge to this paradigm, we will briefly consider a number of reasons why this notion holds such an important place in economic theory. Our aim is not to explain the position of the notion of productivity in economic theory. That would be an impossible task. Our more modest proposal is simply to outline a more or less arbitrary selection of (relatively) recent theories based on this concept.

The notion of productivity is granted a central position in economic theory because it is (or is believed to be) a means of establishing a link between certain fundamental economic variables: first a country's growth and standard of living; second, an economy's competitiveness; and third the level of employment (Harris, 1999; Gamache, 2005; Parienty, 2005).

The Link Between Productivity, Economic Growth and Living Standards

In economic theory, productivity (which is often regarded as synonymous with technical change) is a major determinant of growth. True, the classical economists such as Adam Smith and Ricardo attributed growth to the accumulation of capital, that is to the quantity of means of production made available to workers, but it is clear that such investments increase productivity. Thus for the classical economists, an increase in capital per head led to an increase in wealth per capita. However that may be, virtually all the studies carried out after the Second World War place productivity at the heart of their theoretical systems for explaining growth. We very briefly outline some of these studies below.

Empirical attempts to measure growth and neoclassical theories

It is generally considered that growth in living standards can be explained essentially by increases in labour productivity. A very simple identity is usually adduced in support of this idea. After all, if it is accepted (and it is by no means indisputably the case) that GDP per capita, that is the ratio of real GDP to total population (GDP/H), is a good indicator of a country's standard of living, then it is easy to establish a relationship between a country's standard of living and its labour productivity, as measured by the ratio of real GDP to number of hours worked (GDP/L).

$$\frac{GDP}{H} \quad = \quad \frac{GDP}{L} \quad \times \quad \frac{L}{N} \quad \times \quad \frac{N}{H}$$

| Standard of living | Labour productivity | Working time | Employment rate |

H = total population, L = number of hours worked, N = employment (number of workers)

The preceding identity tends to reinforce the idea that the main lever for raising living standards is increased productivity, since the volume of work performed (which depends on the number of hours worked annually per individual, the employment rate and the economy's demographic profile) is more inert.

Productivity gains impact on living standards through two channels: prices and earnings. Productivity gains lead to falls in product prices (and hence to increases in consumers' purchasing power). They also give rise to increases in the wages paid to workers and the dividends paid to shareholders.

That said, the preceding analysis in no way explains why labour productivity increases. Continuing the pioneering work of Solow (1957), many empirical investigations have sought to advance such analyses by decomposing growth and isolating the effects of different factors. This extensive literature is known as 'growth accounting'.

Taking as its starting point the hypothesis of a technical progress which is autonomous (that is independent of the factors of production K and L) and exogenous (that is 'manna falling from heaven' and unconnected with economic developments), Solow's method (Solow, 1957) consists of decomposing growth $(g_{Y,t})$ very simply into three components: the share explained by the growth in the capital stock $((1-\alpha)g_{K,t})$, that explained by the increase in the stock of labour $(\alpha g_{L,t})$ and the residual $(g_{A,t})$.

$$g_{Y,t} = (1 - \alpha)g_{K,t} + \alpha g_{L,t} + g_{A,t} \tag{1.13}$$

α being the labour elasticity of output.

Thus the so-called Solow residual is the share of growth that is not explained by the growth in the stock of capital and labour. This residual equates to the total productivity of the factors (TFP). It is often regarded as an approximation for technical progress. This identification of the residual and of TFP with technical progress is valid only if technical progress is defined broadly, in such a way as to encompass everything that contributes to increases in production when capital and labour stocks remain constant. If this is not the case, then TFP is a measure not only of technical progress but also of other factors, such as economies of scale, the impact of sectoral shifts, and so on.

It was Denison (1962) who improved Solow's method by decomposing the residual. Denison proposed that a distinction should be made between those components of growth linked to the degree of factor utilization (in particular, the consequences of reductions in working time), those linked to the quality of the factors of production (the consequences of the quality of labour and capital) and those linked to the industrial structure (such as the effects of transfers of resources from low-productivity to high-productivity sectors and those of economies of scale). The share of growth that is not accounted for by any of these factors (residual of the residual) is technical progress (TFP) in the strict sense of the term.

These empirical studies are rooted in theoretical growth models, particularly of course in Solow's (1956), which we do not intend to examine here. One of the significant limitations of Solow's model is that it is based on the hypothesis of an exogenous form of technical change (productivity) that is unrelated to the evolution of the economy. However, contemporary growth is increasingly being explained by productivity (technical progress) and particular forms of technical progress (research and training in particular) that play a key role in growth. This is what endogenous growth models have sought to model.

In such models, technical progress is regarded as endogenous: it does not fall, like manna, from heaven, but rather is the consequence of economic activity itself. For Romer (1986), technical progress has its source in the externalities produced by investments in physical capital. Each investment introduces additional knowledge that enriches the stock of collective knowledge that all firms are constantly augmenting and simultaneously using in pursuit of their activities. These positive externalities enable firms to circumvent the decreasing returns to capital accumulation. Since Romer's seminal paper (Romer, 1986), the number of models has increased rapidly. The main characteristic that distinguishes these models from each other is the nature of the factor that gives rise to technical progress. It may be training, research, international trade, investment in public infrastructure and, more generally, government activities, and so on.

Heterodox growth theories

Among the various heterodox approaches, the French regulationist school, which seeks to link history and macroeconomics in order to explain the evolution and crises of contemporary capitalism, is probably the one that has given greatest prominence to the concept of productivity in its analysis of growth. The concept of 'productivity regime' is used to describe the main determinants of productivity. 'The dynamic of productivity gains (also known as productivity regime) locates the origin of these gains in the production process, whether they be the result of market expansion, of increased substitution of capital for labour or of the diffusion of new organization principles' (Petit, 1998). Thus one of the basic concepts of regulation theory, namely the 'accumulation regime', defines over the long term the set of regularities that constitute 'the way in which, at the level of the economy as a whole, improvements in hourly labour productivity are obtained by changes in the socio-technical conditions of production and a way of utilising that improvement through changes in the population's living conditions' (Billaudot, 2001: 52).

Robert Boyer (2004) has put forward a growth model comprising two equations, one describing a 'productivity regime', the other a 'demand regime'.

The concept of 'productivity regime' reflects the idea that growth (positively) influences labour productivity, in the manner of the Kaldor–Verdoorn law. This influence is expressed initially (in the short term) without additional recruitment (simply through work intensification and substitution of capital for labour) and, in the longer term, by specialization and the establishment of a division of labour between firms.

The notion of 'demand regime' reflects the influence of productivity gains on growth. Regulationists identify and analyse the set of institutional arrangements by means of which productivity gains are distributed in ways that are more or less favourable to growth (modes of pay and investment determination, management rules, and so on).

Thus Boyer identifies two ideal-typical configurations: a classical growth regime and a Fordist growth regime. The 'classical' regime is characterized by a form of growth that has little effect on productivity (lack of increasing returns). In this regime, investment depends basically on profits and wages are determined by the employment situation. The 'Fordist' regime is characterized by considerable increasing returns (made possible by technologies and a mode of organization that favours economies of scale and hence productivity gains). In this regime, investment is driven by the increasing demand generated by mass consumption. This regime is regulated by institutions (wage–labour nexus) that determine, with varying degrees of conflict, the distribution of productivity gains (wages are indexed to productivity).

The Link Between Productivity and Competitiveness

A firm's competitiveness is its ability to generate profits by selling its goods or services in a competitive market. The link between productivity and competitiveness can be considered at both the micro- and macroeconomic levels. If the unit labour cost (that is the wages bill per unit produced) is used as an indicator of competitiveness, the following identity can be used to establish a link between competitiveness and labour productivity.

Unit labour cost = Hourly wage rate × Number of hours worked/Number of units produced
Unit labour cost = Hourly wage rate/Labour productivity

Thus there is an inverse relationship between unit labour costs and productivity.

Since it reduces labour costs, improving labour productivity is an obvious strategy for increasing competitiveness. However, this strategy is not always possible (see Baumol's textbook example of a concert given by a wind quintet (Baumol and Bowen, 1968)). It is not the only possible strategy either, nor is it always desirable (Giles, 2005). It may be more advantageous for a firm to reduce its costs in other ways, by cutting wages, reducing social benefits or contracting out, for example.

This link between productivity and competitiveness does not of course apply to public or government services, to which Chapters 3 and 7 are devoted. Competitiveness and profits are not concerns in such services.

The Link Between Productivity and Employment

There is an obvious relationship between productivity and employment which in the economic literature is often regarded as synonymous with the link between technical progress and employment. Although the existence of such a relationship is undeniable, tautological even, it is not, by its very nature, susceptible of general definitions, particularly when productivity is regarded as synonymous with technical progress.

The question of the link between technical change and employment is indeed a longstanding and fundamentally complex one, both theoretically and empirically, irrespective of the sector in question (for a survey, see Freeman and Soete, 1987; Petit, 1995; Vivarelli, 1995). It brings into play a multiplicity of contradictory causalities, both direct and indirect. It does not seem possible to approach it satisfactorily through a limited number of general mechanisms, nor does it appear to be susceptible of analysis at a single level, whether at the micro-, meso- or macroeconomic level. The debates on 'compensation theory' (according to which market mechanisms are able automatically to compensate for the job losses caused by a labour-saving innovation[2]) give some idea of the complexity of the mechanisms at work. The entangled relationships are further complicated by the fact that employment growth is influenced by variables other than innovation, such as demand and institutional change, among others. The question of the relationship between productivity and employment is a fundamentally complex one, which cannot be dealt with in a general way and to which no general answer can be offered. Rather, the relationship has to be analysed at several different levels (micro, meso and macro).

Thus the studies that have been carried out in this area are contradictory, and it can be concluded that, if there is a link between productivity and employment, then the nature of that link varies as circumstances change. Depending on the level of analysis, productivity gains can have different consequences: some jobs may be lost, others created, skills changed and so on, making it impossible to ascertain for certain whether the productivity gains have damaged or benefited employment.

CONCLUSION: QUESTIONING THE CONCEPT

In the previous section, we stated that the concept of productivity occupies a central place in economics. The concept lies at the heart of many theories and is often equated with technical progress and linked to issues as fundamental as standard of living, growth, employment and competitiveness. However that may be, for some years now a debate has been going on that calls into question if not the concept itself then at least the assumption of many economists that it is universal in scope and significance (Gadrey, 1996a, 2002b; Bonneville, 2001).

The terms of this critical debate, which will be mentioned regularly in the following chapters since services are frequently discussed, can be divided into two groups of arguments, one concerned with errors of measurement and the other, more fundamentally, with its conceptual invalidity. The first set of arguments calls into question the results of studies and suggests corrections; the second challenges the concept itself and suggests it should be abandoned.

The Measurement Error and Correction Argument

These measurement errors have been spectacularly highlighted by some recent studies. In the USA, for example, the Boskin Commission Report (1996) confirmed that the consumer price index had been seriously overestimated and that productivity gains and growth had consequently been underestimated. It goes without saying that all the economic policies and scenarios developed on the basis of these erroneous data are problematic; if not actually doomed to failure, they are subject at the very least to considerable uncertainty.

The measurement errors can be explained by factors that are exogenous or endogenous to the indicators used; these factors may of course be combined.

In a given socio-economic environment (in which the exogenous factors are stable), the endogenous factors are linked to the characteristics of the indicators used and to the difficulty of compiling (reliable) data, particularly on public services. The numerous technical difficulties encountered in defining and measuring output, input and so on and the difficulties of aggregating data (especially but not solely in services) give rise to measurement errors. These problems are the reason why there is such a diversity of techniques for measuring output volumes and productivity, particularly in national accounts. They also cast doubt on some international comparisons. Thus it would seem, for example, that the choices made by various countries in respect of the base year adopted, calculation of the price index and the adjustments required to take account of variations in quality give rise to not insignificant differences in the values for national growth rates (Eurostat, 2001). These differences become problematic, for example, in the context of the 'stability and growth pact' adopted by the European Council in July 1997, which requires member states to keep their public deficit below 3 per cent of GDP. These are fundamental problems in economic and monetary policy that spurred the European Commission to draw up a *Handbook on Price and Volume Measures in National Accounts* (Eurostat, 2001). The doubts raised here relate to the methods and conventions used in the calculations and not the indicator itself. The raising of these doubts has led to the adaptation and harmonization of the statistical tools used and to the correction of the measurement errors.

The exogenous factors, for their part, concern the fundamental changes affecting contemporary economies, which are causing chronic difficulties for the indicators used to measure productivity. To put it very simply, we are dealing here with the transition from a Fordist to a post-Fordist economy based on high-quality production and knowledge. The indicators in use are rapidly being rendered obsolete by the dynamic of contemporary economies (extremely rapid changes in quality, principle of permanent innovation).

These exogenous factors are important sources of measurement errors. The difficulties of constructing indicators are becoming real headaches in 'quality' and knowledge economies. Consequently, all the stops have to be pulled out in order to find technical solutions and to correct the habitual errors. However, these exogenous factors also sometimes cast doubt on the conceptual validity of the notion of productivity.

The (Total or Partial) Conceptual Invalidity of the Notion of Productivity and its Abandonment

In some situations, the concept of productivity quite simply loses its validity. No amount of technical adjustments can resolve this problem. The only solution is to stop using this concept in order to evaluate the performance of an individual, a team or an organization. Such a situation may arise first in areas characterized by considerable informational asymmetries where moral hazard comes into play. This is the case, for example, with certain support functions such as maintenance and IT development, and with intellectual design, planning and steering functions. It also arises in areas characterized by strong service relations (particularly social and civic relations). In these various areas, service quality and productivity may become contradictory objectives. The customer or user qualitative structure has effects on the nature of the service provided and on productivity.

In reality, several different cases can be identified.

1. In the first, the concept of productivity has no meaning, since it is irrelevant to the main issues at stake, which lie elsewhere (creativity, quality of solution, and so on). This applies to the wind quintet concert suggested by Baumol, as well as to all forms of artistic creation, and so on.
2. In the second case, the concept of productivity does not necessarily lose all its validity but no longer retains its position of supremacy. This might be described as a partial invalidation. This case reflects the difficulties that arise when the industrial concept of productivity comes up against what is known as the information or knowledge economy or society. The knowledge society is, after all, characterized by a sharp increase in the cognitive content of economic activities (knowledge being not only their input but their output as well) and by a proliferation of service relationships between providers and clients. The problem this raises is how to measure the productivity of social relations, on the one hand, and of knowledge, on the other. Now in such an economy (which Karpik calls a 'quality economy'), the quantities or volumes of output and prices matter less than their long-term useful effects, otherwise known as outcomes. A lawyer's productivity is of no significance if it ends in judgements that are unfavourable to his clients, that of a doctor is of little importance compared with the results of the treatment provided and a researcher's productivity means nothing

unless it is compared with the quality of the results obtained. In all these cases, in which the outcome is subject to considerable uncertainty (where there is a high level of informational asymmetry), the mechanisms that produce trust are more important than any measurement of output or productivity. The (partial) conceptual invalidity argument now applies to many more economic activities than the total invalidity one. After all, the knowledge society seems to be a universal phenomenon. It manifests itself not only in services but also in manufacturing industry, where there has been an increase in service activities that has been described as an 'intensification of the symbolic activities and social interactions implied by the productive process' (Perret, 1995). Although this partial conceptual invalidity argument may apply to very diverse activities, it particularly affects knowledge-intensive service activities that can be defined as information and knowledge-processing machines (see Chapter 4). Organizations' internal strategic design, planning and steering functions fall into this category. Thus this partial invalidity argument can also be applied to such functions.

3. A third case is that in which the concept of productivity could possibly be meaningful if the environmental variables could be taken into account. In other words, the concept loses its validity when applied to inter-organizational comparisons and benchmarking exercises. However, it could retain its validity if comparable organizations were to be compared or if environmental variables were taken into account (although in doing so we would be replacing measurement by productivity with a multi-criteria evaluation process).

The Need for a Multi-criteria Evaluation

Nevertheless, nobody is suggesting that the criterion of productivity (or, at the macroeconomic level, the closely associated one of growth) should be abandoned completely. The usual recommendation is to abandon the absolute power (whether on the theoretical or operational level) of a single ratio (productivity or growth) and replace it with a pluralist and flexible evaluation system (in which simply abandoning the concept of productivity would, under certain circumstances, be a possible, albeit extreme option).

Abandoning the absolutism of productivity (and of growth) is justified by a number of arguments, outlined above, that cast doubt on the validity of the concept in certain situations. Regardless of the activity in question, indeed, productivity is always inaccurately estimated (although to varying degrees depending on the activity). It suffers from chronic mismeasurement. However, there are other arguments that also cast doubt on the absolutism of productivity (and of growth) and militate in favour of a pluralist approach.

1. Thus, in a given economic activity, performance is not an objective category but rather is considered in different, even contradictory terms depending on the actors concerned (individuals, firms, political authorities). The subjective nature of performance, which certainly applies to tangible goods, is particularly pronounced in the case of the 'goods' produced by the information and knowledge economy, which are based on intangible, abstract and socially constructed factors of production (Bonneville, 2001).
2. Account also has to be taken of the perverse effects of certain goals or targets. For example, at both the macro- and microeconomic level, the drive for growth and productivity generates negative externalities. It may give rise to certain social or environmental costs (stress and other health problems, on the one hand, environmental degradation, on the other) that are not taken into account in estimates of growth and productivity (Jex, 1998; Karasek and Theorell, 1990; Lowe, 2003). At the microeconomic level, the frequently criticized link between overly aggressive productivity strategies and a deterioration in quality is well known. In the administration of justice, attempts to rationalize processes (reduction in time taken to deal with cases) are acceptable only if they can be achieved without detriment to the rights of the accused. A productivist approach could sow the seeds for wrongful convictions, for example by generating excessive pressure to obtain confessions.
3. More generally, the level of production of goods and services is not the only indicator of a society's well-being. Nor is it necessarily the best one. Alternative macroeconomic indicators of development are now being developed, which could be adapted for use at the level of firms and organizations (for a survey, see Gadrey and Jany-Catrice, 2007). One of the best-known of these indicators is probably Osberg and Sharp's index of economic well-being, which is made up of variables associated with the following four components of economic well-being: consumption flows, capital accumulation, inequality and poverty and economic insecurity. Others include the Index of National Social Health developed by the Fordham Institute as an alternative to GDP and various indicators of sustainable well-being (ISEW, Index of Sustainable Economic Welfare). At the microeconomic level, dissatisfaction with the concept of productivity manifests itself in other ways. Stankiewicz (2002), for example, has suggested replacing it with a

concept he denotes by the term *valorité*. This new concept is an attempt to do full justice to the effectiveness of labour, not simply in terms of increasing output but also as a factor in the creation of value. However, *valorité* is not a means of measuring productivity in value terms. Rather it denotes the effectiveness of the production of output in quantitative terms as well as other factors that may be more important than the volume of output produced, such as quality, responsiveness to demand, customer satisfaction, and so on. Shifting from the concept of productivity to that of *valorité* also entails a change in the neoclassical view of the workforce. This new perspective (described as neo-Schumpeterian) includes a recognition that the workforce has more extensive competences that go beyond the ability to influence volumes (traditional neoclassical concept) to include the ability to influence the nature or quality of the output. This capacity for action depends not only on routines but also on capacities for adaptation and creativity that differ from one employee to the next. In order to take account of this neo-Schumpeterian concept of labour and to supplement the concept of the marginal productivity of labour, Stankiewicz proposes and formalizes the concept of 'differential *valorité*' which takes into account differences in individual workers' abilities to make use of routines and to adapt to change.

4. For other activities (particularly at the intra-organizational level), comparisons of productivity are unfair, counter-productive and discouraging for the units in question. This is because they carry out their activities in environments that may differ considerably from each other, making mechanical comparisons very difficult. This applies, for example, to comparisons of post offices or schools located in very different socio-economic environments.

5. In certain cases, finally, the concept of productivity loses its validity or, without losing its relevance entirely, becomes insignificant compared with other aspects of performance. Thus the productivity (technical efficiency) of health and social services is a secondary issue comparing with outcomes as essential as containing outbreaks of chikungunya fever or avian flu, to take just two topical examples.

NOTES

1. This point is important as far as index-based methods are also non-parametric methods.
2. The general view is that the compensation takes place through a number of different mechanisms: the creation of new machines, price reductions, new investments, cuts in wages, increases in earnings and the creation of new products (see Vivarelli, 1995; Petit, 1995).

2. The service challenge

INTRODUCTION

The concept of productivity saw the light of day in industrial and agricultural economies. It can be said to have reached the apogee of its reign in economies dominated by a Fordist growth regime, that is a regime based on productivity gains obtained through increasing mechanization, a deepening division of labour and the exploitation of economies of scale, mass consumption of standardized products and wages indexed to productivity. To a certain extent, therefore, it is the Fordist concept par excellence. As we observed in the previous chapter, the debates it sparks off in such a context are concerned with (incremental) improvements to a notion that is universally accepted (even by the social actors, although they may be at loggerheads with each other over the distribution of productivity gains).

The advent of the service economy (considered from both the functional perspective, that in terms of service functions within manufacturing industry, and from the sectoral point of view) has called into question in a much more fundamental way the methods used to measure productivity, with some commentators even going so far as to question the very validity of a concept adjudged to be outdated and obsolete.

We will begin this chapter by describing, from various points of view, the specificities of services in general[1] and their consequences for the definitions of indicators of productivity and performance. We will then turn to the ways in which productivity is actually measured, making a distinction, once again, between index-based methods and frontier techniques.

THE 'TECHNICAL' SPECIFICITIES OF SERVICES AND THEIR CONSEQUENCES

The literature on the economics and management of services has identified certain specific characteristics that are of undeniable value in any attempt to tackle, in an analytical and simplified way, certain theoretical and operational questions raised by services, whether they concern marketing, human resource management, innovation and R&D or, of course, quality, productivity and performance more generally.

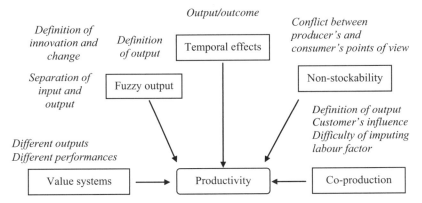

Figure 2.1   The specificities of services and their consequences for the definition of productivity

These characteristics, which are summarized in Figure 2.1, do not exist independently of each other. They are presented separately, sometimes artificially so (in spite of some possible redundancies), in order to link together the sets of indications relating to their consequences for the notion of productivity.

Output is Fuzzy

Services are generally characterized by a relatively vaguely defined, intangible and unstable output. The process of producing a service does not culminate in the creation of a tangible good. Rather what is produced is a 'change of state'. The product is an action, a treatment protocol or a formula – in other words, a process and a way of organizing that process. In many cases, it is difficult to map the boundary of the service.

This first characteristic has several consequences for the definition and measurement of productivity.

1. It is always difficult in services to identify the output (or the unit of output), that is the numerator of the productivity ratio. Thus a computer manufacturer's unit of output is a computer, but what is the unit of output of a consultancy company, a bank or a hospital? This does not mean that there is no answer to this question; rather, there are numerous, contradictory answers, each one as legitimate as the next.
2. It is difficult to separate this output from the factors of production used (in other words, the output from the process). Incidentally, this is

why certain well-known theoretical models, such as that of Baumol (1967), advance the hypothesis that the output can be regarded as identical to the factors of production (and more precisely, in this particular case, to labour). It was this hypothesis that national accountants used until recently to measure the output of certain services, particularly public services. It is still being used for some services.

3. The ill-defined nature of the output also complicates any attempt to identify innovations and improvements to service quality (Djellal and Gallouj, 1999). However, it is essential that innovations and improvements to the output should be taken into account in any measure of productivity.

Output Makes its Effects Felt over Time

Any definition of services must take account of the temporal variable. After all, it is important to distinguish the immediate aspect of a service (the acts involved in providing it) from its effects in the medium and long term. Thus in the English-language literature a distinction is made between output and outcome (the long-term result[2]). Retaining the word output for both cases, Jean Gadrey (1996b) proposes that a distinction be made between the *immediate* output and the *mediate* output. To take the example of a garage mechanic, the immediate output consists of the various tasks he carries out while the vehicle is in the garage for maintenance repair. The mediate output consists of the consequences of those tasks for the vehicle's functioning. In a way, the immediate output equates to what lawyers call the best endeavours obligation, while the mediate output equates more to a contractual obligation to produce a particular result. In the case of a hospital stay, for example, the immediate output consists of the various procedures carried out, while the mediate output equates to the change in the patient's condition, to his or her subsequent state of health or even the additional years of life made possible by the treatment.

Whatever the terminology adopted, this distinction is fundamental to the notion of productivity. Distinguishing between input, output and outcome, as well as taking account of the initial budget (see Figure 2.2), opens the way for performance to be defined in several different ways.

Productivity, in the traditional sense of the output produced by the factor(s) of production (or productive efficiency), reflects the relationship between (immediate) outputs and inputs (Q/F). The relationship between outputs and costs (Q/C) reflects what is generally known as economic efficiency (or cost efficiency). A reduction in costs does not necessarily indicate a gain in productivity. The quest for productivity gains cannot be

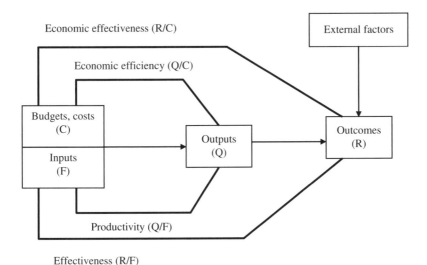

Figure 2.2   The various forms of performance

confused, as it often is in companies and other organizations, with the drive to cut costs.

The outcome of a service also gives rise to two different concepts of performance. The ratio of outcome to inputs (R/F) equates to what we will term effectiveness, denoting the more or less long-term result of the inputs deployed. The ratio of outcome to costs (R/C) expresses the economic equivalent. In both cases, both the measurement and the interpretation of it can be distorted by the intervention of external factors. In the case of health services, for example, the performance of healthcare expenditure as reflected in improvements in lifespan (R/C) or its technical equivalent (R/F) can be blurred by individual risk behaviours. In the case of fire fighting, the outcome (reduction in the damage caused by fire) may possibly be explained by factors unconnected to the firefighters' output, such as improvements in building materials, the installation of smoke detection systems, and so on. Similarly, a student's examination successes cannot be wholly explained by the output of the education system, since there are other contributory factors, such as parental assistance, use of the Internet and public libraries and so on. A decline in criminality, finally, may not be imputable solely to the activities of the police force and the justice system. Other factors play a not insignificant role, including civic education in schools, use of local leisure facilities and so on.

These various concepts of performance are often used (wrongly) as synonyms, which is a source of errors, particularly in the strategies developed to measure or improve them. This applies, for example, to a so-called productivity improving strategy based on a drive to cut costs. A strategy of this kind certainly reduces costs but does not necessarily improve productivity. However, these concepts may also be in competition with each other, with the actors regarding one as more legitimate than the others. Thus, for example, performance judged in terms of outcome might be regarded as more legitimate than performance judged in terms of output, particularly in public services. Another difficulty, which applies to attempts to measure performance in terms of outcomes, is linked to hysteresis, that is the time lag between the improvement in the outputs made possible by the inputs and the improvement in the outcomes. In general terms, this (more or less pronounced) delay may encourage agents to favour more visible short-term solutions over more radical long-term solutions.

At the macroeconomic level (although the argument could be transposed to the microeconomic level), the ratio C/Q is undeniably of value, for public services for example. It measures the cost per unit of output. It is sometimes known as the 'implied deflator' (Pritchard, 2003). Nevertheless, it should not be confused with a productivity indicator. It tells us nothing about the efficiency with which resources are transformed into outputs. After all, since it is expressed in money terms, it reflects both a productivity effect (efficiency with which inputs are transformed into outputs) and the effects of variations in input prices. This means, for example, that an increase in the ratio (that is, in the cost per unit produced) may be perfectly compatible with productivity gains.

It should also be noted that outcomes, to an even greater extent than outputs, are multidimensional and difficult to measure. It is no easy task to add them to each other (Pritchard, 2002).

Output Depends on Value Systems

This assertion is not independent of the other two. In services, the definition of output is not, one might say, 'objective', but subjective. It depends, after all, on the value system or judgement criteria that are favoured; in other words on the output 'convention' that is adopted. This is particularly important for public services, where the principles of continuity, equity and equality play a significant role. Thus, unlike a good, a service does not have an independent existence enshrined in its technical specifications. It is a *social construction* (reference world) that exists in various ways in *time* (time horizon) and in the *material world* (degree of materiality or tangibility).

The consequence of the 'socially constructed' or conventional nature of the output of a service activity is that various types of 'products' and different types of performance can be identified, depending on the evaluation criteria adopted. Furthermore, these criteria vary in space and in time. The third section of the present chapter is devoted to this important question.

Output is Interactive (or Co-produced)

The idea that customers or users take part in the production of a service has often been put at the heart of definitions of services. Some authors have even suggested that customers should be incorporated into the production function as inputs. One such is Oï (1992), who proposed the following production function for retailing: $X = f(L, K, N)$, in which N is the volume of labour provided by consumers. The analysis could be extended by adding the volume of capital provided by customers. After all, particularly in the case of NICTs and networks, consumers use not only their own labour forces but also their own technologies (computers, Internet and so on) in order to co-produce the service. This characteristic has several implications for the definition and measure of output and productivity.

1. The interactive nature of service production is one of the factors that make it difficult to define and identify the output (or the 'standardized' unit of output). After all, the customer's part in the process means that the output is always different, since it adapted to specific needs. This characteristic is not peculiar to high-level services but also affects less knowledge-intensive services. For example, as Hulten (1985) notes, the number of haircuts is not a good indicator of a hairdresser's activity. The first reason is that each cut is different, depending on the customer's wishes and personal characteristics. The second reason is that a purely volume-based indicator takes no account of the customer's perception of the haircut. Broussole (1997), in his comments on this example, rightly states that what matters from the point of view of measuring output is 'the average performance to which producers commit themselves and not the diversity of particular services provided'. In the opposite case, all industrial products (cars, computers, and so on) can be regarded as different from each other, largely as a result of the vicissitudes of the production process (which may impact on its operational life, potential faults, and so on).
2. Customers can have a positive or negative influence on a service organization's productivity (and, more generally, on its performance). Thus good pupils or students have a positive influence on the productivity and performance of schools and universities, while competent customers can improve the performance of any consultants they might hire.

3. Depending on the type of service in question, various strategies can be put in place that seek either to exclude customers as far as possible by making available only standard products that eliminate the degree of variability introduced by customers' interventions. In this case, the producer's efforts are focused on the numerator of the productivity ratio. Conversely, at the other extreme, customers can be made to do part of the work themselves (self-service) (see Chapter 6).

4. This interactivity makes it difficult to impute the labour factor to the production unit (this is particularly true of service relationships with consultants, subcontractors, and so on).

Output is not Stockable

The non-stockable nature of services (that is their immediateness) means that they are consumed as they are produced. Since services produce changes of state, such changes cannot be stocked (Hill, 1977). This characteristic can be used to understand the nature of the output of service activities. The consumer's point of view (what he or she considers they have consumed) can, after all, be added to that of the producer (what he considers himself to have produced) in order to define the output. These two points of view do not always coincide.

ANALYZING THE SPECIFICITIES OF SERVICES AND THEIR CONSEQUENCES FOR PRODUCTIVITY: A DIFFERENT PERSPECTIVE

Although it is useful, the preceding analysis, which isolates certain characteristics of services, is inadequate since it amounts to mutilation. It seeks, as it were, to highlight certain consequences or elementary effects in a laboratory environment, whereas observable reality is more complex and systemic.

Thus the characteristics considered – intangibility, interactivity, immediateness – are not sufficient to distinguish a good from a service. The first reason for this is that a not inconsiderable number of services do not possess these technical characteristics, or they no longer do so or do so only to a certain extent. Activities such as catering, large-scale retailing, cleaning and transport have an obvious 'tangible' content, while the relational dimension does not always seem to be very significant. Some authors, seeking to reflect this 'loss' of specificity in services, have no hesitation in speaking of industrialization (see Chapter 6). The second reason is that increasing numbers of goods also possess these characteristics to a certain extent, as a result of the increasing prominence of the service dimension in industrial production ('servicization'). Two conclusions can be drawn from these observations. The first is that the consequences of these characteristics for the notion of productivity are not confined to services. The second is that, for certain services (which will have to be identified), the effects of these characteristics on the definition and measurement of productivity have to be put into context. In other words, each service will have to be considered on a case by case basis.

The specificities of services can be tackled by adopting a more systematic definition that gets round the limitations of an approach based on the identification of intrinsic technical characteristics (and in particular the problem of the inescapable exceptions to the definition). The Hill–Gadrey definition is authoritative in this respect. We outline it briefly below, before examining its implications for the analysis of productivity in services.

The Service Triangle

It was Hill (1977) who first formulated such a general definition of services, based in particular on an analytical dissociation between the customer and the medium of service provision and a distinction between a service as process and a service as outcome. Thus for Hill a service is 'a change in the condition of a person, or a good belonging to some economic unit, which is brought about as a result of the activity of some other economic unit, with the prior agreement of the former person or economic unit'. Gadrey (1996b) extends and clarifies this definition and provides a diagrammatic representation of it in the form of the 'service triangle' (Figure 2.3).

The vertices of the triangle denote: (a) the service provider (whether public or private, an individual or an organization); (b) the customer, consignee or user, again regardless of institutional form (households, individuals, firms, organizations, communities); and (c) the service medium, which is defined by the target or reality modified or worked upon by the service provider on the customer's behalf.

Thus a service is defined (Gadrey, 1996b) as a set of processing operations carried out by the service provider on a medium linked in various ways to the customers, but not leading to the production of a good able to *circulate economically independently of that medium*. The purpose of these processing operations is to transform the medium in various ways.

The sides of the 'service triangle' represent particular relationships: the various ties between the customer and the medium (ties of ownership, use and identity), the operational links between the service provider and the

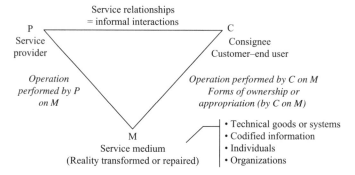

Source: Gadrey (1996b).

Figure 2.3   The service triangle

medium and, above all, the service relationship between the service provider and the customer in respect of the proposed interventions.

The main mediums (M) envisaged are the following: technical goods or systems, codified information, individuals (customers, users) themselves with their physical, intellectual or locational characteristics, and organizations, again in their various aspects (technologies, structures, collective competences and knowledge). The nature of the processing operations (repairs, transport, maintenance, transfer, management, analysis and so on) depends of course on the type of medium that is the target of the processing.

This diversity of possible mediums for the transformation or processing operations is of particular value for the analysis of productivity. First, it serves as a basis for developing a relatively simple typology of services activities, in which the various types differ depending on the extent to which the concept of productivity retains its validity. Second, it makes it possible to penetrate the 'black box' of any activity in order to identify internal functions, which also differ with regard to the applicability of the concept of productivity.

A Typology of Services Suited to Analysis of Productivity

The value of the preceding definition (and in particular of the distinction by type of medium) is that it can be used to identify different groups of services to which the traditional definitions and methods used to measure productivity apply to varying extents. Thus Gadrey (1996a) suggests that services can be divided into four groups, with the main distinguishing feature being the extent to which their output is standardized, stabilized and identifiable; in other words the extent to which the traditional concept of productivity can validly be applied to them.

These four groups are as follows (see Table 2.1):

1. services that mainly involve the physical processing of technical mediums;
2. intellectual services applied to organized productive knowledge;
3. services applied to individuals' knowledge and capabilities, in the actual final consumption; and
4. internal organizational and management services.

As Gadrey (1996a) notes, most services in group 1 differ little from the conventional production of physical goods, which is the category to which the statistical conventions would in any case have assigned them. This is why it is to this group that the traditional notion of productivity can be most easily applied. In most of the corresponding sub-categories, after all, the processing operations applied to the medium are generally standardized, reproducible acts (which makes it possible to estimate volumes of output) and the mediums in question can generally be isolated and identified (a good, a person, a piece of codified information).

The services (or service functions) in group 2, which are often called 'intangible' or 'pure' services because, unlike those in the previous group, they are not targeted mainly at goods, are less well suited to the traditional measures of productivity. They are generally the source of indirect or induced productivity among their customers (they are determinants or levers of productivity in other activities), but that tells us nothing about their own productivity. With the exception of some very specific cases (standard surveys, standard contracts, and so on), it is difficult to identify the output and, even more so, to find an appropriate way of measuring it. Thus those strategies based on applying the traditional measures (value added at constant prices, deflated wages, and so on) come what may do not give any real indication of the productive efficiency of these activities and usually lead to tautologies. For this reason, Gadrey (1996a) warns against methods of measuring engineering output in volume terms that involve deflating value added (more than 80 per cent of which is accounted for by wages) by a price index equating to the index of engineering consultancy fees. This amounts, after all, to putting more or less the same thing in the numerator and the denominator, or in other words evaluating outputs in terms of inputs. Ultimately, this can only lead (for example, in the extreme case in which value added consists solely of the fees of consultant engineers) to a measure of productivity that is always equal to unity, regardless of the evolution of quality and productive efficiency.

Group 3 (services applied to individuals' knowledge and capabilities, in final consumption) also poses significant problems with regard to the

*Table 2.1   A typology of services by degree of validity of concept of
productivity (after Gadrey, 1996a)*

Group of services or functions*	Sub-categories and/or definition	Examples
1. Services mainly involving the physical processing of technical mediums	A: Services (regardless of recipient) applied mainly to physical goods or systems with a view to modifying or restoring their (technical, social or spatial) use characteristics or to make them available to users for codified purposes.	Transport, repair and maintenance of goods, catering, hotel and accommodation services. But also including: transport and distribution of mail, telecommunications networks, wholesale trade.
	B: Services (regardless of recipient) *applied mainly to physical goods or coded information* in order to ensure their availability, sale, exchange or change of owner, transmission or hire, *without any significant modification of their use characteristics*.	Retailing, real estate transactions and rentals, various rentals, standardized processing of codified information (e.g.: some of the functions of banks and insurance companies).
	C: Services intended for individuals or households, applied mainly to their material structure or physical form for the purposes of transport, bodily hygiene or routine maintenance (distinguished as far as possible from medical or paramedical services).	Hairdressing, beauty treatments, transport.
2. Intellectual services applied to organized productive knowledge	These are (market or non-market services) intended for companies and government bodies and departments and applied principally not to goods but conditioning the organization and management of the production of goods or services.	Engineering, consultancy services, certain aspects of financial, banking, legal and insurance services intended for businesses, R&D, software production and advertising/PR services and so on.
3. Services applied to individuals'	Services consumed by households and targeted not at their physical	Education, health, leisure, culture.

Table 2.1   (continued)

Group of services or functions*	Sub-categories and/or definition	Examples
knowledge and capabilities, in the actual final consumption	property or their day-to-day physical maintenance but rather at less tangible realities that are less easily distinguishable from their own personalities: their educational/ training and personal capacities, knowledge, health and physical development, leisure and cultural activities, as well as their social rights and obligations.	
4. Internal organizational and management services	Administrative activities (office activities) within companies and other organizations.	

* The same activity may fall within the scope of several different functions.

identification and measurement of output and the traditional measures of productivity are, consequently, difficult to implement. Although the boundaries between this group and the previous one are not always easy to draw, they differ from each other in various ways. In group 3, for example, results cannot be separated from individuals, who may take part to varying degrees in the provision of the service. It is also probably in this group that the distinction between output and outcome proves to be essential. After all, the indirect results of these services are just as important, if not more important, than their direct results.

Group 4 comprises administrative (office) activities within companies and other organizations. Consequently, the analytical level is different from that of the preceding categories. The output of these services is essentially intangible and is difficult to reduce to reproducible acts. Thus the measures of volumes and productivity pose the same problems as in the case of intellectual services (consultancy, engineering, expertise). After all, as Gadrey (1996a: 87) notes, 'the output – "corporate management" – is not a standardized product or a given result: it changes as modes of management and organizational forms change'. Thus the question of the productivity of document typing on computers is much more problematic than it appears. It cannot be concluded from the time gained to produce a given document that productivity has improved. The difficulties arise out of the fact that the

Table 2.2   Functional decomposition of immediate services (adapted from
            Gadrey, 1991)

'Tangible' operations [M]	Contactual or relational service operations [R]
'Informational' operations [I]	
'Methodological' operations [K]	

output is no longer the same (Gadrey, 1996a): corporate managers (the
authors of the documents) now put a document through many more successive correction stages (improved quality), while some managers now do some
of the typing themselves rather than leaving it all to their secretaries.

Government services and, within that category, the steering and planning and design services that are our particular concern in this book, fall
into the categories that pose most problems in terms of productivity. After
all, government services belong in category 3. Internal steering and planning (design) services, for their part, belong in category 4 but have much in
common with services in category 2.

Functional Decomposition of Services and Productivity

The preceding typology is of value at the sectoral level, with each sector being
approached and defined in terms of the principal medium of service provision. In reality, all services are combinations, to varying degrees, of operations
performed on a number of different mediums. It is important to take this into
account at the microeconomic level when seeking to achieve productivity
gains. After all, different activities (operations) have different reserves of productivity to be tapped, and they cannot all be exploited in the same way.

As we have already noted, a service (that is, its immediate output) can be
provided through various mediums: tangible goods, codified information,
knowledge or individuals themselves (considered in their various aspects –
physical, aesthetic, emotional, location in space, and so on). Thus a service
can be regarded as a combination of various functions or operations
intended to process each of these mediums in some way or to solve problems associated with them (see Table 2.2):

- 'tangible' operations or functions [M] that involve the 'processing' of
  tangible objects, that is transporting, transforming, maintaining,
  repairing them, and so on;
- 'informational' operations or functions [I] that involve the 'processing' of 'codified' information, that is producing, capturing, transporting it, and so on;

- contactual or relational service operations [R], whose principal medium is customers or users themselves and which consist of a direct service, that is one provided in immediate contact with the customer; and
- 'cognitive' or 'methodological' operations or functions [K] that involve the processing of knowledge by various means (codified routines, intangible technologies).

Every service activity combines the 'tangible', 'informational', 'methodological' and 'relational' functions in varying proportions that differ over time and in space. The question of productivity must be considered from different points of view depending on the nature of the operations in question and the dominant component in a given output. After all, the tangible and informational components ([M] and [I] respectively) can be measured using the traditional methods. The cognitive or methodological components [K] and the relational components [R], on the other hand, are more difficult to measure.

MEASURING PRODUCTIVITY IN SERVICES

Just as we did when investigating the measurement of productivity in general, we will examine index-based, data envelopment and parametric methods. In the first three sections, the emphasis will be on attempts to extend the traditional methods outlined in Chapter 1 to services. In the fourth section, on the other hand, we will examine more critical alternative frameworks, some of which go so far as to question the very relevance of the notion of productivity.

Index-based Methods

All the general difficulties outlined in Chapter 1 apply to services, and in many cases even more strongly. We will confine ourselves here to mentioning the new difficulties (in order to construct indices specific to services). Most of the new problems can be said to revolve around measurement of the numerator, since the difficulties linked to the factors of production are largely the same as those encountered in manufacturing.

As we noted in Chapter 1, the methods of measuring productivity in terms of volume (or constant prices) require either appropriate price indices for the units produced or direct indicators of the physical quantities produced (duly weighted). In many services, the problem is that the ill-defined nature of the output makes it difficult to decompose the evolution of the *value* produced so that it can be expressed in terms of *volumes* and *prices*. When defining the output and determining its boundaries are themselves problematic tasks, how can unit prices be identified or determined (unit prices of what?)? In this case, volume is an abstract category that cannot easily be given a concrete content. Let us examine two standard examples: retailing and banking. Thus the 'retail service' or the 'production of retail services' is still valued in terms of the volume of goods sold. Indeed, there is currently no other means of identifying 'units' of retail service to which unit prices might be linked. Now the 'retail service' cannot be reduced to volumes of goods sold. In varying proportions depending on the type of outlet and the country in question, it consists of a certain number of characteristics that play a part in defining the 'retail service' (and which also explain consumers' preferences for one type of outlet over another). These characteristics include, for example, product quality, the range of products on offer, the quality of the service provided, geographical accessibility, and so on. These characteristics have to be taken into account in any attempt to calculate a volume of retail service. Failure to do so means that productivity will be underestimated in the case of those retail outlets that provide enhanced levels of service. This is unacceptable, since different outputs are then being compared in time or in space. Similarly, the production of banking services is still valued by means of an indicator known as 'net banking income'. However, net banking income does not reflect a volume of output but rather a value that is extremely sensitive to the financial and monetary context. Thus a bank may be particularly efficient in terms of its technical operations (number of transactions, cheques and files processed) while scoring poorly in terms of net banking income.

Statisticians have displayed prodigious imagination in attempting to resolve these difficulties. Numerous solutions and expedients, of varying degrees of sophistication, have been proposed in order to produce volume-based data for different types of services. As far as the deflator is concerned, for example, several types of indices have been tried out: general prices index, consumption indices, wage indices, sale price index of a related service, price index for an industrial good linked to the service in question, and so on.

The OECD (1995) compiled an international survey of methods of measuring value added in volume terms in services. This survey is still topical and shows that international practices are extremely diverse. We will limit ourselves here to outlining some general solutions to the problems of evaluating the output of service industries in volume terms. The following are some of the solutions that have been adopted (Gadrey, 1996a):

1. deflation (of the value produced by the industry) by the general prices index in the economy as a whole;
2. deflation by a wages index for the industry in question (or by a wage index regarded as similar);
3. use of the numbers employed in the industry in question in order to estimate the output volume;
4. deflation of the value produced by the price of a manufacturing activity linked to the service activity in question;
5. deflation by the price of certain related but more easily identifiable and codifiable services (basic service acts or operations); and
6. counting the beneficiaries of a service.

The limitations of these various methods are well known (Gadrey, 1996a). Deflation by the general prices index cannot take account, in a given industry, of the productivity gains accompanied by a fall in the unit price of the outputs produced by the industry in question (and it may even reverse the sign). Deflation by the industry's wages index is problematic when most of the value added is made up of wages (as is the case in consultancy, for example). It can only lead to a productivity ratio close to 1. Making the number of people employed in an industry (or, more generally, its inputs) a proxy for its output similarly amounts to fixing the value of productivity once and for all. The numerator and denominator are identical. This is a method that is frequently used in some services (particularly public services). Deflation by the prices index of an industrial activity similar to the service activity in question is based on a weak hypothesis. For example, if the output of architectural consultants is deflated by the construction costs index, it is being assumed – questionably – that the unit price of a service of this type is proportionate to the cost of construction. The same doubts can be cast on the deflation of a service's value (a banking and financial service, for example) by the prices index for related but more easily identifiable services (renting of safe deposit boxes, portfolio management, placing of securities). These doubts are all the more serious since these related services are not representative of the service being valued. Finally, the method based on using the number of beneficiaries as a proxy for output volume clearly takes no account of any variations in the volume of service provided for customers.

Methods of measuring real output vary within countries, as has already been noted, depending on the industries under consideration, and, within the same industry, from country to country. Thus in 2001, after a three-year investigation of the various practices in use across Europe, Eurostat and the OECD published a handbook devoted to the measurement of prices and volumes in national accounts. This manual, which seeks to harmonize measurement practices, makes a certain number of recommendations based on an examination of each major section of the CPA product classification (Classification of Products by Activity). The various possible methods of measuring prices and volumes are divided into three categories:

1. the most appropriate methods (A methods);
2. less appropriate but acceptable methods (B methods); and
3. unacceptable methods, not to be used (C methods).

Table 2.3 shows some examples of methods for a number of service activities classified according to these categories.

Data Envelopment Methods

Numerous attempts have been made to apply DEA methods to services. Clearly there can be no question here of surveying at any great length an extensive and highly technical literature. We will confine ourselves to some general comments, with a particular emphasis on the diversity of objectives pursued in the studies listed.

The first feature differentiating these numerous applications of the DEA method from each other is the criteria adopted to compare the production units under investigation. Some studies compare the public and private sectors, others units within the same organization and yet others adopt a geographical criterion (local, regional, national, international). Some studies are strictly methodological in nature and include no measurement of any kind. Others go on to compare the results produced by the DEA method with those produced by other methods. Another distinguishing feature, of course, is the type of industry analysed. Virtually all service industries have been covered, as Table 2.4 seems to show.

Econometric Methods

Many studies using econometric methods (and particularly stochastic frontier analysis) have also sought to extend methods developed elsewhere to services. They have also sought to investigate the consistency and compatibility of parametric and non-parametric approaches. We confine ourselves here simply to providing some examples in the recent literature (see Table 2.5). Once again, it is apparent that these methods can be applied to any service industry.

Table 2.3   Methods of deflating and measuring output in volume terms for various service activities (after Eurostat, 2001)

Service activities	A methods	B methods	C methods
Wholesale and retail trades	• Difference between deflated sales and deflated purchases	• Volume of sales, assuming that the volume of trade margins evolves in line with the volume of sales	• Method whereby trade margins are directly deflated by a sales price index
Hotels and catering	• Deflation of output by Producer Price Index (PPI) (if it is suitable) • Deflation by CPI (consumer price index) when the prices charged to business and private customers evolve in the same way and consumption patterns are comparable	• Volume indicators such as 'bed nights' and meals served • Deflation of output by a only partially representative PPI • Deflation by CPI when the prices charged to business and private customers evolve differently and consumption patterns are different	• Any method based on the use of input data or crude output volume data (for example number of customers in a hotel or bar)
Passenger transport	• Deflation by appropriate	• Use of CPI adjusted to the basic prices provided it takes sufficient account of variations in quality • Volume indicators based on passenger kilometres	• Volume indicators based on number of passengers carried
Freight transport	• Deflation by appropriate PPI	• Volume indicators based on the number of tonne-kilometres transported	• Volume indicators based only on the number of tonnes transported
Banks	• For FISIM (financial intermediation services indirectly measured): no A method	• For FISIM: – input-based methods – detailed output indicators that must cover all	• Other financial services: – producer prices – volume indicators reflecting a

Table 2.3   (continued)

Service activities	A methods	B methods	C methods
	• Other financial services: when there are separate prices for the services invoiced for, deflation by means of a PPI of a representative set of these services	activities generating FISIMs (number of bank accounts, number of cheques processed, number and value of loans and deposits, and so on) – apply base period interest margins on loans and deposits to the stocks of loans and deposits revalued in order to obtain the prices corresponding to the base period • Other financial services: producer price index not adjusted for quality	limited range of financial products or services – input-based methods – use of a general prices index
Insurance	• None	• Use of a volume indicator based on detailed indicators, such as the acquisition and administration of policies and the administration of claims • Non-life insurance: number of policies broken down by product (household, motor vehicle, third party liability, and so on) and by type of purchaser	• Life insurance and pension funds: number of policies broken down by product and type of purchaser

Table 2.4   Application of the DEA method to services: some examples

Service activity (excl. public services)	References and principal objective
Insurance	Mahlberg and Url (2003): the consequences of the single market for the productivity of insurance services in Austria
Aircraft maintenance	Rouse *et al.* (2002): development of an integrated performance measurement system in the engineering services division of an international airline
Financial services	Worthington (1999): evolution of the productivity of Australian financial services; Drake and Hall (2003): efficiency in Japanese banking
Restaurants	Reynolds and Thompson (2007): comparative productivity of 62 restaurants in a chain
Retailing	Donthu and Yoo (1998): productivity in retail stores belonging to a restaurant chain; Keh and Chu (2003): retail productivity and scale economies
Hotels	Barros and Santos (2006): efficiency measurement in Portuguese hotels
Consultancy, professional services	Nachum (1999): productivity of management consultancy in Sweden; Dopuch *et al.* (2003): efficiency of audit productions of an accounting firm (comparison SFA, DEA)

Beyond Productivity: Performance? Beyond Measurement: Evaluation?

The transition from an economy that might be described as an industrial or Fordist economy to a post-industrialist information and knowledge economy calls into question the indispensability of the concept of productivity. When there is no longer any consensus as to what constitutes, at a given moment, the output or performance of a given activity and, consequently, no one definition or indicator can be regarded as technically better than the others, it becomes necessary to some extent to abandon *measurement* in favour of *evaluation*. This is particularly true in the case of service activities, which make up the core of the information and knowledge society. In other words, the definition of output and the construction of performance indicators must be based on valuation conventions. This is the purpose of the worlds of production framework outlined in the following section. However, taking account of the plurality of worlds and value systems in defining and evaluating performance should not be regarded as a strictly intellectual and

Table 2.5   *The application of econometric methods to the measurement of productivity in services: some examples*

Service activity (excl. public services)	References and main objective
Services in general	Hempell (2005): measuring the impact of ICTs on productivity; He *et al.* (2007): the relationship between productivity, consumer satisfaction and profits
Insurance	Mahlberg and Url (2003): the impact of the single market on productivity in insurance services in Austria; Fuentes *et al.* (2001): productivity in Spanish insurance; Greene and Segal (2004): efficiency in the US life insurance industry
Retail trade	Ratchford (2003): the productivity paradox in large-scale retailing
Banking	Shu and Strassman (2005): ICTs, productivity and profits in banking; Fernandez *et al.* (2005): alternative efficiency measures for multiple output production; Williams and Gardener (2003): the efficiency of European regional banks
Hotels	Barros (2004): efficiency of hotel industry in Portugal; Anderson *et al.* (1999): efficiency of hotel industry in USA
Travel agency	Barros and Matias (2006): econometric frontier model to evaluate the efficiency of Portuguese travel agencies
Audit, accountant	Dopuch *et al.* (2003): efficiency of audit productions of an accounting firm (comparison SFA, DEA)

academic exercise. After all, the different worlds interact with each other (either strengthening or clashing with each other) and these influences are sources of very real disruptions (that is they can be perceived in work units and raise problems). To cite just one frequently mentioned example, the emphasis on productivity can give rise to many perverse effects on quality.

The distinction between several 'worlds' of production
We hypothesize that the various purposes or 'outputs' of service activities can be linked to different 'worlds' (that is sets of outputs or of concepts of outputs and criteria for evaluating those outputs). Drawing freely on the work of Boltanski and Thévenot (1991), it is suggested that services can be defined and evaluated on the basis of different sets of justificatory criteria, which equate to the following six worlds:

- the industrial and technical world, the outputs of which are described and estimated mainly in terms of volumes, flows and technical operations;
- the market and financial world, the 'output' of which is envisaged in terms of value and monetary and financial transactions;
- the relational or domestic world, which values interpersonal relations, empathy and relationships of trust built up over time and regards the quality of relationships as a key factor in estimation of the 'output';
- the civic world, which is characterized by social relations based on a concern for equal treatment, fairness and justice;
- the world of innovation (the world of creativity or inspiration);
- the world of reputation (the world of brand image).

Figure 2.4 illustrates this framework, which does justice to the multiplicity of service 'products' or 'outputs' by combining space–time analysis with symbolic space. Taking account of the diversity of these 'worlds' is particularly important in services and the tertiary sector in general, and especially in public services. After all, to a greater extent than in any other economic activity, the qualities of the output are justified (reference worlds) on a number of competing and frequently ambiguous registers.

A multi-criteria framework for evaluating service performance
This digression on product diversity is intended to highlight what is our primary concern here, namely the diversity of performance. After all, if the 'generic outputs' are different, and given that performance is defined as the improvement in the 'positions' or 'operating efficiency' relative to the various outputs, it is not difficult (at least in theory) to accept the existence of a plurality of (generic) performances associated with (generic) outputs considered in their two facets ('volume' and quality).

Just as with outputs, therefore, several types of performance can be identified, depending on the 'families' of criteria adopted for the purposes of definition and valuation: industrial and technical performance (in which the main criteria are volumes and flows), market and financial performance (in which the emphasis is on monetary and financial operations), relational performance (in terms of interpersonal ties), civic performance (in terms of equality, fairness and justice), innovation performance (in terms of the design or planning and implementation of innovative projects) and reputation performance (in terms of brand image). The question of performance can also be considered in terms of the time frame of the evaluation (short term, long term) or even from the point of view adopted in making the evaluation (the user's or the service provider's).

	Industrial and technical world	Market and financial world	Relational or domestic world	Civic world	Innovation world	Reputational world
Direct output (short term)						
Performance relative to direct output						
Indirect output (long term)						
Performance relative to indirect output						

Figure 2.4   A multi-criteria framework for analysing service output and performance

Contrary to certain prejudices, civic, relational, reputational and innovation performance are not immune to all forms of quantification. True, it may seem paradoxical, for example, to consider social or civic relations (which are generally associated with disinterested attitudes or the gift/counter-gift principle) in terms of performance (a notion with strong technical and commercial connotations). The intention is not of course to measure relationship intensities, particularly since sociologists have drawn attention to the composite nature of the service relationship, which is regarded as a locus for the verbal exchange of technical and market information and signs of civility and mutual esteem (Goffman, 1968). On the other hand, there is no reason why the length of time spent in the relationship or even, once the content has been examined, the quantity of relations of each type cannot be measured. Thus improvements in (internal or external) customer satisfaction indicators and reductions in user turnover can be regarded as indicators of relational performance, while the evolution of the production and share of social quasi-benefits make it possible to some extent to monitor the evolution of civic performance. Similarly, the rate of (incremental) innovations introduced and the resolution rate for problems encountered during the test phase of an innovative project or even the share of solutions codified (routinized) and transferred to a generalized application can serve as indicators of innovation performance.

Figure 2.4 depicts 12 different concepts of performance, which may mutually reinforce each other or, conversely, contradict each other, or at least may do so once a certain threshold has been crossed. For example, an increase in technical performance may give rise to an increase in market performance. It is likely, therefore, that an increase in the number of accounts opened per employee in a bank will be accompanied by an increase in net banking income per employee. Similarly, an improvement in relational performance (manifested, for example, in an increase in the customer retention rate) may have a positive influence on market performance. These different types of performance may also be negatively linked, since individual pairs of them may clash with each other. For example, a good civic performance (high rate of social quasi-benefits) may lead to a deterioration in a competitiveness or productivity (technical performance) indicator. Similarly, an improvement in technical performance may impact negatively on market performance. The phenomenon may occur, for example, when bank cards are issued as a matter of course (volume effect) without regard for certain 'security' conditions.

As we shall see in the remainder of this book, a framework of this kind has particular implications for public services. However, it can also be applied without difficulty to market services. Table 2.6, taken from Gadrey (1996a), illustrates this perfectly in the case of insurance services. It shows, in particular, that technical productivity is but one aspect of performance and that public services do not have a monopoly on civic performance. After all, a private insurance company can also pursue performance targets in this area, for example by imposing limits on its trawling for private information from customers' past histories or adopting a premium structure that evens out differences between the generations or social classes.

CONCLUSION

In this chapter, the concept of productivity has been subjected to trial by (market) services. The main conclusion to be drawn from this examination is that we should be wary of cognitive irreversibilities or lock-ins (or what is known in management sciences as the 'competence trap'), which serve to perpetuate (inappropriate or even obsolete) practices or ideas, not out of necessity but out of mere habit.

When applied to services, the notion of productivity comes up against certain analytical difficulties. In some cases, particularly when it is possible to identify relatively homogeneous units of output that are only weakly interactive, these difficulties can be resolved technically and the concept remains relevant. Thus when a firm focuses its efforts on delivering

Table 2.6   An application of the multi-criteria framework to insurance (Gadrey, 1996a)

	Industrial and technical world	Market and financial world	Relational or domestic world	Civic world
Direct output (short term)	'Volume' of claims, 'volumes' of contracts (by homogeneous groups of cases)	Premiums, compensation claims paid out	Quality of direct relations between staff and customers (business relations, relations with experts, and so on)	Refusal to go too far in the search for private information on the insured (health, history, and so on)
Performance relative to direct output	Technical productivity, ability to process technical operations more quickly, to settle claims more efficiently, reductions in waiting periods and error rates, and so on	Increase in premium levels, improvement in the claims/ premiums ratio, yield on short-term investments, and so on	Improvement in customer satisfaction indicators in respect of the service relationship	Proportion of contracts in which the company agrees to accept additional risks for civic reasons or to avoid discrimination
Indirect output (long term)	Concepts of little relevance except perhaps for evaluating the impact of insurance on the technical performance of insured companies and hence on economic growth and innovation	Financial stability and security (of customers and of the company)	Customer loyalty/retention	Premium structures that equalize, for example, differences between the generations or social classes (Michel Albert's 'Rhenish' model)
Performance relative to indirect output		Company's long-term financial yield indicators	Reduction in customer turnover	Support for a form of financial solidarity

Table 2.6 (continued)

	Industrial and technical world	Market and financial world	Relational or domestic world	Civic world
		Contribution of insurance to the financial health of customers and of the economy		through inter-class or inter-generational pooling of risks

standardized products, its strategy can be said to come to the rescue of the concept (see Part II of this volume). In other cases, it is debatable whether the concept should be retained, either because a particular indicator is taken – wrongly – to represent productivity, even though the technical solutions adopted mean that it falls outside the scope of that concept, or because continued use of the concept is tantamount to keeping alive an invalid indicator. In both cases, particularly when measures of productivity are required for strategic purposes, a cautious approach makes multi-criteria evaluations of performance mandatory.

NOTES

1. Nevertheless, the emphasis here will be on market services; we will consider other characteristics peculiar to non-market services in Chapter 3.
2. In some studies, the outcome is decomposed temporally, with a distinction being made between short-term, medium-term and long-term outcomes.

3.   Public services: a new challenge

INTRODUCTION

Non-market services constitute a new challenge to the concept of productivity. After all, in addition to the difficulties posed by the very nature of a service activity, they add others linked to the activity's public or non-market characteristics.

The definition of non-market or public services and of their scope is also a question to which no immediate answer can be given. Nevertheless, we will not be entering this debate here. For simplicity's sake, we will confine ourselves essentially to three types of public services: first, public service enterprises (such as national postal services or railway companies); second, public services such as health and education; and third, public administration (central and local government). Although the second and particularly the third group are the main objects of investigation in this book, we will not be completely ignoring the first one. After all, concerns about productivity have infiltrated the public sphere, starting with public service enterprises, which have many points in common with service companies in the market sector. Consequently, these public enterprises constitute an interesting test bed for investigating the notion of productivity in services, located at the intersection between the productivity-related issues that have traditionally been a concern in the market sector (see previous chapter) and those raised by the public sector. Thus for those seeking to examine the question of productivity, they represent an interesting area of transition between market services and government services.

Once again our aim here will be to examine, first, the implications of the 'public' nature of such services for productivity and then to examine a number of tools developed to measure productivity in this sector and some of the attempts that have been made to implement them.

THE SPECIFICITIES OF PUBLIC SERVICES AND THEIR CONSEQUENCES

Public services are services. Thus all the technical characteristics examined in the previous chapter (and their consequences for the definition and

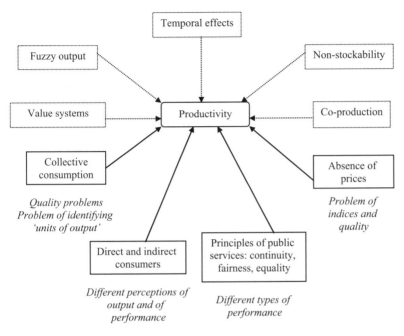

Figure 3.1   The specificities of public services and their consequences for the definition of productivity

measurement of productivity) apply to them as well (see Figure 3.1). However, the public or non-market nature of these services introduces other characteristics, the consequences of which for the definition and measurement of productivity will be examined here. These new characteristics too are regarded as technical and intrinsic – at this stage we are not dealing with characteristics, such as the quality or nature of the labour supply, that are associated more with the levers or factors of productivity. These characteristics will be examined in the second part of the book.

Public Services are Services

All the specificities considered previously in the case of services in general also apply to public services. The definition represented diagrammatically by the service triangle can be applied to public services without the slightest difficulty. The specific characteristics of public services (which will be examined in greater detail in the following section) do not alter this definition in any fundamental way. At most, they might help to make the representation a little more complex. In the case of a hospital for example, the triangle could be expanded to incorporate the regulatory system and institutions (R), or even the wage relationship between direct service providers (P), such as doctors, nurses, nursing auxiliaries and so on, and the organization (O) to which they belong (hospital, or even department). The service triangle then becomes the service pentagon (Figure 3.2).

In hospitals, as in any other public service activity, the introduction of supervisory bodies and regulatory institutions has a considerable influence on the concept of performance. After all, the service-providing organization, the individual service providers and the supervisory bodies may be pursuing different performance targets, with the medical and nursing staff focusing on quality of care and effectiveness targets (that is outcomes), while the service-providing organization and the supervisory bodies may be more concerned with efficiency targets.

We do not intend here to re-examine the various characteristics of services one by one. We shall confine ourselves here to three that are of fundamental importance in public services, namely the definition of output, the diversity of value systems and the question of time horizon.

The difficulty of defining output

It seems even more difficult to define output in public services than elsewhere. Furthermore, when experts on services are looking for illustrations of how difficult it is to define output, it is often to public services that they look for examples, whether in education, hospital services or R&D. Thus as we shall see, the subterfuge that involves evaluating the output of public services in terms of inputs is not due simply to the absence of prices but also to the difficulty of defining the output. This difficulty is particularly evident in services such as national defence (the output of which can be regarded as dissuasion, at least in times of peace), police or even the administration of foreign policy. Given this difficulty – although this is also true of market services – it is activity indicators (intermediate stages or components of the final output) that are usually used to give an indication of the output as a service delivered by the provider and consumed by the end user (Eurostat, 2001; Yu, 2003).

Thus in Table 3.1, all the indicators listed are, for want of anything better, activity indicators. In the case of hospitals, the activity consists of treatments and bed days, whereas the output should be defined as the number of cancers or heart problems treated or, more generally, as the volume of care received by a patient. In the case of the police, the number of patrols carried out or arrests made are examples of activity indicators.

Although activities are an appropriate approximation for output, ultimately it is output itself that ought to be measured. After all, counting up activities can give rise to obvious misinterpretations. For example, if a

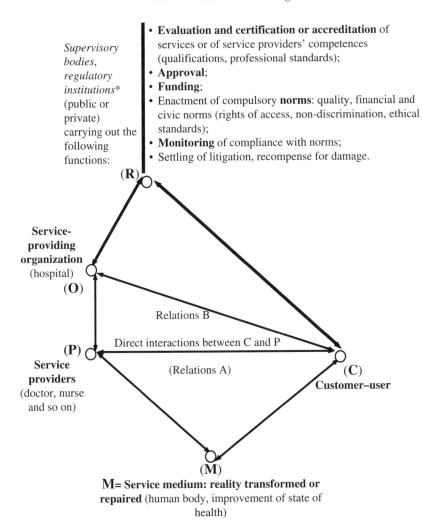

Supervisory bodies, regulatory institutions* (public or private) carrying out the following functions:

- **Evaluation and certification or accreditation** of services or of service providers' competences (qualifications, professional standards);
- **Approval**;
- **Funding**;
- Enactment of compulsory **norms**: quality, financial and civic norms (rights of access, non-discrimination, ethical standards);
- **Monitoring** of compliance with norms;
- Settling of litigation, recompense for damage.

(R)

Service-providing organization (hospital) **(O)**

Relations B

Direct interactions between C and P

(P)

Service providers (doctor, nurse and so on)

(Relations A)

(C)

Customer–user

(M)

M= Service medium: reality transformed or repaired (human body, improvement of state of health)

* In France, health conferences, regional hospital agencies (ARHs), National Agency for Accreditation and Evaluation in Healthcare (ANAES), National Health Insurance Funds for Wage Workers (CNAMTS), Regional Offices of Health and Social Affairs (DRASS), conciliation committees and so on.

Figure 3.2   The hospital services pentagon (after Gadrey, 1994)

hospital introduces a technique that reduces the number of days' stay, the relevant activity indicator (number of days' stay) will show a decline in productivity, which does not reflect reality. Similarly, when the crime rate falls, police productivity can only decline if it is defined by the number of arrests

Table 3.1   Some examples of output and outcome indicators in public services

Public service activity	Output indicator	Outcome indicator
Health	Number of treatments, number of bed days	Additional years of life (QALY: quality adjusted life years) Life expectancy
Education	Number of students, number of hours' teaching	Investment in human capital calculated on the basis of lifetime earnings Education level of the population
Police	Number of fines, number of arrests	Reduction in crime rate
Justice	Number of trials	Reduction in crime rate
Prisons	Number of prisoners	Reduction in crime rate
Fire services	Number of fires put out, number of people rescued	Reduction in damage caused by fires

made. However, it is true that the dividing line between activities and output is not always very clear. The definitions of activities and output that are adopted obviously have significant consequences for the evaluation of output and of productivity.

The question of time horizon
The question of the time horizon to be adopted in any definition of output seems to be even more important in public services than elsewhere. In other words, the question of the distinction between output and outcome or between mediate output and immediate output is absolutely fundamental in public services.

The two concepts of output reflect different concepts of performance. Performance viewed in terms of outcomes can be regarded as much more important than performance in terms of output. This is particularly true in some public services, as a quick comparison of the indicators shown in Table 3.1 will confirm.

Thus without calling into question the value of the notion of productive efficiency, effectiveness seems to be a much more important issue in public services than in market services. What matters fundamentally, after all, is not the number of days' stay in hospital, hours of teaching, arrests made or judgements handed down but rather the reduction in mortality, the unemployment rate, crime rate and so on.

The question of value systems

The question of value systems is closely linked to the previous one, in the sense that giving preference to outcomes or to output also implies privileging one way of representing the world over another. In reality, this question can be extended beyond the choice of time horizon; as we have already noted, both output and outcomes can also be considered in terms of a multi-criteria framework for evaluating different 'worlds' or value systems.

The hypothesis advanced here is that public services are more deeply affected than other services by the existence of complementary or contradictory value systems. In the case of health services everywhere, for example, the evaluation of output and performance brings into play two visions that are difficult to reconcile: that of public authorities, with its emphasis on cost cutting, and that of medical personnel, which emphasizes quality of care.

The Public Dimension of Public Services

Public services have specific characteristics that require specific analysis. These specificities relate to their public or non-market aspect. We will begin by briefly outlining the justifications to be found in economic theory for their public or non-market character. We shall see that it is performance (whether defined in terms of efficiency or fairness) that constitutes the basic justification. We will then consider some of the general characteristics of public services and their implications for productivity.

Market services versus non-market services: a brief detour via economic theory

In economic theory (and particularly in public economics), the existence of public services is justified by two arguments based on performance (efficiency and fairness).

The first argument is that non-market services are more efficient than market services in certain specific circumstances known as market failures. These market failures can manifest themselves in the following different forms:

1. High levels of informational asymmetries between producers and consumers, which mean in particular that consumers are not in a position to formulate their needs and assess the quality of the services provided. This situation is common in health services.
2. A (natural) absence of competition, that is the existence of a natural monopoly, which means that a single company can provide

one or more products more efficiently than a number of different companies.

3. The existence of production or consumption externalities, which manifest themselves when the consumption (or production) of a good affects not only the consumer (or producer) in question but others as well. For example, a given worker's investment in human capital increases not only his or her own utility but also that of the work group to which he or she belongs. Another example is vaccination, which not only protects the person being vaccinated but also reduces the likelihood that he or she will infect others.

4. When the product under consideration is a 'pure public good'. A product (good or service) is said to be a 'pure public good' when it possesses the twin characteristics of being non-rival and non-excludable. This means that first, consumption of the good by one individual does not deprive anyone else of that good (there is no limit to the number of individuals who may consume the good in question simultaneously); and second, nobody can be excluded from consuming the good. Clearly it is difficult for this type of good (national defence, justice system, street lighting, fire service), which is susceptible to opportunistic behaviour of the kind described as 'free riding', to be provided by the market.

Some public services are affected by only a limited number of failures, while others seem to be affected by all of them. It is generally reckoned that the first group (which some people believe could be transferred in whole or in part to the tender mercies of the market) poses performance problems similar to those posed by normal market services, while the second group poses different problems and should be treated differently. Transport, telecommunications, energy and postal services belong to the first group, while government services belong to the second group. Health services and education constitute a group apart.

The second argument is based on the pursuit of fairness and social justice. After all, the equity principle demands that those who cannot afford to pay for them should not be excluded from certain services that are regarded as basic human rights (education, health, justice and so on). Thus non-market services are more effective than market services when it comes to civic performance. We will return to this question in the third part of this chapter.

The specific characteristics of public services and their consequences for productivity

The characteristics that might be regarded as specific to public services can be summarized in the following four statements (see Figure 3.1):

1. the output has no price;
2. it is (in certain cases) consumed collectively;
3. a distinction has to be made between direct and indirect consumers; and
4. it adheres to the public service principles of equality, fairness and continuity.

Our next step is to assess the consequences of these various characteristics for the definition and measurement of public services.

The output has no price The main characteristic of public services is that they are provided, for the most part, free of charge or at modest prices that do not cover the costs of production. This characteristic has fundamental consequences for the definition and measurement of productivity. In contrast to market goods and services, we do not have a market price that can be used, on the one hand, to measure volumes of output and, on the other, to weight the various outputs in order to calculate an aggregate output when a public organization provides several outputs.

Irrespective of the usual technical problems of measurement and quality (see Chapter 1), the absence of prices also makes it impossible to take account of changes in the quality of the output of public services. In other words, the (fundamental) problem of how to take account of quality when measuring productivity is even trickier in the case of these services.

The output is consumed collectively (in some cases) The non-rival nature of the output of some public services has consequences for the measurement of productivity. For example, if the number of pupils in a class is increased, the teacher's productivity might be said to have increased as well. However, the additional work may give rise to problems with quality, and so on.

Of course not all public services share this characteristic. However, those services whose output is consumed collectively are generally those in which productivity is most difficult to measure, since they are the ones in which the 'units of output' are most difficult to identify. Olson (1972: 362, after Le Pen, 1986), for example, takes the view that 'the fundamental characteristics of a public good that mean that no one can be effectively excluded from consuming it also make it a good whose output does not take the form of divisible units that can be easily counted'. For the opposite reason, it is less difficult to identify the output (and hence to measure productivity) in those public services that are consumed individually.

The various levels of difficulty in defining and denoting output can be revealed by making a distinction between three types of output (Caplan, 1998; OECD, 1999):

1. Services consumed by individuals, such as health, education and certain social services aimed at individuals. They are services for which the market supply is smaller than the non-market supply but is, nevertheless, significant and can, therefore, be used as a reference point for measuring outputs, particularly as far as the prices index is concerned.

2. Government administrative services (which are held to produce outputs consumed by governments). Examples include administration of the tax system, the central administration of health and social affairs and the provision of advice to ministers. In some cases, when the constituent acts can be identified, the output can be easily defined (for example, the number of tax declarations processed by the tax authorities or the number of beneficiaries of a particular social welfare programme). In others, it is more difficult to identify units of output. This applies, for example, to the provision of advice to ministers and the steering and planning (design) functions found in most central government departments. However this may be, the problem seems to be no different from that encountered in some market services, such as consultancy (which can be used as reference points).

3. Public goods and collective services (national defence, foreign affairs, environmental protection). These services, which are collectively consumed, are the most problematic from the point of view of measuring output and productivity. The textbook example here is probably national defence, for which it is virtually impossible to establish a unit of output. In this case, the most appropriate approach is to devise a method of measuring outcomes.

Direct and indirect consumers   A distinction is often made between two types of consumers of public services (Greiner, 1996): *direct* consumers (those who benefit directly from the service provided, that is users) and *indirect* consumers (that is, the public at large, taxpayers, citizens). Although they are ultimately the same group of individuals, their perceptions of the output and performance can be said to be different. After all, direct consumers emphasize the nature and quality of the service provided and its mode of delivery, whereas indirect consumers are more concerned by the economic and financial aspects (as taxpayers) and the long-term socio-economic effects (as citizens).

This distinction, it should be noted, is not simply a reflection, at the level of consumption, of the distinction between direct and indirect output already mentioned above. Direct consumers can be just as concerned with the direct output as with the indirect output. On the other hand, this distinction reinforces the notion that a number of different value systems exist and may contradict each other. Thus depending on the perspective adopted (consumers as actual users of the services or as abstract entities), the criteria for the defining output and performance differ.

Output consistent with the principles of public services The principles in question are continuity of service, equality of treatment and financial consistency. These principles are usually regarded negatively from the perspective of the levers of productivity. After all, whether applied to human resources or to investment, they are the basis for very precise rules and a high degree of centralization, which may serve to make procedures more cumbersome when the drive for productivity gains demands rapid and flexible responses. We will return to this question in Chapter 7. However, as far as defining output and performance is concerned, which is our focus here, these public service principles may, on the contrary, be interpreted very positively. After all, this public dimension (embedded in the principles of continuity, fairness and so on) is reflected in the production of *value added*, which might be described as *social* or *civic*, which is not usually included in any measures and is often regarded as a cost or an additional cost, particularly (and increasingly) in public service enterprises. The great advantage of the worlds of production framework, which has been mentioned on several occasions, is that it also includes this social or civic value added and the corresponding performance.

MEASURES OF PRODUCTIVITY IN PUBLIC SERVICES

Compared with other activities, fewer attempts have been made to measure productivity in public services, whether by national or international statistical institutes or academic researchers. In this regard, therefore, we are in a pre-paradigmatic phase, in which various approaches are being tested without any one methodology being regarded as superior to any other. This also means that comparisons of public service productivity in time and space are often relatively risky. It should also be noted that not all public services are treated in the same way. There is, after all, a relatively well-established tradition of studies of productivity in health or education services. The same does not apply to other public services, particularly government services.

However that may be, in reviewing the main methods used to measure productivity in public services (or the attempts that have been made to do so), we will make a distinction as before between non-parametric (index-based, DEA) and parametric (econometric) methods.

Index-based Approach

The indices used in public services and particularly in government services, which involve measuring output in terms of input, are particularly questionable. Nevertheless, they are still widely used. In the absence of any more direct indicators of output, strategies have been developed for replacing output-based measures with measures based on activities.

Measuring output in terms of input
In the absence of market prices and given the impossibility of constructing volume indicators (and faced with the theoretical hypothesis that services can be reduced to the deployment of human resources), statisticians for a long time measured the output of services in terms of the inputs. It was only relatively recently that they stopped doing so, and indeed still use this method for some services. Thus the output of public administration was evaluated by summing the production costs at current prices (labour costs, intermediate consumption and capital amortization). In order to obtain an estimate of output at constant prices (in volume terms), the various costs are deflated. Clearly, this is not a satisfactory way of estimating output, since it means that the same value figures in both the numerator and denominator of the productivity ratio. It is hardly surprising that this method shows no variation in productivity, since that is the implicit hypothesis on which it is based. Statisticians have begun to abandon this approach, which is known as the input approach.

Measuring output in terms of activities
The idea that output indicators based on inputs should be abandoned in favour of more direct output indicators is the subject of an ongoing debate. Advocating such a shift amounts to calling for the standardization of output and productivity measurement methods, on the assumption that, with the exception of collectively consumed services, public services differ little from market services. The international statistical institutions have been notably vocal in advocating this approach. Chief among them have been the OECD (1999), whose Statistics Directorate and Committee for Public Management (PUMA) have put forward ideas for improving the measurement of output and productivity in public services, and Eurostat (2001, Chapter 4) which, concentrating on health and education services and general public administration, has proposed ways of improving price and volume estimates for non-market outputs. The European Commission, through the ESA (European System of Accounts) 95, has also advised national accounting offices to adopt output indicators for public services.

Despite these general positions, attempts at national level to measure productivity in public services are still few and far between and diverse in nature. The OECD (1999) and Handler *et al.* (2005) have both conducted preliminary assessments. The results are as follows. Most countries have only very recently introduced output indicators into their national accounting systems, and some have not even begun to introduce them at all. Some countries, such as the UK, where output indicators were introduced as early as 1986, are exceptions to the rule. Most of the measures introduced relate to a small number of public service activities, among which health and education feature very frequently. Some countries, such as Finland for example, have covered virtually all public services (including collective services). In all countries, strategies are being developed with a view to gradually incorporating new sectors. Government services are often among the last on the lists. Consequently, it is for these services that output indicators are, for the moment at least, scarcest and least unanimous. For example, it was not until 1998 that the UK, despite being one of the leaders in this area, stopped measuring output in terms of input in most government services (Ashaye, 2001). When countries have not (yet) succeeded in defining a unit of output, as is the case, for example, with certain collective services such as national defence, the old method, in which output continues to be identified with the volume of inputs, is still applied.

To summarize the efforts made to date in the various countries (particularly the UK, the Netherlands, Australia and the USA) to implement this general strategy of adopting methods based on output indicators, they can be said to have consisted of the following steps (Fisk and Forte, 1997; Baxter, 2000; Ashaye, 2001; Northwood *et al.*, 2001; Pritchard, 2003): first, compiling lists of the main activities in the various types of public services under investigation; second, identifying a volume-based measure for each type of activity (for example, the number of incidents or cases in a given period); and third, identifying a weighting unit in order to be able to aggregate the various volume-based measures. In the absence of prices, the relative production costs for each type of activity in a given reference year are generally used, it being assumed that the weightings must be proportional to the production costs for each activity. One commonly used method of carrying out this weighting is to calculate the cost of one case for the reference year and then multiply it by the number of cases in that year. This general process is described in the UK as the construction of a cost-weighted activity index (CWAI) for each sphere of public services. Although it does not claim to be exhaustive, Table 3.2 shows some examples of output indicators used very recently for various types of public services in the UK.

Despite their numerous shortcomings, these experiments, which have involved identifying the output of public services, constitute significant

Table 3.2   Examples of output indicators used for public services (adapted from Handler et al., 2005)

Type of public service	Output indicators used
Health services (Caplan, 1998; Pritchard, 2002, 2003)	Identification of 14 types of activity: number of treatments provided for patients for each type of activity Weighting: relative cost of the various activities
Education (Caplan, 1998; Pritchard, 2002, 2003)	The basic unit of output is the lesson given to a pupil. Thus a class of 30 equates to double the output of a class of 15 (assuming the quality is unchanged)
Local personal social services (Caplan, 1998; Ashaye, 2001)	Three activities: 1) residential homes for the elderly; 2) home help services for the elderly; 3) children's services Number of activities carried out for clients Weighting: cost of each activity
Social security (Pritchard, 2002)	Payment of benefits: number of applications of each type processed and payments paid Weighting: relative cost by type of application
Police (Pritchard, 2003)	Number of crimes cleared up by type (degree of seriousness)
Prison (Baxter, 2000; Pritchard, 2003)	The basic unit of output is the custody of one prisoner for one day. It is planned to identify different categories of prisoner at a later stage
Justice (Baxter, 2000; Pritchard, 2003)	Courts: number of cases processed by type of court Legal aid: identification of 10 types. Number of cases by type
Fire service (Ashaye, 2001; Pritchard, 2003)	Three activities: 1) fire fighting, 2) fire prevention, 3) special services (not linked to fire fighting/prevention) • Fire fighting: number of fires (of different types) and false alarms • Prevention: number of hours spent on various prevention activities (inspections, training, etc.) • Special services: number of road accidents and rescue operations etc. Weighting: average number of hours' work for each type of incident

steps towards a method of measuring productivity, particularly when they are compared with input-based methods.

However, the indicators used are indicators of the *activity* of public services and not of their *output*. Moreover, another major difficulty has to be resolved, as the Atkinson Report suggests (Pritchard, 2004). The problem in question is how to identify the equivalent of value added, as in other activities (cf. Chapter 1). No such notion of value added is visible in the output indicators used, whether it be the number of pupils receiving a lesson or the number of patients treated in a hospital. However, this is an absolutely fundamental notion and is an important area of research for the future.

The headache of variations in quality

The main methods of taking account of variations in quality are based on price, on the assumption that, in a situation of perfect competition, differences in price between products reflect differences in quality (that is differences in the products' characteristics). In other words, a higher price indicates higher quality. In the case of tangible goods and market services, this is always a difficult exercise, as we have already noted. With computer systems, for example, it is not unusual for a system of significantly higher quality than previous systems to be sold at a considerably lower price.

When it comes to non-market services, the difficulty is increased by the absence of market prices. In the light of these difficulties, the *Eurostat Handbook on Price and Volume Measures in National Accounts* (Eurostat, 2001) identifies three methods of adjusting for quality:

1. *Direct measurement of the quality of the output itself.* This measurement is carried out by means of regular surveys of the quality of public services. These surveys (for example, regular reports of schools inspections) give some idea of the variations in quality over time. Their main limitation is that the information thus gathered tends to reflect the quality of the production process rather than the quality of the output and is often subjective and not necessarily consistent over time or between units.

2. *Measuring the quality of the inputs.* The hypothesis on which this method is based is that 'the quality change of the inputs leads automatically to a quality change of the output'. In this case, of course, it is the labour input that is the object of the principal measurements. Thus differences in employees' pay are held to reflect differences in the quality of the workforce, which have to be included in the volume component.

3. *Using outcomes.* The hypothesis underlying this type of method is that the quality of the output lies in its results, that is in the outcome. The most appropriate way of adjusting for quality, therefore, is to investigate changes in outcome indicators. Thus all things being equal, the quality of police output is reflected in a fall in the crime rate and the quality of university output in an increase in the number of graduates

while the total number of students remains unchanged. This method of adjustment has obvious difficulties, which have already been mentioned. First, it is difficult to 'neutralize' the exogenous factors (it can hardly be claimed that the quality of university output has improved if universities have lowered their standards). Second, there may be a time lag between the change in output quality and its results (outcomes). For example, an improvement in the quality of police output is not immediately reflected in a fall in the crime rate.

DEA Approaches

Non-parametric methods (particularly the DEA method) have been applied very successfully to public services. The main reasons for this success have already been mentioned, in a general way, in Chapter 1. We will briefly outline again here those that particularly concern public services. These methods are particularly well suited to multi-output and multi-input activities, for which no price information is required. All that is needed is information on the quantities of inputs used and the quantities of outputs produced in the various organizations under investigation. It is assumed that the output quantities can be measured directly. We will confine ourselves here to providing a few examples of inter- or intra-organizational comparisons, at national and then international level (there are currently far fewer studies at the latter level).

Examples of comparisons at national level

Without carrying out any bibliometric studies, it can be said with absolute certainty (although the same applies regardless of the method used to measure productivity) that health services and then education are the areas in which the DEA method is most commonly applied. However, it may be applied to any public service activity (and at various levels of aggregation), as Table 3.3 shows.

Examples of international comparisons

Given the heterogeneity of the data and calculation methods used, there are very few international comparisons of the productivity of public services. We will look here at two recent exceptions, which are based on non-parametric frontier techniques (DEA and FDH: free disposable hull[1]). The studies in question are by d'Afonso *et al.* (2005) and by Afonso and St Aubyn (2005).

Afonso *et al.*'s (2005) study introduces a distinction between public sector performance (PSP) and public sector efficiency (PSE). PSP reflects the outcome of public services. It is measured by a series of seven aggre-

Table 3.3   Some illustrations of the application of the DEA method to public services

Type of public service	Reference and perspective adopted
Health	Hollingsworth *et al.* (1999): survey of non-parametric methods and their applications
	Maniadakis *et al.* (1999): impact of the internal market on hospital efficiency, productivity and service quality
	Ouellette and Vierstraete (2002): technical change and efficiency in the presence of quasi-fixed inputs: application to hospitals
Universities	Worthington and Lee (2004): efficiency, technology and productivity in Australian universities
	Johnes and Johnes (1993): comparison of the research performance of UK economics departments
Justice	Lewin *et al.* (1982): comparison of the efficiency of courts
Post offices	Tulkens (1986): definitions and methods of measuring productive performance: application to the Belgian Post Office
Public enterprises in general	Young-Yong *et al.* (2000): the impact of competition on the efficiency of public enterprises
Vehicle inspection services	Odeck (2000): the increase in productivity and efficiency in vehicle inspection services in Norway
Airports	Sarkis (2000): comparative efficiency and productivity of the principal American airports
Central banks	Gilbert *et al.* (2004): evolution of productivity at the American Federal Reserve
Police	Drake and Simper (2003): a comparison of several parametric and non-parametric methods of measuring police force productivity
Local government	Stevens (2005): comparison of DEA and SFA
Public library	Hammond (2002): efficiency of the public library system in the UK
Public administration in general	Yaisawarng (2002): development of strategic plans for improving performance

gated socio-economic indicators (with the same weighting), selected from the spheres of public administration, education, health, infrastructure, income distribution, economic stability and economic performance. PSE reflects the relationship between outcomes and the inputs used, estimated on the basis of public expenditure. Alfonso *et al.* estimate performance and efficiency indicators for 23 OECD countries in 2000.

Their analysis produces two interesting results. First, few differences are observed between countries as far as performance is concerned. Second, on the other hand, the differences in efficiency are much more pronounced. The analysis reveals that those countries with relatively small public sectors are significantly more efficient than those whose public sectors are larger. The highest PSE scores were recorded for Japan, Switzerland and Australia, while the lowest were recorded for Italy, Sweden, France and Belgium.

Alfonso *et al.*'s study is index-based. It is supplemented by an FDH analysis that aims to measure the level of waste in public expenditure in the various countries or the efficiency of public expenditure in terms of inputs and outputs. In order to achieve this objective, public sector output is measured by the PSP indicators and input by the ratio of public expenditure to GDP in the year 2000. The analysis suggests that the most efficient countries, that is those located on the production possibilities frontier, are the USA, Japan and Luxembourg (followed by Australia, Ireland and Switzerland). Most EU member states could obtain better results while using fewer inputs – they are, after all, located well within the production possibilities frontier. Thus the average input efficiency coefficient for the EU 15 is estimated to be 0.73. This means that the same level of output could be produced with 27 per cent fewer inputs.

Another international comparative study using the FDH and DEA methods was carried out by Afonso and St Aubyn (2005). This study does not investigate the whole of the public sector but focuses on education and health only in a number of OECD countries.

In the case of health services, the output indicators adopted are either the infant mortality rate or life expectancy, while the input indicators are either per capita health expenditure (in PPP) or the number of doctors, nurses and beds. Educational output is estimated using data from the OECD's PISA (Programme for International Student Assessment) survey, which investigates the performance of pupils aged 15+. The input indicators used are, on the one hand, physical inputs (such as the number of hours' teaching per year and per school in 2000 or the number of teachers per 100 pupils) and, on the other hand, financial inputs, namely annual expenditure (in PPP) per pupil on secondary education in 1999.

In the education sector, the study found that on average, for all the countries in the sample, the same level of output could be obtained while using between 11 and 48 per cent less input. The average input efficiency coefficients[2] (in terms of outputs) vary from 0.52 to 0.89 (depending on the method of estimation). The results for each country differ depending on whether the input is defined in financial or physical terms. Thus Hungary is inefficient if the inputs are measured in physical terms but efficient if they are measured in financial terms. Exactly the opposite is the case for Sweden and Finland. These differences reflect the relative prices of resources in the various countries.

The results are largely similar for the health sector. On average, the same level of output could be obtained with between 4 per cent and 26 per cent fewer inputs, since the input efficiency score (in terms of outputs) varies from 0.74 to 0.96 depending on the country. Again because of the differences in the relative prices of resources in the various countries, it is found that the Czech Republic and Poland are efficient in financial terms but not in technical terms and that Sweden is efficient only when the inputs are measured in physical terms and that it is some distance from the efficiency frontier when they are measured in financial terms.

Econometric Approaches

In an article published more than two decades ago, Le Pen (1986) reported on the development of a new and promising approach to the measurement of productivity in non-market public services, namely econometric analysis. In doing so, he was drawing attention to the work of Scicluna *et al.* (1980) on the productivity of police services in Canada. This study used a sample of 99 local authorities as the basis for estimating a multi-output production function for municipal police forces, linking the factors of production used to outcome indicators ('offence rate for crimes of varying levels of severity, ranging from violent crimes to infringements of the highway code'). As Le Pen (1986) notes, the value of this econometric approach is twofold. First, it is concerned with outcomes and not activity, as is often the case when productivity in public services is investigated. Second, it is capable of determining the proportion of the change in the crime rate that can be attributed to the factors of production used by the police (police officers, equipment, and so on) and the proportion that can be attributed to factors in the social environment. It can be regarded as a relatively satisfactory measure of productivity.

Since then, the econometric approach to the analysis of productivity has spread to all public service activities. Given the scale of this expansion, here too we can do no more than provide some illustrations, listing the services covered and, where possible, the types of questions investigated (Table 3.4).

It should be noted that econometric studies focus less frequently on measurements of productivity than on analyses of the relationship between productivity (measured, for example, by a ratio of the total factor productivity (TFP) type) and the explanatory variables. This emphasis fits better with the second part of the book, in which we examine the determinants of productivity.

Table 3.4   Some examples of the application of econometric methods to public services

Type of public service	Reference and perspective adopted
Urban transport	Karlaftis and McCarthy (1999): effect of privatization on productivity and costs in urban transport; Farsi *et al.* (2006): efficiency of regional bus companies; Roy and Yvrande-Billon (2007): the consequences of ownership structure and contractual choices on efficiency in the urban public transport sector in France
Health	Menon and Lee (2000): the effects of IT and regulatory changes on productivity; Rosko and Mutter (2008): analysis of 20 SFA studies of hospital inefficiency in the USA
Education	Stevens (2005a): efficiency of 80 English and Welsh universities as suppliers of teaching and research
Fire services	Jaldell (2005): fire service productivity and performance
Police	Drake and Simper (2003): study of police force productivity that compares the results of several measurement methods (both parametric and non-parametric)
Airports	Oum *et al.* (2003): comparison of the productivity of the main international airports from a benchmarking perspective
Local government	Stevens (2005b): comparison of DEA and SFA
Tax offices	Barros (2005): SFA to benchmark the tax offices
Telecommunications	Nemoto and Asai (2002): economies of scale, technical change and productivity growth in local telecommunications services in Japan
Electricity	Coelli (2002): comparison of different methods of measuring productivity (DEA, SFA)

BEYOND PRODUCTIVITY

In the light both of the sometimes insurmountable measurement difficulties examined above and the particular nature of public services, a pluralist approach to performance seems even more essential in public services than elsewhere. Here more than anywhere, the notion of performance is (or has to be) a social construct, a convention subject to debate. A pluralist approach to performance should not be regarded simply as an epistemological choice. As we have observed on several occasions, it is technically necessary given that, in some cases, the concept of productivity has become meaningless.

Once again, the framework based on the work of Boltanski and Thévenot provides a useful heuristic for examining performance in public services. By way of illustration, we will look at three cases, all of which have been investigated either by ourselves or by members of our team: first, the financial and postal services provided by the French Post Office; second, the French national employment service ANPE; and third business incubators, which are often service organizations set up by local authorities. We will also tackle the question of performance measurement in French family welfare offices (known as CAFs), using another multi-criteria framework based on a conventionalist approach, namely that developed by Salais and Storper (1993).

Productivity and Performance in the French Post Office

As has already been noted, the heuristic framework on which we draw identifies 'several families or groups of characteristics or criteria for investigating activity and its outputs and performance'; taken together, these characteristics constitute the industrial world, the market or financial world, the relational or domestic world and the civic world. The first two worlds can be described as *computational worlds*, which revolve around the counting of volumes or values; the last two can be grouped together under the heading *relational worlds*, where the watchword is not counting but 'counting on'.

In Table 3.5, the 'outputs' of the Post Office's two main areas of activity (financial and postal services) are identified and described. The table is constructed by combining the four worlds (families of characteristics, criteria or states of 'grandeur') and two time horizons (the short term and the long term). In all, eight different types of outputs are identified and illustrated.

Outputs and Performance of the French National Employment Service

Delfini (1999) uses this multi-criteria framework in a study of productivity and performance in the French national employment service (ANPE). The ANPE's output is not in fact easy to identify. There are a number of possibilities, none of which is undeniably more convincing than the others. They include (Delfini, 1999): the number of users benefiting from the ANPE's services, the number of individual or collective services provided by ANPE staff, the number of jobseekers placed or vacancies filled, the ANPE's contribution to social cohesion and the fight against social exclusion, and so on.

Table 3.6 shows some examples of output and performance indicators for various possible worlds. Productivity is an assessment of performance based on the direct output and the industrial world.

Table 3.5 The worlds of 'production' or 'families of criteria' for defining Post Office outputs (Gadrey, 1996a)

(Indicator of)	Industrial world	Market world	Relational or domestic world	Civic world
Direct (short-term) output Postal services	• Indicators relating to mail logistics, volumes of mail delivered, collected and sorted by category of mail • Industrial quality indicators (errors, operational problems)	• Post Office revenue (mail), revenue by type of operations • Value added and possible margins • Competitiveness of the various segments	• Development of personal relationships in postal services division (particularly delivery) • Individualization of postal services • Interpersonal arrangements	• Equal treatment for users (counters, delivery rounds) • Equal access • Non-discrimination (young people, non-nationals) in customer contacts • Assistance to marginal populations • Special rates for disadvantaged groups
Financial services	• More or less the same indicators as for banks: transactions completed, accounts managed (by type), industrial quality indicators (errors, operational problems)	• Net banking income and associated notions • Deposits (total amounts) • Competitiveness of the various activities	• Same for financial services	• Social banking services: agreement to open accounts for people on low incomes, 'humanized' penalties, advice to people in difficulty
Indirect (long-term) output (outcome)	• Post Office's contribution (mail function) to national or local economic output, to mail	• Degree to which the development of postal services is self-funded • Contribution of	• Development of loyalty (to the Post Office and/or certain agents) and of mutual trust	• Contribution to national or local solidarity with respect to the most deprived

Postal services	order business and other economic activities, to production and delivery times and to the efficiency of other activities	postal services to the long-term profitability of client firms and other external effects that can be measured in monetary units	• Contribution to regional and local development (rural areas, urban districts)
Financial services	• Currency creation and circulation by the Post Office (technical indicators)	• Same for financial services	• Same

Table 3.6 The ANPE's worlds of production (Delfini, 1999)

(Indicator of)	Industrial world	Market world	Domestic world	Civic world
Direct output	• Increase in employability through access to labour market information, vacancies, training courses: – on a self-service basis (advertisements, Minitel, vocal servers, interactive information terminals) – via interviews, services • Filling vacancies registered with the ANPE	• Services free of charge to users (photocopies, Minitel, registration of vacancies) • Paying job acclimatization costs for subsidized jobs	• Quality of the service relationship (adaptation to user demand) – personalized response – follow-up, possible support in job	• Equal and fair treatment for jobseekers (positive discrimination principle): individualized support for disadvantaged jobseekers
Performance (in terms of efficiency)	• Productivity indicators, industrial quality indicators (time taken to fill vacancies, waiting times, reduction in operational problems)	• Volume increase in costs	• User satisfaction indicators • Volume of direct interactions	• Volume and share of disadvantaged jobseekers in support services and in specific programmes
Indirect output	• Contribution to labour market fluidity	• Contribution to development of certain specific employment forms and to reduction of wage costs	• Contribution to preservation of social cohesion	• Contribution to fight against social exclusion

| Performance (in terms of effectiveness) | • Micro: through reintegration of jobseekers into labour market
• Macro: reduction of frictional unemployment | • Proximity of services in rural or deprived areas | • Micro: placement rate for disadvantaged groups (long-term unemployed, those on national minimum income, handicapped workers, and so on)
• Macro: reduction in very long-term unemployment and its relative share in total unemployment |

81

Output and Performance of Business Incubators

Business incubators are organizations set up, usually at local level, in order to encourage and support start-up companies. For more than 20 years now they have been an important tool in policies designed to assist the regeneration and strengthening of local economic systems. These organizations can be classified as service providers since they provide their 'customers' (individuals seeking to set up their own businesses) with material and human resources in a number of different ways.

These organizations are neither static nor homogeneous. They have developed in the course of their history. Today, therefore, they differ in various ways, including the identity of their sponsors, mode of organization and funding, the nature of the services they provide and the type of clients or projects in which they specialize. If we confine ourselves to these last two criteria, business incubators can be said to provide both simple and high-level services, that is material processing services (real estate, catering and reprographic services, for example) and knowledge-processing services (various types of advice, training, and so on). There are also generalist incubators and specialist incubators (concentrating, for example, on particular industries, types of clients or stages in the business start-up process). Those that promote entrepreneurship in the Schumpeterian sense of the term (that is the establishment of a company in order to introduce an innovation) are important actors in local innovation systems or what is known as the interactive innovation model, that is assisted by a service provider (Gallouj, 2002).

As for most other service activities, it is difficult to define and measure the output of incubators. Any investigation of this output has to take into account a number of different time horizons and worlds of production. It is a social construct, embedded in a space that is not only physical but also symbolic and temporal. Thus the output is a construct based on convention.

Table 3.7 sets out a framework that takes account of the diversity of 'outputs' of incubators by combining space–time analysis with symbolic space. As far as the temporal dimension is concerned, it can be assumed that the short term (that is the period of time required to provide the direct output) equates to the company's time in the incubator, while the long term (indirect output) begins when the company leaves the incubator.

Judged by the industrial and technical criteria, an incubator produces certain direct outputs, such as accommodation, advice and training. These direct outputs are intended to generate indirect, long-term outputs, such as company formations and job creation.

Judged by the market and financial criteria, incubators can be said to offer access to services at lower cost (shared costs) and to sources of finance.

Table 3.7   A multi-criteria framework for analysing the output and performance of business incubators

	Industrial and technical world	Market and financial world	Relational or domestic world	Civic world	Innovation world	Reputational world
Direct output (short term) during a company's time in the incubator	• Accommodation (office provision) • Basic services • Advice, assistance, training • Market visibility?	• Services at reduced cost • Access to finance • Turnover managed during time in incubator	• Individualized answers • Interpersonal arrangements • Trust • Personalized advice • Breaking down of isolation • Integration into internal network • Integration into external networks (consultants) • One-stop shop	• Support for particular populations or industries	• Addition of new (innovative) services • Support for innovative projects	• Short-term image of the locality, department or region
Performance relative to the direct output	• Productivity gains • Economies of scale • Improvement in industrial quality • Incubator occupancy rate • Failure rate	• Improvement in 'financial health' indicators • Competitiveness relative to rival organizations (cost of creating one job compared with other organizations)	• Improvement in organization's relational qualities (service relationships, integration into networks)	Improvement of civic qualities	Improvement of innovation quality	Improvement of reputation and image

Table 3.7 (continued)

	Industrial and technical world	Market and financial world	Relational or domestic world	Civic world	Innovation world	Reputational world
Indirect output (long term) on exit from incubator	• Company formation • Creation of direct and indirect jobs	• Generation of turnover (direct and indirect) • Generation of wages (direct and indirect) • Generation of local taxes	• Establishment of loyalty to local area	• Regeneration of disadvantaged areas • Redeployment	• Creation of a local innovation system • Creation of an entrepreneurial culture	• Long-term image of the locality, department or region
Performance relative to the indirect output	• Improvement of contribution to (local, national) economic growth • Evolution of number of business start-ups • Evolution of the number of jobs created • Evolution of the quality of these jobs • Rate of surviving companies after x years	• Improvement in the generation of the various types of revenue	• Consolidation of a local system or network of services (long-term integration into this system)	• Long-term improvement of civic qualities	• Consolidation of local innovation system and long-term integration into that system	• Long-term improvement of reputation and image

In the long term, the various actors foresee the generation of income: turnover and profit in the case of companies, wages in the case of employees and local taxes in the case of local authorities.

As far as the relational or domestic world is concerned, incubators can be regarded as loci for the establishment of formal and informal relations that are consolidated over time (trust relationships, empathy, integration into internal and external networks). These types of relations help to generate loyalty to the local area.

From the point of view of the civic criteria, incubators provide support for particular (socio-economically disadvantaged) populations or geographical areas. They also contribute to long-term civic outputs, which can be described as social cohesion, regional development, and so on.

The innovation world encompasses a number of outputs, such as the introduction of new services by incubators and support for innovative projects. The establishment of a culture of entrepreneurship and innovation and the consolidation of local innovation systems are examples of this world's indirect outputs.

From the point of view of the reputational world, finally, incubators produce an output best described as the image of the locality, department or region in question, whether in the short or long term.

These different 'worlds' of outputs have their corresponding 'worlds' of performance. Table 3.7 identifies and illustrates 12 different concepts of performance, which may mutually reinforce or, conversely, contradict each other, at least from a certain point onwards.

Productivity and Performance in Family Welfare Offices

In attempting to explain and illustrate the question of productivity and performance in family welfare offices, we will draw not on Boltanski and Thévenot's (1991) framework but rather on that developed by Salais and Storper (1993). These two frameworks are closely related and based on similar hypotheses. What particularly sets them apart from each other is that the first has its origins in political philosophy and seeks to characterize value systems, while the second is concerned with the more economic characteristics of production, markets and labour.

Just like Boltanski and Thévenot's construct, Salais and Storper's framework identifies a number of possible worlds. However, it is much narrower in scope than its predecessor: rather than seeking to cover all human and social activities, it attempts only to account for the plurality of productive systems. Consequently, it focuses on conventions relating to output or, more precisely, output quality (in reality, such conventions also conceal conventions on labour quality).

The fundamental difficulty in any production and consumption activity is, after all, uncertainty about the quality of the output. This uncertainty can be dispelled by two mechanisms that were very well described by Knight (1921). They are *consolidation* (that is amalgamation into the same category of objects with similar characteristics) and *specialization* (that is recourse to the work of professionals and experts). It is these two uncertainty-reducing mechanisms that Salais and Storper use to identify the various possible types of output qualities and the plurality of the corresponding worlds of production. According to Salais and Storper, output quality can be measured by two different scales (or conventions): on the one hand, the extent to which demand is consolidated, that is the degree of dedication, and, on the other, the extent to which the productive activity is specialized.

On the basis of these two scales, the following kinds of outputs can be identified:

- dedicated outputs (that is those for which demand is weakly consolidated; these are products specific to the needs of a given customer or group of customers);
- generic outputs (that is products that are independent of their users, whose 'destination is anonymous');
- specialized outputs (fruits of the work of 'specialists');
- standard outputs (fruits of the work of non-specialists).

By combining the degree of dedication of the product, on the one hand, and the degree of professional specialization of the work, on the other, four 'pure' types of production world can be identified (see Table 3.8):

- the market world of standardized dedicated outputs, that is outputs that are the result of a standardized work process but aimed at a targeted, clearly identified clientele (flexible production);
- the industrial world of standardized generic outputs, that is mass products aimed at an undifferentiated clientele that are the result of standardized Fordist work processes;
- the interpersonal world of specialized dedicated outputs, that is customized or 'made-to-measure' products aimed at a clearly identified customer and satisfying his particular requirements that are created by professionals in possession of idiosyncratic expertise (craft industries, specialist equipment);
- the intangible world, in which specialized generic outputs are produced and consumed, that is anonymous products (in this case, in fact, 'public goods' knowledge) that are the fruit of the labours of high-level experts (research activities).

Table 3.8   The worlds of production (after Salais and Storper, 1993)

	Specialized outputs (the fruits of specialist work processes)	Standardized outputs (the fruits of standardized work processes)
Dedicated outputs (intended for identified consumers)	Interpersonal world of production	Market world of production
Generic outputs (intended for anonymous consumers)	Intangible world of production	Industrial world of production

Drawing on a modified version of Salais and Storper's framework, Adjerad (1997, 1999) identifies four worlds of production within family welfare offices which are differentiated from each other by the degree of flexibility characterizing the output and the extent to which it is co-produced by benefit recipients. They are the bureaucratic–Taylorist world, the neo-bureaucratic–Taylorist world, the world of relational bureaucracy and the world of adhocracy within a government body.

The bureaucratic–Taylorist world is characterized by the mass produc-tion of standardized outputs. The work process here is highly standardized and routine (strong division of labour and automatic application of predefined procedures) and benefit recipients play only a very reduced role. It is the 'standard file' that constitutes the basic reference point for the output. Productivity (based on measured time management) and a concern for the rigorous application of legislation constitute the main performance indicators here.

The neo-bureaucratic–Taylorist world is characterized by flexible pro-duction and industrial quality. This model provides a diversified range of standardized services. Benefit recipients play a greater part here, which is reflected in the use of a mix of standard cases in order to take account of their requirements, but without abandoning the traditional industrial mode of production. In other words, efforts to take account of client expectations do not take the form of customized services. Performance assessment is based on industrial-type productivity and quality ratios (accessibility, reg-ularity of payments).

The world of relational bureaucracy is one of the paths taken in the mod-ernization of certain mechanistic or Taylorist bureaucracies (the other path being neo-Taylorist bureaucracy). The service relationship occupies a key place in this world, in which mass production is gradually abandoned in favour of personalized or customized services.

Table 3.9   The CAF and its worlds of production (Adjerad, 1999)

Degree of output flexibility Degree of co-production by benefit recipient	Non-standardized services	Standardized services
High	World of open professional and paraprofessional bureaucracy or relational bureaucracy	Neo-bureaucratic–Taylorist world or world of consensual bureaucracy
Main characteristics	Emphasis on the service relationship	Emphasis on industrial-type quality: waiting times, accuracy of payments and so on
Work and work rules	Recognition that management operational staff has some degree of autonomy, with some signs of institutional recognition of their professional knowledge. Professionalism of social work agents. Quality judged by professional criteria	Recognition that operational staff have some degree of autonomy (but no institutional recognition of their professional knowledge)
Concept of public service	To facilitate the implementation of public policies. To interpret the rules in order to satisfy users. To organize users' 'voice' in order to obtain feedback	Oscillation between uniform treatment of service users and differentiation by broad category of benefit recipients
Concept of output and performance	Output: personalized services, customized outputs Performance indicators: currently non-existent	Output: diversified ranges of services or quasi-products Performance indicators: productivity and indicators of industrial quality (accessibility of services, regulatory of payments and so on)

Table 3.9 (continued)

Degree of output flexibility Degree of co-production by benefit recipient	Non-standardized services	Standardized services
Low	World of adhocracy within a public body	Bureaucratic–Taylorist world
Main characteristics	Emphasis on creation	Emphasis on routines
Work and work rules	Favoured mode of non-management social work. Freedom to create. Work not prescribed	Standardized work. Management coding. Strict application of regulations. Little autonomy for staff. Work prescribed
Concept of public service	To devise individual or collective responses to the various problems	Uniform treatment of citizens, continuity, equality
Concept of output and performance	Output: novel solutions, specific actions Performance indicators: degree of novelty, originality of responses	Output: mass, standardized Performance indicators: productivity, accuracy of implementation of legislation

The organization's staff are no longer mere performers of procedures but professionals enjoying a certain degree of autonomy. Adjerad notes that the CAF has no indicators that can be used to evaluate the relational dimension, which is an essential component of this world's output. His explanation is that it is difficult to measure the degree of trust between an official and a user or an official's degree of devotion. Nevertheless, our analyses of the Post Office and business incubators and so on provide some theoretical leads that might enrich analysis of this particular aspect of the CAFs' performance (relational performance).

The world of adhocracy within a public body, finally, is reduced by Adjerad to social workers. In this world, the emphasis is not on the service relationship but on the creation of service. Thus Adjerad shows that, in social work, 'each new problem is met by attempts to innovate and devise original solutions. Thus the basic "state of greatness" that structures this world is creation. Projects may concern individuals, families or communities (an urban district, for example). They may concern family, social or housing problems. The particular difficulty lies in the fact that they very often concern unique cases'. This world seems even less well equipped than the previous one for assessing performance and the notion of productivity seems to have little relevance here.

CONCLUSION

In the previous chapter, having subjected the notion of productivity to the service test, we called for a cautious approach to the definition, measurement and use of the concept. When it comes to public services, that caution needs to be redoubled, since the general difficulties that apply to services are further compounded, in this case, by the specific difficulties associated with the characteristics of public services.

Thus in the absence of market prices, national accountants and statisticians have shown little reluctance to measure output in terms of input, confirmed in their actions by the theoretical assumption that the output of services can be reduced to labour. For want of any better solution, they continue to use this approach for certain government services, while at the same time acknowledging its vacuity. Given the nature and objects of the public service relationship, not only is productivity difficult to measure but it also conflicts with other concepts of performance. In this area more than in others, the distinction between output and outcome or, in Claude Rochet's words (Rochet, 2002), between 'doing things well' and 'doing the right things', seems to be absolutely fundamental. It is probably in this area that multi-criteria analytical frameworks based on a definition of output as a social construct turn out to be most promising.

NOTES

1. FDH is another widely used non-parametric production frontier technique. It involves constructing a piecewise linear 'envelope'. The FDH method does not require the convex production frontier implied in the DEA method.
2. The input efficiency scores or coefficients indicate the possible percentage reduction in input for the same level of output, while the output efficiency scores or coefficients indicate the possible percentage increase in output that could be obtained with the same volume of input.

4. Internal steering, planning and design departments in public organizations: the ultimate test

INTRODUCTION

This chapter marks a shift in the general organization of the book. Up to this point, we have examined the question of productivity, first in a general way (irrespective of sector). We then investigated it in the context of market services and then of public services, with a special emphasis on the institutional dimensions (firm/organization) or sectors of activity. Our intention now is to penetrate the 'black box' of the organization, and in particular of government services. Thus this chapter, like the previous one, focuses on public and government services, but the emphasis now is on the intra-organizational dimension. It can be regarded as an extension to or supplementary section of Chapter 3.

The intra-organizational level is of particular interest to decision-makers in firms and public bodies, particularly when they are seeking to compare performances with a view to allocating resources, for example. At this level of analysis as at the others, identification of the output and of the relevant outcome poses certain difficulties. There is also the difficult question of the links between the resources committed and outputs. The output in question here is an intermediate and not a final output.

Our starting proposition, which will be analysed in the course of this chapter, is that, as the productivity issue gradually spreads through the government services, it comes up against various difficulties, depending on the type of activity concerned. After all, some functions pose fewer difficulties than others when it comes to defining and measuring output. Much of the debate on their external equivalents also applies to internal functions such as cleaning, security or advice services.

However, it can also be said that, in most of the government services in France, the actual implementation of productivity strategies (as we shall see in Chapter 7) seems to focus on the steering and planning (design) functions and (in various ways and to varying extents) ignores other activities. Thus the use, definition and relevance of the notion of productivity (in the strict sense of the term) are affected by a law of diminishing returns. Productivity strategies become increasingly difficult to implement and gradually decline in relevance depending on the service remit and issues at stake.

Our intention in this chapter is to examine the intra-organizational levels that are useful in ascertaining the varying degrees to which the notion of productivity is applicable, to illustrate them and to analyse the difficulties they pose.

THE VARIOUS POSSIBLE INTRA-ORGANIZATIONAL LEVELS

There are many intra-organizational levels that can be considered in any attempt to tackle the question of productivity. We will draw here on Mintzberg's well-known model (Mintzberg, 1979) in order to represent them in a simplified way. We will use the example of the French Department of Health and Social Affairs to illustrate this model.

Mintzberg's Model

Mintzberg's model provides an interesting heuristic for considering, in a simplified way, the question of productivity at various organizational levels. After all, in its canonic formulation (see Figure 4.1), Mintzberg's model breaks down organizations into five parts.

The first part is the *operating core* (the base of the configuration). It is made up of operational personnel whose activities are 'directly linked to the production of goods and services'. Thus it is the operating core that fulfils the organization's principal remit (producing its output). It is their activities that define the final product. Without this core, the organization as a whole has no *raison d'être*. Mintzberg notes that it is in the operating core that standardization is most advanced, although the diversity of types of operational personnel (car mechanics, university professors, and so on) means that the degree of standardization varies.

The second part is the *strategic apex* (top management), which is the principal decision-making centre. Its function is to manage the organization ('give it an overall direction') in order to ensure that it fulfils its remit effectively (the production of goods or services). The work of the strategic apex is abstract, not repetitive or susceptible to standardization and characterized by a high degree of freedom and long-term thinking.

The third part is the *middle line*, which provides an uninterrupted though not necessarily scalar link between the strategic apex and the operational

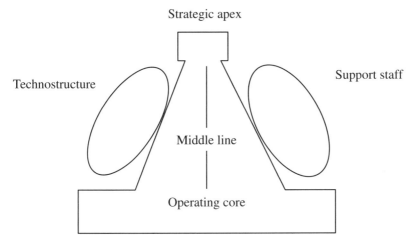

Figure 4.1   The canonic form of Mintzberg's organizational configurations model (Mintzberg, 1979)

core. The further down the hierarchy one goes, the less abstract the work is, the more easily it can be standardized and the shorter the time horizons become.

The fourth part is the *technostructure*. It houses experts who organize, monitor and control the work of other personnel. The technostructure's role is to influence the work of others and to make it more effective, but without taking part in it directly. It is the key agent in the organization's standardization. The technostructure comprises three groups of experts, each of which has a corresponding type of standardization (standardization of work, of outputs and of qualifications):

1. work analysts (example: methods specialists), experts in the standardization of work;
2. planning and control analysts (long-term planning, budgeting, accounting), experts in the standardization of results;
3. personnel analysts (recruitment, training and so on), experts in the standardization of qualifications.

Not all of the activities of the experts in the technostructure are directed towards the operational core. Their work on standardization may be aimed at different levels of the hierarchy. Thus at the lower levels in a manufacturing firm (see Figure 4.2), the analysts standardize work flows (production scheduling, methods, quality control). At the intermediate levels, they help to standardize the organization's intellectual level (training of middle

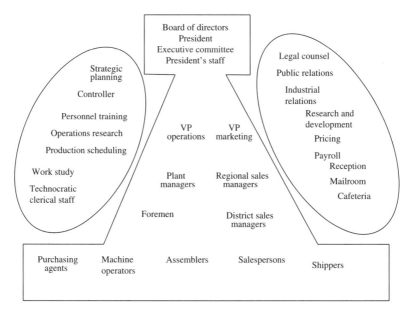

*Figure 4.2   Some members and units in the various parts of a
manufacturing company (Mintzberg, 1979: 33)*

managers, for example) and carry out operations research studies. At the
higher level, these analysts engage in strategic planning and develop management control systems.

Mintzberg notes two interesting paradoxes. The first is that specialists in
standardizing the work of others coordinate their own work not by standardizing it (with the possible exception of a certain degree of standardization based on qualifications, since the technostructure experts are highly
qualified) but rather through mutual adjustment and informal communication. The second paradox is set forth in a short footnote (Mintzberg, 1979:
30). The technostructure's *raison d'être* is change. 'The technostructure has
a built-in commitment to change, to perpetual improvement. The modern
organization's obsession with change probably derives in part at least from
large and ambitious technostructures seeking to ensure their own survival.
The perfectly stable organization has no need for a technostructure.' We will
return to this paradox in Chapter 7 when we examine productivity strategies
in government departments and public organizations.

The fifth part is made up of *support staff*. It houses all the logistical
support functions that intervene indirectly in a firm's activities (unrelated
to work flows). These logistical support functions are very diverse, ranging
from legal advice to in-house catering, via mail and cleaning services and

R&D (see Figure 4.2). Thus these logistical support functions are no different from the technostructure functions in their information and knowledge-intensiveness. After all, the logistical support functions include both intellectual functions (legal advice, R&D, public relations) and more operational functions (catering, cleaning, reception), which are easier to standardize. Logistical support functions can be located at various levels of the hierarchy, depending on who their main 'clients' are. Since the main clients of legal advice and public relations departments are located at the strategic apex, these functions are themselves located at the top of the hierarchy. Their activities are more difficult to standardize. Lower down the hierarchy, on the other hand, are activities in which the work is more standardized (catering, mail, reception, payroll) (see Figure 4.2).

A Model of the French Department of Health and Social Affairs

The aim of this section is to sketch out the current general organization of the French Department of Health and Social Affairs (*Administration des affaires sanitaires et sociales*), making free use of Mintzberg's canonic model.[1] In carrying out this exercise, we draw in particular on an internal document (DAGPB, 2003) that sets out the Department's remits and structures.

One of the Department's distinctive features is that it combines responsibilities that in other countries are sometimes separated, for health services, on the one hand, and for social affairs, on the other.[2]

The minister, the principal private secretaries and their close collaborators are positioned at the strategic apex. The middle line begins with all the directors of the central departments and finishes at the core operator level, that is the administrative officers in the offices of health and social affairs in the *départements* and regions of France (*directions départementales et régionales des affaires sanitaires et sociales* or DDASS/DRASS), and so on.

The technostructure is made up of various departments in both the health and social affairs sectors. They include, in the health sector, the Directorate-General for Health (*Direction générale de la santé* or DGS), the Directorate for Hospital Services and Healthcare Organization (*Direction générale de la santé l'organisation des soins* or DHOS) and the Directorate-General for Nuclear Safety and Radiological Protection (*Direction générale de la sûreté nucléaire et de la radioprotection* or DGSNR) and, in the social affairs sector, the Directorate for Social Security (*Direction de la sécurité sociale* or DSS), the Directorate-General for Social Action (*Direction générale de l'action sociale* or DGAS), the Directorate for Population and Migration (*Direction de la population et des migrations* or DPM) and the Department for Women's Rights and Equality (*Service des droits des femmes et de l'égalité* or SDFE). The main function of these departments is to develop strategies and policies for providing good health and social care to the French people. The Directorate for General Administration, Personnel and Budget (*Direction de l'administration générale, du personnel et du budget* or DAGPB) occupies a particular position in this organizational structure, since its activities can be divided between the technostructure and the logistical support functions, whether intellectual or operational. After all, the DAGPB fulfils planning, design and steering functions as well as support functions. These latter functions cover the following six areas: human resources, real estate resources, current operating resources, information systems, documentary resources and legal expertise resources.

The logistical support functions presented in the document on which this section is based are intellectual functions, namely the Directorate for Research, Surveys, Evaluation and Statistics (*Direction de la recherche, des études, de l'évaluation et des statistiques* or DREES) and the Department of Information and Communications (*Service de l'information et de la communication* or SICOM). However, this government department, like any other department of this size, also has catering, cleaning, reception and security services, among others. They are provided in part by the DAGPB in its support functions role.

Figure 4.3 shows two elements of the Department of Health and Social Affairs: first, the central administration (which is the object of our study), which houses the strategic apex, the technostructure and the logistical support functions and employs some 2500 officials; and second, the operating core, which comprises the decentralized departmental and regional offices in which a total of 12 500 officials are employed.

Figure 4.3 shows a third important level, located outside the boundaries of the Department of Health and Social Affairs as such. It consists of all the entities to which the Department delegates all or part of the management of its policies. They include:

1. public bodies and organizations, whether at national level, such as the French Institute for Public Health Surveillance (*Institut de veille sanitaire* or InVS), the French Agency for the Safety of Health Products (*l'Agence française de sécurité sanitaire des produits de santé* or AFSSAPS), the French Food Safety Agency (*l'Agence française de sécurité sanitaire des aliments* or AFSSA), the National Agency for Health Accreditation and Evaluation (*l'Agence nationale d'accréditation et d'évaluation en santé* or ANAES), and so on, or at local level (public hospitals);

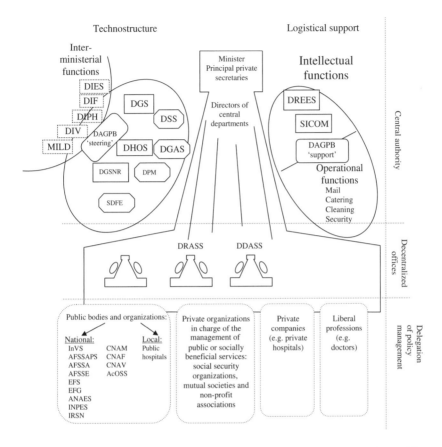

Figure 4.3   A graphic representation of the French Department of Health and Social Affairs

2. private organizations entrusted with the management of a public or socially beneficial service: for example the social security organizations, non-profit associations, mutual societies, and so on;
3. private companies (for example private hospitals);
4. the liberal professions (for example doctors).

In total, this level comprises almost 80 000 entities of various kinds and 1000 social security organizations. It provides about 2.4 million jobs.

Mintzberg's canonic configuration is certainly useful for our present purpose, but it also raises certain difficulties. The first is that many of the central departments and decentralized offices (particularly beyond a certain size) could themselves be described in terms of this canonic model, since they also comprise a strategic apex, a technostructure, a middle line and operational staff. Thus the DDASS and DRASS, for example, are also engaged in significant planning, design and steering activities at local level, which is not without consequences for the difficulty of measuring productivity and implementing the corresponding strategies, as we shall see.

Mintzberg does not ignore the existence of such organizational structures when they manifest themselves at the level of the operating core (here the decentralized offices); he alludes to the possibility, in this case, of a multidivisional structure. However, it would appear that such a structure can also be identified in some of the directorates that we have positioned within the technostructure. This observation (the consequences of which will be investigated in greater detail in the second part of the book) may have implications for the question of the productivity of 'technostructure' services. After all, the 'functional services' located in the technostructure are often in the front line when efforts are made to achieve productivity gains. It is often easier to entrust these functional services to other providers, 'more or less external' to the central administration (subcontracting), on the grounds that they have little connection with the organization's core business.

THE QUESTION OF PRODUCTIVITY AT THE INTRA-ORGANIZATIONAL LEVEL

Put simply, several lessons concerning productivity at the intra-organizational level can be drawn from the analysis of Mitzberg's model.

The Question of Productivity at the Various Levels of Mintzberg's Model

The productivity question must be posed differently depending on the intra-organizational element under consideration (see Figure 4.4). Until recently, efforts to increase productivity in government services and the discourse on productivity were directed for the most part at staff in the operating core (the bottom of Mintzberg's model). This is, after all, by far the largest group in any organization and the one whose activities, qualifications and even outputs can be most easily standardized. It constitutes the main reservoir of productivity in government departments, and the difficulties of defining, measuring or legitimating this productivity are the same as those described at some length in the previous chapter. It should not be forgotten, indeed, that it is the activity or output of this operating base that ultimately constitutes the final output of the department in question. The output of the operating bases is, quite simply, the output of the organization as a whole.

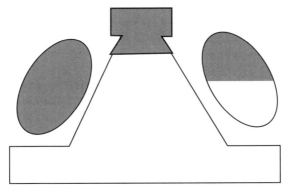

The shaded areas represent those components in which the productivity question is most problematic

Figure 4.4   Mintzberg's configuration and the topography of the difficulties of measuring productivity

The question of productivity seems more problematic in the activities of the technostructure than in those of the support functions. After all, all the technostructure's functions are intellectual and intangible and not easy to standardize. Its tasks are diverse and non-repetitive. However, closer examination of the support functions reveals that they can be divided into two totally different groups. The first group is made up of intellectual support functions, which have the same characteristics of intangibility and non-standardization as the functions of the technostructure (public relations, R&D, and so on). In this group of functions, the question of productivity is just as problematic as it is in the technostructure functions. The second group is made up of operational support functions, which are less intellectual and more tangible in content, more easily standardized and more likely to be a source of productivity gains.

The productivity question is also problematic, of course, at the level of the strategic apex and the upper part of the middle line. Here too, the functions are eminently intellectual and difficult to standardize and have a long-term perspective.

The Question of Productivity for Any Given Level

For any given component in an organization, the question of productivity becomes all the more problematic the higher up the configuration it is located (see Figure 4.5). The concept of productivity seems to lose its relevance the further upwards one moves from the base towards the apex,

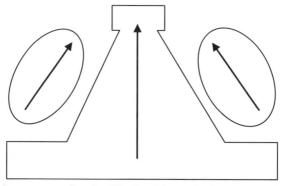

The upward movements reflect the difficulty of the productivity question

Figure 4.5   *Mintzberg's configuration and the topography of the difficulties encountered in measuring productivity (a dynamic view)*

whether in the middle line, the technostructure or the logistical support functions.

The more the activities in question are intended for clients in the upper reaches of the hierarchy, the more the question of productivity becomes problematic. The examples put forward by Mintzberg in the case of a manufacturing firm are very explicit (see Figure 4.2). Thus the technostructure's strategic planning or budgetary control functions pose greater difficulties than its role in organizing production. Similarly, as we have already noted, support functions such as legal advice or public relations, which provide services for the upper part of the middle line, are more problematic than cleaning or catering functions.

Application to the French Department of Health and Social Affairs

Application of the model to the Department of Health and Social Affairs leads us to qualify some of the preceding statements while retaining the general argument.

If the general argument is applied to this French government department, then it follows that it is easier to define and measure productivity in the decentralized departmental and regional offices (DDASS, DRASS, and so on) than in the technostructure, the support functions or the strategic apex. It also follows that the difficulties are greater in the upper reaches of the technostructure and support functions (the DREES and SICOM, that is the intellectual support functions, as opposed to the operational support functions). It also follows, finally, that the notion of productivity becomes less relevant the further up the middle line one goes, that is the closer one gets to ministerial level.

Nevertheless, this general argument is in need of qualification.

As we have already noted, even though it does indeed become more difficult to measure productivity as one moves from the decentralized offices to the central departments, we should not lose sight of the fact that the departmental and regional offices (DDASS and DRASS) are themselves increasingly taking on steering, design and planning functions. As a consequence, it is becoming increasingly difficult to measure productivity here as well.

Some units in the technostructure that undoubtedly belong in that part of the configuration may, nevertheless, engage in activities that fall more within the scope of the (intellectual) logistical support functions. This does not make it any less difficult to define and measure productivity but may have consequences for productivity strategies (for example, it may be easier to outsource the support functions).

As far as the logistical support functions are concerned, the rule that productivity is more difficult to measure the higher up Mintzberg's model one goes seems to be confirmed. After all, the logistical support functions can clearly be divided into intellectual functions (which are resistant to attempts to measure productivity) and operational functions (which are better suited to such measures). It should be noted that, in its 'support roles', the Directorate for General Administration, Personnel and Budget (DAGPB) straddles these two sets of functions. On the other hand, the rule that the level of difficulty rises the higher up the configuration one goes seems to be less operant when applied to the technostructure, unless the various design, planning and steering sections of the central administration can be hierarchized on the basis of their conceptual and strategic content, which is unlikely. Thus in the Department of Health and Social Affairs' technostructure, it is probably more useful to make a distinction between those entities that provide services for both the decentralized offices and the other entities in the technostructure (for example the DAGPB) and those that provide services only for the decentralized offices than to classify the entities according to whether they serve the top or bottom of the configuration. Thus that part of the DAGPB that belongs to the technostructure (that is, its planning and steering functions) has the task of controlling certain aspects of the decentralized offices' activities but also, and more importantly, supports and assists in the control of the other technostructure entities (all of the Department's directorates).

It should be noted that some entities or functions are inter-ministerial entities. This is why parts of other ministries' technostructures are shown in Figure 4.3. However, this question of joint entities can, from now on, be considered at all levels of the organization (logistical support functions, and so on).

DEFINING AND MEASURING PRODUCTIVITY AT THESE VARIOUS LEVELS

What does productivity mean at these various intra-organizational levels and how can it be measured? In answering this question, one of the lessons that must be drawn from the general discussion above of the organizational structures is that a distinction has to be made between two groups of analytical units:

1. material or operational support functions, and
2. intellectual functions, broadly defined to include both planning (design) and strategic steering functions (carried out by the various entities in the technostructure, the strategic apex and the upper part of the middle line) and intellectual support functions.

The first group, which we will only mention here, is the internal equivalent of external operational service providers (catering, mail services, buildings and vehicle fleet management, equipment maintenance, cleaning, security, and so on). The material processing aspect that dominates and defines these activities makes the productivity question less problematic than in other areas, as has already been noted several times. These activities are particularly prone to outsourcing and the use of technical systems.

The second group of functions (to which most of the following analysis will be devoted) is the internal equivalent of external intellectual services (research, audit, consultancy, and so on). Gadrey *et al.* (1992) suggest that the definition of consultancy activities reveals the linkage between two functions associated with two types of competences: '(a) an intellectual function involving analysis, research and expertise that draws both on high-level *specialist knowledge* and *experience* of solving problems in a certain field of knowledge; (b) an intellectual function, characteristic of consultancy, involving the identification and formulation of problems and of plans, the adaptation and transmission of knowledge to other agents (belonging, in this case, to a company or organization), assistance with decision-making and, increasingly, assistance with the implementation of all or some of these decisions'. Gadrey *et al.* also note that consultancy (in the strict sense) makes greater use of type (b) competence, even though type (a) competences are indispensable. Indeed, it is type (b) competences that distinguish consultancy in the strict sense from investigation or research activities. They also separate out audit services, which involve verifying that all functions (legal, organizational, IT, sales, and so on), and not just accounting and financial functions, are fulfilling their remits 'efficiently and effectively, and in conformity with certain quality standards' (control functions (c)).

The Department of Health and Social Affairs' intellectual functions, which is what we are concerned with here, are consistent with these various definitions. The technostructure, which is concerned mainly with design, planning and steering, performs type (a), type (b) and type (c) functions, with the last two types (identification and formulation of problems and transmission of solutions, on the one hand, and verification and control functions, on the other hand), being probably the most important. Within the support functions, the DREES, for example, basically falls within the scope of type (a) investigation and appraisal functions.

Thus it can be assumed that the definition and measurement of productivity in these intellectual functions can be considered here in the same terms (and with the same difficulties) as those applied to external research, audit and consultancy services. The analogy can also be used to consider strategies for improving the productivity and performance of design, planning and steering functions (see Chapter 7).

Intellectual Functions (of Professional Advice, Design, Planning and Strategic Steering): (Internal) Knowledge-intensive Services

The Department of Health and Social Affairs' intellectual functions are internal 'knowledge-intensive services'. These are research, consultancy and engineering services that encompass the whole range of functions making up companies' activities and are the driving force in various environments (economic, legal, social, scientific, technological, and so on). Although they are heterogeneous in nature, they are often regarded as the archetypical services and labelled 'pure', on the grounds that they best illustrate the characteristics of intangibility, interactivity and immediacy that are often used to define services. Thus it is to this type of activity that the general framework of service specificities and their consequences for the definition and measurement of productivity (Chapter 2, Figure 2.1) best applies. Nevertheless, these particular service activities have another fundamental characteristic that complicates even more the problem of how to define and measure productivity. This is their cognitive dimension. Thus knowledge-intensive services (whether internal or external) bring together two problematic areas of economic theory (particularly from the point of view of measurement), namely the *service* economy and the *knowledge* economy.

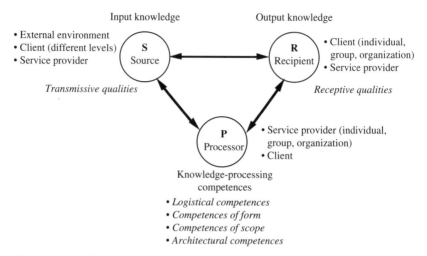

Figure 4.6   The provision of knowledge-intensive services as a knowledge-processing activity

We will not examine in detail here the consequences of the particularities of consultancy work as a service activity: as we have already noted above, they reflect and illustrate, in an ideal-typical way, the analysis conducted in Chapter 2. On the other hand (and these two aspects are closely linked), we do intend to give greater prominence here to the consequences of knowledge-intensive services, which will be considered from the point of view of their informational and cognitive dimension. After all, knowledge-intensive services can be defined as 'machines' for processing and producing information and knowledge on behalf of a 'client'. Thus knowledge is both their main input and their main output. Furthermore, this cognitive output is an intermediate consumption in their clients' production processes (Gallouj, 2002; Nachum, 1999; Toivonen, 2004).

Knowledge-intensive Services: 'Machines' for Processing and Producing Knowledge

From a cognitive perspective, any transaction involving knowledge-intensive services brings three elements into play (Figure 4.6):

1. the source (S) of the input knowledge;
2. the recipient (R) of the output knowledge; and
3. the processor (P) of the input knowledge and the (co-)producer of the output knowledge.

This simplified model conceals many relatively more complex configurations. Thus the recipient of the knowledge (R) may denote an individual client, a group within the organization or the client organization as a whole. The service provider itself is also a recipient, since it makes every effort to store the knowledge resulting from each new transaction in its organizational memory in order to use it subsequently as input knowledge. The source of the knowledge (S) is also a heterogeneous category, which can include: (a) the client (recipient) in its various forms; (b) the client's external environment; and (c) the processor, considered as a database of knowledge accumulated in the course of repeated acts of service provision. While just one of these source elements may be brought into play in the provision of a knowledge-intensive service, it is more usual for all of them to be involved. The processor (P) is the service provider, which may also be considered as an individual, project group or organization. The client is also a processor of knowledge, particularly when the service is co-produced and not simply subcontracted.

If this model is applied to the French Department of Health and Social Affairs, the knowledge processors can be identified as the various directorates in the central administration (those that we positioned in the technostructure in Mintzberg's configuration, for example the DGS, DHOS and DSS), as well as the intellectual services provided by the support functions (the DREES, for example). Their main tasks are to produce intellectual solutions to problems of different kinds (created by the environment's dynamic) and to implement and monitor those solutions. Table 4.1 at the end of this chapter provides some general illustrations of these entities' responsibilities. The main recipients of knowledge are those that might be described as the Department's internal 'clients', that is the decentralized offices (DDASS and DRASS) and the various agencies to which aspects of health and social policy implementation are delegated. As far as the sources of knowledge are concerned, they can include, for any given directorate, the external environment, other directorates, internal clients, and so on.

The main activity of internal or external knowledge-intensive service providers (as knowledge processors) is to transfer, under the best possible conditions, a set of knowledge embodied in a solution from a source to a recipient. This transfer involves the circulation of knowledge, both physically and, in the case of market services, economically (with all the difficulties of transferring property rights inherent in this particular commodity in the case of external knowledge-intensive services). We will first describe the modalities of this transfer before going on to examine, in strictly analytical terms, their implications for the definition and measurement of productivity. These modalities equate to the operations performed by the service provider on various aspects of the knowledge, namely its (physical) circulation, its form, its scope and its structure.

Modalities linked to the circulation of knowledge
Knowledge can be circulated in a very simple basic form that we describe as the *linear transfer of knowledge* or *basic logistical competence*. In this case, knowledge is reduced to the status of information. The service provider is regarded as a mere processor of information, a simple intermediary that confines itself to transferring the information ('physically') from the source at which it is located to the recipient. In this case, the knowledge is not modified as it moves from S to R; the input knowledge is the same as the output knowledge. Services such as market research, the use of on-line databases, certain aspects of recruitment consultancy or of the transfer of technical systems by IT consultants and, in the case of government services, the issuing of a regulatory circular can all be described in these terms.

Modalities linked to the form of knowledge
This pair of modalities describes the ability to modify the (codified or tacit) form that the knowledge may take. In essence, it covers (and indeed extends beyond) the conversion mechanisms that Nonaka (1994) denotes by the terms externalization and internalization. *Externalization* is synonymous with formalization and codification. It denotes the transformation of tacit knowledge (at the source) into codified knowledge (on reception). This transformation of the knowledge makes it easier to manipulate and gives it a certain degree of stability. The development by a knowledge-intensive service provider of a software program specific to a given client may, for example, be interpreted as the implementation of externalization competences. After all, the development process involves translating a number of organizational routines or processes into computer codes. *Internalization*, on the other hand, denotes the transformation of codified knowledge (at the source) into tacit knowledge (on reception). In this case, the service provider acts as a support for the client's learning process (teacher). Internalization cannot take place without close interaction between client and service provider. It enables the client to appropriate the knowledge more easily.

Modalities linked to the scope of the knowledge
The second pair of modalities reflects the evolution of the scope of the knowledge. It contrasts generalization competences with localization competences. *Generalization* denotes the transformation of specific knowledge (at the source), whether tacit or codified, into tacit or codified general knowledge (on arrival). This competence makes it possible to extend the range of application or the audience for the body of knowledge in question. *Localization* (or differentiation or specification) denotes the transformation of general knowledge (at the source) into knowledge adapted to the

local context (on arrival). As before, this knowledge can be both tacit and codified. Localization increases the degree to which the client can appropriate the knowledge.

Modalities linked to the structure or morphology of the knowledge
In the course of a transaction, a knowledge-intensive service provider may also modify the architecture of the knowledge. This can take place in two different ways: by association or by dissociation. Association involves supplying the recipient by combining knowledge sets that were initially independent of each other. Although this is an essential principle in the production of novelty in the Schumpeterian approach to innovation, we are considering association here more generally and more mechanically as one of the basic knowledge-processing mechanisms that does not necessarily produce innovation. Thus different activities can be described by means of this basic mechanism: not only R&D, which involves the production of new (tacit or codified) knowledge by combining old (tacit or codified) knowledge sets, but also the association of organizations (collaborations, mergers, and so on). Dissociation, conversely, involves splitting up a set of knowledge (whatever form it may be in) in order to produce different knowledge with which to supply the client. As in the previous case, the knowledge may be embodied in individuals, in technical systems or in organizations, and the dissociation may relate to the knowledge itself or to the mediums through which it manifests itself.

The Consequences of the Cognitive Nature of Knowledge-intensive Services for the Productivity Problem

In privileging such a definition of knowledge-intensive services (and particularly of consultancy), that is regarding them as knowledge-processing activities, the literature is brought face to face with the difficulty of defining and measuring productivity. Methods of measuring productivity that have their roots in the world of manufacturing (that is those based on the notion of standardized output and input units and the possibility of taking account of variations in quality) become problematic when the output of the activities in question is heterogeneous and quality is difficult both to define and to measure.

After all, given the diversity of their clients and of the internal and external environments they are dealing with, the solutions offered by knowledge-intensive service providers are generally specific and bespoke. Some of these solutions are particular innovations, sometimes described as *ad hoc* innovations (Gallouj, 2002). An *ad hoc* innovation is defined as a solution that throws a certain degree of new light on a firm's (legal, organizational, strategic or technical) problem but which cannot necessarily be transferred (totally) to other firms. It is, as it were, an incremental product innovation in which the product is not a tangible entity but an intellectual solution to the client firm's problem.

Taking account of variations in quality is not simply a problem of measurement. It is also a basic conceptual problem, since it is particularly difficult to assess variations in the quality of cognitive solutions. As far as output quality is concerned, two problematic scenarios can be identified:

1. in this first scenario, quality evolves much too rapidly to be taken into account (NICTs being the emblematic example here); and
2. in this second scenario, quality necessarily differs from one transaction to another, because of the bespoke nature of the service. This is the case with knowledge-intensive services. For example, when a strategy consultant develops strategies for two different companies, they cannot really be regarded as the same product.

In consultancy, the labour input is by far the most important factor of production. In this type of activity, the essential aspect of that labour is its capacity for creativity and innovation in knowledge processing. The qualitative aspect of the input is more important than its quantitative aspect. This quality is not fixed, for a given factor, since it can vary considerably from one commission to the next, depending on a number of variables such as the individual's health, his or her affinity with the client, different experience from one commission to another, and so on).

In all service activities, input quality is strongly linked to productivity and, more generally, to performance. This link is even more fundamental in knowledge-intensive services. In this particular area, it is, moreover, subject to considerable informational asymmetries, which have been very well described in the literature (Gallouj, 1997; Karpik, 1989). After all, it is difficult to evaluate the quality of high-level experts' work and to establish the relationship between the work carried out and the results obtained.

Clients and their knowledge of their environment and their problems often constitute an input in service provision, particularly when the service provided is strategic in nature. The quality of this input can have a considerable influence on a knowledge-intensive service provider's quality and productivity. Thus the productivity and, more generally, the performance of the service depend on the recipient's qualities. These receptive qualities include cognitive aptitudes and 'technical' conditions as well as attitudes (behaviours and strategies) favourable to knowledge acquisition. They reflect the additive and complementary character of knowledge. The quality of a knowledge-intensive service provider's output depends on the quality of their reception. The better the receptive qualities, the more communication is facilitated and the more informational asymmetries are reduced. These receptive qualities are weakened when a client organization does not have an internal department made up of specialists in a given function (for example a legal department when a legal service is being provided). These receptive qualities can also be affected by internal conflicts or unfavourable individual or group behaviour (refusal to learn), particularly when the recipient feels threatened by the new knowledge.

The source of the knowledge itself may also have certain characteristics that facilitate the flow of knowledge to a greater or lesser extent. These transmissive qualities describe a source's propensity to deliver up its knowledge. They also denote a source's cognitive aptitudes, technical conditions and attitudes and the degree to which they encourage the transfer or, conversely, the retention of knowledge. Thus these transmissive capacities are dependent on the nature of the knowledge and on the cognitive characteristics (aptitudes) of the source's various component parts, as well as on the attitudes of those component parts to sharing the knowledge. The source's transmissive qualities are generally enhanced when the knowledge is codified. They are diminished when this knowledge is regarded by the source (or its component parts) as strategic or when the purpose for which the knowledge is to be used is likely to call the source into question in one way or another. Such mistrust is not uncommon in audit services and, more generally, in 'therapeutic' knowledge-intensive services, that is those that seem to provide answers to what Kubr (1988) calls 'corrective problems'.

The question of the consequences of knowledge-intensive service providers' cognitive characteristics can also be approached by examining the consequences of the basic knowledge-processing mechanisms already alluded to above. Some of these basic mechanisms seem to be more amenable than others to the notion of productivity. Thus the measurement of productivity and the implementation of productivity strategies would seem to be less problematic in the case of the logistical, externalization and generalization mechanisms, since they involve codified knowledge (from the various points of view already mentioned). On the other hand, the internalization, localization and association–dissociation mechanisms are not conducive to productivity measurement (the first two because they help to make the cognitive solution unique and personalized, the other two because they involve creation and novelty). These mechanisms call for different performance evaluation systems. Of course, with the exception of certain extreme cases, the preceding (strictly analytical) observations cannot serve as a basis for directly interpreting any given knowledge-intensive service transaction, since such activities (whether internal or external) often combine these different basic principles.

Measuring Productivity in these Activities

Although the cognitive dimension is an obstacle to the measurement of productivity in all knowledge-intensive services, there are, nevertheless, significant differences depending on the type of service in question. The difficulties are less acute in accountancy than in advertising or strategy consultancy. As for other services (see Chapter 2), the productivity of knowledge-intensive services has essentially been measured by comparing turnover with the number of hours worked or the cost of labour. Such methods have obvious limitations, which concern both input and output.

Output

Measuring output in terms of turnover poses many problems (Nachum, 1999). As has already been noted, the output of knowledge-intensive services is particularly difficult to define because it is both a service and cognitive in nature. It encompasses both the production of solutions (which are always different and sometime innovative) to problems of various kinds, the implementation of these solutions and, perhaps most importantly, the (objective or subjective) effects of the preceding aspects of the output on the client. In some cases, nevertheless, homogeneous 'output' indicators can be identified; these are never totally satisfactory but they do make it possible to get close to certain commonly used techniques. They include standard contracts in legal consultancy, software packages in IT services and patents in R&D. Prices do not necessarily reflect the output received by a client, because that output is so heterogeneous. In some knowledge-intensive services, moreover, the prices are fees that are not linked to the output produced (examples: architects, advertising agencies). Turnover, second, is sensitive to a number of external factors, such as the economic situation and the evolution of demand and competition. Finally, the price set by some knowledge-intensive service providers depends not on the output but on the provider's reputation. The output created for the client, that is the improvement in the client's situation produced by the service provider's work, is an essential aspect of the output of knowledge-intensive services. This improvement can be measured by variations in the client's output or turnover or by more subjective satisfaction indicators. Although it is fundamental, its evaluation poses considerable difficulties, because these effects cannot be easily separated out from a number of other environmental factors.

Input

Given the particular nature of knowledge-intensive services, the input of both service providers and their clients has to be taken into account.

Clearly, the labour factor occupies a central position on both sides. However, the traditional method of estimating the labour (which is used even in consultancy companies) in terms of the volume of hours worked is problematic. It takes no account of labour quality, which is, as we have already noted, an essential factor in the productivity of knowledge-intensive services. For this reason, the volume of hours worked is often replaced by wages, on the assumption that wage differentials within consultancy companies reflect differences in labour quality, with the highest paid being presumed to be the most experienced and most competent. However, the limitation of this method is obvious and has already been pointed out: since most of the value added or turnover of knowledge-intensive services is accounted for by employees' remuneration, the productivity ratio produced by this method amounts to putting the same number in both the numerator and denominator.

Output and Productivity of Planning and Steering Functions in the French Department of Health and Social Affairs

To the best of our knowledge, there are very few studies of productivity (strictly defined) in internal intellectual functions. However, this is not true of performance evaluation in the broad sense of the term. Malleret (1993) offers an interesting review of them, in which methods based on the search for the cost function occupy a central position.

We have already suggested that external intellectual functions might be a source of inspiration for our investigation of productivity in internal functions. Nevertheless, there are significant differences between the two types of functions, which may alter their relationship to the question of productivity.

The first significant difference is the nature of the clientele. In the case of internal functions, the clientele is a captive one. The entities in question are decentralized, their responsibilities devolved; the relationships between them and the planning and steering functions are not always horizontal and based on co-production but rather vertical and, to varying degrees, hierarchical. They have absolutely no freedom to exercise the 'exit' option, that is to terminate the service relationship. And their ability to 'voice', that is to communicate grievances, complaints or proposals for change, may be thwarted by the vertical nature of the relationship. Apathy or demotivation, which is obviously prejudicial to performance, may in some cases be the only mode of expression available to them. Although it is constantly growing as a result of decentralization, deconcentration and delegation, the diversity of this clientele is, nevertheless, less pronounced than that of external consultants.

A further distinction has to be made between direct and indirect clients at various levels. In many cases, the performance of planning and steering functions has to be considered at the level not only of the direct clientele but also, and most importantly, of the indirect clientele (and in particular of the end customer, that is the user).

The structure of the labour input has few points in common with that of external functions. External knowledge-intensive services, for example, are often characterized by forms of association (partnerships) that determine pay structures and mobility rules (for example the 'up or out' strategies found in some consultancy companies) that have nothing in common with the world of the civil service, in which pay and promotions are determined by different criteria.

Another significant difference between external and internal knowledge-intensive services is the existence among the latter of horizontal service relationships. After all, the production processes of the various directorates in the central administration are not independent of each other, since the directorates are obliged to cooperate with each other. Consequently, the performance of a given directorate in conducting its vertical relationship with a decentralized office may depend on the performance of a horizontal relationship with another central directorate. The 'control' principle on which the evaluation of centres of responsibility is based is not always respected (Malleret, 1998).

As far as steering functions (and particularly strategic steering functions) are concerned, it is not certain, given the other issues at stake, that productivity should be the overriding objective. Incidentally, there is often a confusion with these intellectual functions (and indeed with operational functions as well) between productivity gains and cost savings. These two categories do not necessarily overlap completely, as we have already noted, and if productivity drive is regarded as synonymous with cost cutting, then the whole notion of productivity might as well be abandoned, since it loses most of its analytical value. Consequently, it is often necessary to stress other aspects of performance, particularly outcomes.

We will not raise here the question of the productivity of the strategic apex (the Minister in government departments). Nevertheless, however difficult it may be to answer, the question can be posed in respect of the other entities in the department, particularly the technostructure (if only, as Malleret (1993) notes, because the other entities in the organization and users would find it difficult to understand why one entity should not be subject to the appraisal that is compulsory for all the others and which it requires the others to undergo). The answer to this question is closely linked to the nature of the remits (that is the outputs) of these various entities. Table 4.1 (compiled on the basis of an internal DAGPB document, 2003)

Table 4.1   *The various entities in the Department of Health and Social
Affairs (technostructure and support functions) carrying out
intellectual functions and their outputs or remits (excluding the
inter-ministerial units attached to the Department of Health
and Social Affairs)*

Entity	Remit
Health Directorate-general for Health (DGS)	• To plan, implement, coordinate and evaluate national health policy • To analyse the health needs of the French population • To set targets and priorities for health policy, coordinate and evaluate programmes, plan prevention and health promotion policy and formulate intervention strategies • To encourage research and the development of expertise in public health • To develop the health indicators required for drawing up health programmes • To handle questions concerning the demographics of the health professions and professional ethics and determine their training needs • To define standards and reference systems to ensure the quality and safety of professional practices • To promote the quality and safety of healthcare procedures • To contribute to the formulation of medicines policy • To develop disease prevention, monitoring and risk management measures • To reflect on ethical questions • To ensure that users' rights are respected and that the healthcare system is democratic • To lead and coordinate the work of the decentralized offices and other regional actors • To follow European and international developments • To act as the supervisory authority for public healthcare establishments
Directorate for Hospital Services and Healthcare Organization (DHOS)	• To organize the provision of healthcare • To respond more effectively to the population's needs by optimizing resources • To ensure the quality, safety, continuity and proximity of the healthcare system • To plan, implement and monitor pricing and financial regulation policy • To organize and manage health professionals' careers • To provide guidance on and give impetus to HR policies

Table 4.1   (continued)

Entity	Remit
	• To draw up rules relating to the public hospital service and practitioners and to ensure that they are applied • To exercise its powers relating to the authorization regimes for dispensing pharmacies and medical analysis laboratories
Directorate-General for Nuclear Safety and Radiological Protection (DGSNR)	• To draw up and monitor the application of the general technical regulations relating to the safety of basic nuclear installations • To develop and implement measures for preventing the health risks associated with exposure to radiation • Authorizations relating to basic nuclear installations • To organize and lead the supervision of installations • To monitor sources of radiation • To monitor the transport of radioactive materials for civil use • To organize environmental radiological surveillance for the whole country • To draw up and implement the regulations • To make plans for setting up an emergency organization in the event of incidents • To organize the distribution of information on these subjects to the public and media • To take part in the activities of international organizations
Social protection	
Directorate for Social Security (DSS)	• To develop, implement and evaluate policies relating to social security • To draft the legislation governing the funding of social security and to monitor its implementation • To develop and implement policies for regulating the health insurance system • To develop and implement policies relating to the fiscal and social resources of the social security regimes • To develop and implement policy relating to the application of NICTs in the sphere of social security • To act as the supervisory body for social security organizations and to implement target-based and management agreements • To negotiate and monitor France's international commitments in social security matters
Social affairs and solidarity	
Directorate-General for	• To develop and manage the implementation of policies on social services

Table 4.1 (continued)

Entity	Remit
Social Action (DGAS)	• To coordinate the actions of the social affairs departments on non-contributory social benefits and to draw up and monitor the implementation of the regulations relating to its sphere of responsibility • To carry out the financial monitoring of these benefits and to evaluate them • To take responsibility for the training of professionals, the conditions under which they operate and the ethical rules to which they are subject • To draft legislation relating to the setting up and operation of establishments and services • To ensure that the rights of users and staff in these establishments are respected
Directorate for Population and Migration (DPM)	*To contribute to policy development by:* • taking part in the drawing up of immigration and integration policies • implementing, monitoring and evaluating anti-discrimination policy • taking part in the drawing up of demographic, international migration and co-development policies *To organize reception and support by:* • processing applications for permission to work and family reunification • taking charge of the reception and accommodation of asylum seekers and refugees • administering civic integration contracts *To promote integration by:* • developing and driving forward integration programmes • managing applications for French nationality
Department for Women's Rights and Equality (SDFE)	• To put into practice government policy promoting equality between men and women • To organize, coordinate and evaluate the decentralized network • To support the development of associations
Joint entities Directorate for General Administration, Personnel and Budget	• To develop and implement policies on HR management, professional development, training, recruitment, social action and social dialogue • To implement a policy for monitoring and reviewing the careers of senior managers

Table 4.1   (continued)

Entity	Remit
(DAGPB)	• To coordinate implementation of legislation relating to the finance acts • To draw up and implement the budget and to drive forward and coordinate procedures for distributing resources • To develop and implement the Department of Health and Social Affairs' policy on information systems and NICTs • To draw up logistical and real estate policy and documentation policy • To provide legal advice and assistance, to defend the Department and to provide legal protection for its officials • To lead deliberations on the Department's development and to steer the decentralization and modernization of its organization, methods and management tools • To facilitate work with the decentralized offices
Directorate for Research, Surveys, Evaluation and Statistics (DREES)	• To develop part of the statistical apparatus and to collect data for, analyse and diffuse the results of the major surveys • To take part in determining the direction of research policy, to contribute to the development of researchers' work and to make full use of the results • To compile synthesis reports and other documentation to aid decision-making and to produce socio-demographic, economic and financial studies and projections • To contribute to the development, validation and implementation of methods of evaluating social policies
Department of Information and Communication (SICOM)	• Institutional communications for the Department of Health and Social Affairs • Ministerial information and communication campaigns • Editorial policy (institutional publications, and so on) • Events policy (organization of conferences and seminars, and so on)

Source: DAGPB document, 2003.

describes the remits of the main entities in the Department of Health and Social Affairs.

Examination of the remits of the various entities in the central directorates of the Department of Health and Social Affairs (Table 4.1) shows that they can be divided into four areas of responsibility: (a) provision of professional advice and expertise; (b) strategic steering; (c) regulation; and (d) monitoring and evaluation. We will see in Chapter 7 that the general trend in the Department's development (one that is not yet at an end) is towards a concentration on these steering and planning functions.

In order to measure the productivity of these various entities, an acceptable output indicator has to be developed. Clearly, however, in view of the diversity of their remits, their constantly evolving and non-standardizable nature and the impossibility of aggregating them in order to calculate a volume of activity, this is a virtually impossible task. Furthermore, the constant improvement in the quality of these activities in recent years is difficult to incorporate into an output indicator. Finally, these entities' productivity (in the strict sense of the term) may well be regarded as a less important issue than the performance they induce in others, whether they be the decentralized offices, those bodies and organizations to whom certain responsibilities are delegated or other central departments.

CONCLUSION

Our attempts to tackle the question of the productivity of organizations' internal services mark a break with the analytical approach adopted in the preceding chapters. Paradoxically, however, these attempts to penetrate the black box of the organization by focusing on a government department's internal directorates come up against the whole range of difficulties already mentioned. However, they may also produce some solutions. After all, within these organizations there are service activities similar to those we have already examined in the light of the problems they pose when it comes to applying the concept of productivity. Thus the organizations are made up of knowledge-intensive service functions, such as legal advice, accounting, HRM, design, planning and strategic steering, and of operational service functions, such as catering, cleaning, caretaking and so on. Productivity is easier to define and measure in the case of operational services than in that of knowledge-intensive services, since the outputs have a tangible content and are more standardized. Furthermore, knowledge-intensive services are not homogeneous, since they include some activities that are more codifiable than others, such as legal advice and accounting, for example, compared with, design, planning and strategic steering. Finally, government departments tend to concentrate on the activities that are most difficult to measure and to outsource operational services. This further compounds the difficulties in measuring productivity, and their performance is more accurately reflected in the effects they produce than in their output.

More generally, our main concern in the first part of the book has been to evaluate the performance of organizations (at different levels of analysis), with productivity occupying a central position in our deliberations. However, there is a need also to investigate the purpose of such evaluations. In 1996, the French High Council for Evaluation identified three purposes in the case of public services:

- information: to apprize citizens of the results of government actions in the interests of transparency and democracy;
- sound management: evaluations provide a basis for the rational allocation of resources;
- learning and mobilization: the aim here is to encourage government officials to identify performance objectives and levers and to appropriate them (training, motivation, and so on).

In other words, although one of the objectives of evaluation is certainly audit, the two purposes outlined above it also provide a basis for action. It is to this second objective that the second part of the book is dedicated.

NOTES

1. We are not making any judgements here as to the precise form of the configuration (mechanistic bureaucracy, professional bureaucracy, and so on).
2. More generally, it should be noted that in France, to a greater extent than in other countries, the number of ministries and their remits seem to change according to election results and not necessarily to fulfil public policy objectives. This unstable ministerial landscape can effect the measurement of performance as well as improvement strategies.

PART II

Productivity: determinants and strategies

5. The traditional factors influencing productivity

INTRODUCTION

Intensive efforts have been made in the economic and management literature to determine the origin of productivity gains. As a result, it has been possible not only to identify, enumerate and classify, in increasing detail, the levers of productivity but also to develop a number of theoretical models. Some of these models have already been examined in Chapter 1, when we investigated the reasons why the productivity question lies at the heart of economic theory.

Excluding the effects of sectoral reallocations of factors (labour mobility, migration, and so on), it is generally agreed that six generic factors influencing productivity can be identified (see Figure 5.1); they are not, of course, independent of each other (CBO, 1981; Harris, 1999; Gamache, 2005):

1. technical factors;
2. human factors;
3. organizational factors;
4. economic factors;
5. political and institutional factors; and
6. social factors.

Of these six groups of generic factors, the last three (economic, political and social factors) are macroeconomic and macro-social factors. They are general environmental factors which are particularly 'inert' in the short or even medium term. No one firm or organization can change them, but they exert fundamental influences at the microeconomic level. In the case of two of them (political and social factors), any attempt at quantification faces certain difficulties, at least with regard to some of their component parts.

The first three groups of generic factors (technical, human and organizational factors) can be considered at both the macroeconomic and microeconomic level. It is these factors that firms and other organizations can influence in their efforts to improve productivity.

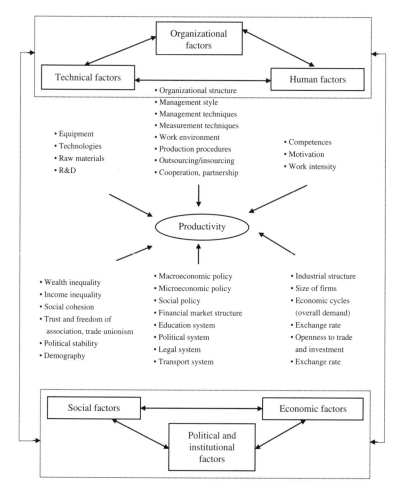

Figure 5.1   The factors influencing productivity

The aim of this chapter is to investigate each of these groups of factors, in a general and theoretical way and independently of sector. We will be focusing in particular on the most 'flexible' factors, namely technical, human and organizational factors. These three groups of factors are considered separately, but at the same time they are obviously linked; in particular, it can be difficult to separate organizational factors from technical and human factors.

TECHNICAL FACTORS

Three technical factors seem to influence productivity:

1. investment in equipment (machinery and tools),
2. technological innovation, and
3. R&D.

The explicit aim of investing in equipment and technological process innovation is to achieve productivity gains by substituting machines for human labour. There are many examples in economic history of workers rebelling against competition from machines, including the uprisings staged by the Lyonnais silk workers, or canuts, and the Luddite movement in nineteenth-century England. The productivity question also arises in respect of other forms of technological innovations (particularly product innovation). These forms of innovations are generally considered to affect the numerator of the productivity ratio. Information and communication technologies (ICTs), of course, now play a central role in this technological innovation. Very many studies have investigated the links between information technologies and productivity (Gordon, 2000, 2002; Schreyer, 2000; Bassanini *et al.*, 2000), whether they have been concerned with: (a) the contribution of ICT producers to the growth in productivity at the macroeconomic level; (b) the productivity gains associated with the diffusion and use of ICTs in the other sectors of the economy; or (c) the productivity gains (without additional investment for a network member) associated with club effects or network externalities.

Technological innovation is not necessarily based on R&D activity. However, such activity is itself a source of productivity gains, as has been shown in numerous empirical studies (Mansfield, 1961; Griliches, 1964).

Table 5.1 shows a number of estimates of the R&D elasticity of output for various countries (or groups of countries) and different levels of analysis (firm, industry, total economy, and so on). In France, the studies by Cunéo, Mairesse and Mohnen (Cunéo, 1984; Mairesse and Cunéo, 1985; Mairesse and Mohnen, 1990) are authoritative in this area. By introducing a new factor, namely technological capital (cumulative investments in R&D), into a production function in addition to capital and labour, these authors calculate a number of research elasticities of productivity. There are also many studies that have attempted to measure the relationship between patent applications and productivity growth. As far as the theoretical models are concerned, several models have been constructed that draw on endogenous growth theories, to which we referred in Chapter 1, and incorporate research as a factor influencing growth.

Table 5.1   Estimates of the R&D elasticity of output (after Cameron
(1998) based on a compilation of different syntheses)

Reference	Elasticity	Reference	Elasticity
United States		Patel and Soete (1988)	0.13 t
Griliches (1980a)	0.06 f	Mairesse and Hall (1996)	0.00–0.17 f
Griliches (1980b)	0.00–0.07 i	**Germany**	
Nadiri and Bitros (1980)	0.26 f	Patel and Soete (1988)	0.21 t
Nadiri (1980a)	0.06–0.10 p		
Nadiri (1980b)	0.08–0.19 m	**UK**	
Griliches (1986); Patel and Soete (1988)	0.09–0.11 f	Patel and Soete (1988)	0.07 t
Nadiri and Prucha (1990)	0.06 t	**Netherlands**	
Verspagen (1995)	0.24 i	Bartelsman *et al.* (1996)	0.04–0.12 f
Srinivasan (1996)	0.24–0.26 i	**G5**	
Japan		Englander and Mittelstädt (1998)	0.00–0.50 i
Mansfield (1988)	0.42 i		
Patel and Soete (1988)	0.37 t	**G7**	
Sassenou (1988)	0.14–0.16 f	Coe and Helpman	0.23 t
Nadiri and Prucha (1990)	0.27 i	**Countries in the Summers-Heston data base**	
France		Lichtenberg (1992)	0.07 t
Cunéo and Mairesse (1984)	0.22–0.33 f		
Mairesse and Cunéo (1985)	0.09–0.26 f		

Note: The estimates are calculated at different levels: f: firm; i: industry; t: total economy; m: total manufacturing sector; p: private sector.

The relationship between technical factors and productivity gives rise to certain paradoxes. The best known is that identified by Solow, who observed that productivity stagnates as investment in information technologies increases. Several explanations for this paradox have been put forward in the literature. The first is the one that was developed at some length in the first part of the book. It concerns the difficulty of defining and measuring productivity in a post-industrial or post-Fordist economy characterized by intangible outputs and subject to extremely rapid qualitative changes and innovation cycles. The second explanation is based on the notion of 'roundabout' production or hysteresis. After all, a technical factor does not impact immediately on productivity. There is in fact a time lag, which may be explained by the time required for an organization to absorb the new technology (reorganization time). At the macroeconomic level, this time lag can also be expressed in another way, namely in terms of the time required to ensure consistency between the various elements of the technical system, which may mean it is several decades before the rewards can be reaped in the form of increased productivity. The idea is that it is enough, as it were, to show patience for the effects of information technology on productivity to manifest themselves, whether at the micro- or macroeconomic level. If the previous explanation ('roundabout' production) is considered from a purely mechanical perspective, that is if the gradual reduction of the time lag is regarded as an automatic mechanism, then a third explanation can be envisaged (one that is only a particular form of the previous one if a broader meaning is attributed to it). This explanation is based on sociological factors that indicate a rejection of change (a refusal to reconfigure information and communication circuits). One last interpretation of the paradox involves challenging the hypothesis that there is a link between ICTs and productivity. According to this explanation, there is a tendency to exaggerate the consequences of ICTs and to be mistaken about their advantages. In many services, after all, only a small part of the production processes in question is altered by the ICTs. Furthermore, the costs of operating computer systems are significantly underestimated and limit the benefits in terms of productivity increases (CENV, 1998). This argument could be presented for a different point of view, by noting, for example, that the reasons for introducing computer systems extend well beyond the search for productivity gains and include a concern to improve quality, establish 'one-stop shops', introduce new services and so on.

Another paradox associated with productivity can be identified. Given the inadequacy of the various definitions, it may well be that investment in R&D will prove to be much higher than it currently is (Djellal *et al.*, 2003). Under these circumstances, a new paradox may be observed, whereby increased investment in R&D in services is not reflected in significant productivity gains.

To conclude this point, it should be remembered that productivity growth is frequently used in order to investigate technical change, although in this case technology is defined more broadly (by combining the elements mentioned above and some elements of the human and organizational factors).

HUMAN FACTORS

Human capital plays an essential role in productivity. Many theoretical models have highlighted the relationship between various aspects of human capital and productivity. Excluding the quantitative aspect, for simplicity's sake, two generic dimensions of human capital can be identified: first competences; and second effort.

Improving Competences: Training, Learning and Productivity

The quality of human capital (competences) plays an essential role in productivity gains. It influences productivity through two channels in particular: an enhanced aptitude for innovation and the introduction of innovations into an organization and an increased ability to transmit these competences to work groups. This question can be considered equally well at the microeconomic or macroeconomic level.

Many characteristics of human capital can give rise to differences in productivity; they include age, health, level of education, gender, and so on. We will focus here on two particular characteristics. In particular, the quality of human capital can be enhanced first by education and training; and second by learning phenomena.

Education and training
The main economic models that link education and training to growth and productivity can be divided into two groups:

- one group that links the rate of growth in output per capita to the rate of growth in the level of education;
- and one group that links this growth to the *stock* of human capital (and not to its rate of growth).

The model developed by Lucas (1988), which is regarded, along with that developed by Romer (1986), as the precursor of the endogenous growth models, belongs to the first group. In Lucas's model, the population decides, at any one time, between output and training. Training (the acquisition of human capital), which in this model is clearly dissociated from learning by doing, is regarded as roundabout production, the aim of which is to increase productivity in later periods.

Learning phenomena
This concept of learning is often associated with the observations made in the American aircraft industry during the inter-war period. A constant reduction in assembly times (and hence in unit production costs) was observed when output increased, this reduction being due not to returns to scale but to learning effects (repetition of movements, and so on).

This concept was subsequently developed into a theory by K. Arrow (1962), who links the overall productivity of the factors of production to cumulative gross investment. This cumulative investment is regarded as a good indicator of experience, since the introduction of a new piece of machinery creates a new atmosphere in production, which stimulates learning and knowledge. Barro and Sala-i-Martin (1995) use the expression 'learning through investment' to describe this positive impact of experience on productivity.

However, learning by doing is not the only form of learning. Contemporary economists (particularly evolutionary economists) have sought to highlight many other forms of learning (Malerba, 1992): (a) learning by using (Von Hippel, 1976; Rosenberg, 1982) or by trying (Fleck, 1994), which ultimately reflects the repetition of a person's own actions during the interaction with a given technical object; (b) learning by interacting (Lundvall, 1988; Von Hippel, 1988) or by consulting, which is based on repetition of the relationships with others; and (c) learning by searching (Cohen and Levinthal, 1989). All these forms of innovation also have an impact on productivity, and many of them could be said to be more appropriate for services than learning by doing (which has an industrialist connotation of repetition during the process of manufacturing a standardized and homogeneous good).

In evolutionary theory, these various forms of learning are considered to be the source of incremental innovations, which lead in turn to productivity gains which, in their cumulative effect, are much more significant than those produced by radical innovations (particularly those produced by research and development). Furthermore, individual learning is incorporated into so-called collective or organizational learning, which assumes that a firm or organization is able to learn more (or less) than the sum of its members. Organizational learning abilities also influence productivity.

Work Effort and Intensity

Work effort and intensity are human factors influencing productivity. However, the production of this effort and intensity often requires other factors to be mobilized, whether they be human (for example skills, learning), technical, organizational or social. It is this diversity and the indeterminate nature of the sources that suggested to Leibenstein the term X-efficiency (see Box 5.1). Thus any attempt to investigate the generic factors influencing productivity can approach this question of work intensity in different contexts and from different points of view. In other words, there are very many different routes, both direct and indirect, to increased productivity through work intensification (Burchell, 2002; Gollac and Volkoff, 1996; Green, 2001; Valeyre, 2002). Figure 5.2 presents some illustrations, although it is hardly exhaustive.

There is evidence in the recent literature to show not only that work has intensified in the developed economies but also that the form of this

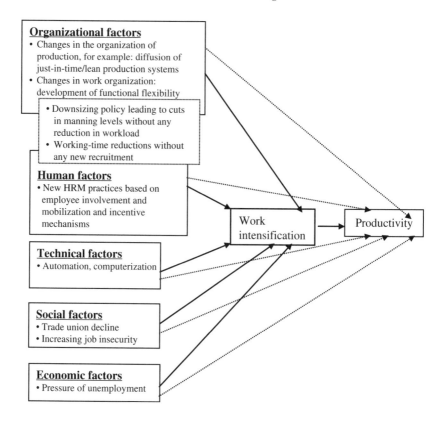

Figure 5.2   Work intensification and productivity

intensification has changed (Green, 2001; Valeyre, 2002). The Taylorist
forms of intensification (based on increased work rates and the elimination
of downtime) are still in evidence, often in a more relaxed form. However,
new forms of work intensification have emerged. Some of these might best
be described as market-driven forms, since they reflect strategies for rapid
adjustment, at any point in a company's production process, to pressures
generated by demand or by changes in the market or the competitive environment. Others are more event-driven and reflect the extreme urgency
with which any dysfunction (breakdowns and so on) must be treated. Thus
in its working conditions survey, DARES identifies six forms of work
intensification (work rate constraints):

1. automatic constraints imposed by machines, work flows or assembly
    line work;

2. event-driven constraints arising out of the urgent need to deal with dysfunctions;
3. constraints arising out of production standards and deadlines (when these have to be met in less than a working day);
4. management constraints impacting on work rates and resulting from the checks and controls carried out by managerial and supervisory staff;
5. horizontal constraints imposed by work groups; and
6. market-driven constraints generated by customer demands.

Specialists in management sciences have developed a theoretical corpus in the area of work effort and intensity entitled 'mobilization practices', which are examined in relation to performance (Barraud-Didier, 1999; Lawler, 1986). Mobilization is defined as effort or commitment directed towards a performance target by means of an increase in work motivation.

In management, mobilization practices stand in contrast to control and monitoring practices. They are based on the sharing out among all the members of an organization of the various factors that contribute to the organization's success, namely rewards, knowledge, power and information (Lawler, 1986).

BOX 5.1   X-EFFICIENCY THEORY

In 1966, Harvey Leibenstein published an article in the *American Economic Review* entitled 'Allocative efficiency vs X-efficiency'. In the article, he develops a very simple but resonant idea. According to Leibenstein, traditional microeconomic theory emphasizes allocative efficiency (that is efficiency in the allocation of resources) to the detriment of other sources of efficiency, which he regards as much more important and in which motivation and incentive occupy a central position.

X-efficiency is a reflection of managerial quality (good or bad). Managers, after all, determine not only their own productivity but also that of the production units for which they are responsible, since effort, which is an a priori variable in neoclassical theory, becomes a discretionary variable in X-efficiency theory.

Leibenstein provides a number of examples that tend to support the existence of X-efficiency. Thus a firm that has been facing productivity problems for many years sees it rise following a change of manager (without any other change).

Similarly, Hawthorne's effects suggest that, simply by taking an interest in a group's work, management can increase the group's output.

The psychological factors linked to motivation exert considerable influence over productivity. It would seem, for example, that:

1.   small production units are more productive than large ones;
2.   units made up of friends are more productive than those that are not;
3.   units that are supervised in a general way are more efficient than those supervised too closely; and
4.   units that understand the importance of their work are more efficient than those that are left in ignorance.

Explicit mention is also made of the role of consultancy services in improving management efficiency. In other words, some service activities play an important role in X-efficiency. Leibenstein even provides a justification for the use of consultants, since he shows that, in the cases he studied, the return to investment in consultancy is high: the productivity gain generated by consultants is considerably greater than the cost of hiring them.

ORGANIZATIONAL FACTORS

Organizational factors are not, of course, independent either of human or of technical factors. They are often determined (induced) by the latter and they influence the former.

We are dealing here with intra- and inter-firm organizational factors and not structural factors linked to market organization (which fall within the scope of economic factors). Organizational factors reflect a firm's internal organization: its mode of governance, type of division of labour or production method, recruitment techniques and payment systems. They also encompass the type of relations it maintains with its environment, whether with suppliers of goods and services, consultants, competitors, the public authorities, and so on.

These organizational factors could also include certain aspects, both tangible and intangible, of the way in which employees' working spaces and other facilities are organized. They encompass architecture and ergonomics (which may contribute to employees' physical, visual, aural and aesthetic comfort) as well as the provision of a large number of supplementary services (car parks, crèches, food or drink dispensers, canteens, sports facilities, and so on).

Another important factor is the measurement of productivity and, more generally, of performance. Measurement systems themselves (whether their purpose is to set targets and measure results, to calculate the necessary resources or to allocate those resources, and so on) can also be regarded as organizational factors influencing productivity.

This brief listing of the organizational factors influencing productivity illustrates the broad scope of a question that brings into play not only economics and management sciences but also psychology, architecture, ergonomics and physiology. From this general list of productivity factors, we will confine ourselves here to examining, largely from a theoretical perspective and in terms of their relationship to productivity, the following three factors, which once again are somewhat arbitrarily separated:

1. the organization of the production process;
2. the nature of firms' external relations; and
3. incentive systems (contract and incentive theory).

The Organization of the Production Process

To anyone investigating the organization of production processes (or indeed work organization) and its impact on productivity, three names come to mind immediately: Adam Smith, Taylor and Ford.

After all, it is Adam Smith, with his celebrated example of the pin factory, who is generally regarded as the begetter of the notion that specialization and the division of labour have a powerful influence on productivity. The productivity gains generated by the division of labour are, according to Adam Smith (1960), realized by means of three mechanisms: first, an increase in each worker's dexterity; second, the saving of the time required to move from one task to another; and third the use of machines to replace human labour.

Increasing returns to scale (economies of scale) are also important determinants of productivity. Numerous sources of economies of scale can be identified: the indivisibility of inputs, the laws of physics or geometry, the existence of fixed costs, the principles of bulk buying, of multiples, of accumulated reserves, and so on.

It was by exploiting this 'basic factor' (division of labour and productivity gains) that Taylor and Ford developed their work organization systems, which inspired (and continue to inspire) the development of a very large number of (productivity) management techniques in all sectors of the economy.

Taylorism (and the scientific organization of work) can be defined in a simplified way by reference to two major principles:

1. the horizontal division of the work process (Adam Smith's principle), in which each worker is allocated a simple, specialized task that represents just a small part of the overall operation. The productivity gains are generated by the manual dexterity engendered by repetition and the elimination of down time, whatever its cause: tool changes or change of action, deliberate ('systematic soldiering') or natural slacking;
2. the vertical division of labour, in which there is a strict separation between execution tasks and planning and control tasks. The planning or layout department plays an essential role, since it is here that the actions and postures most likely to increase productivity are defined. By measuring the time elapsed for each component operation of a work process, the planning department lays down standard times for each task and hence defines the target work rate.

Fordism was to add two further principles to the Taylorist principles of the horizontal and vertical division of tasks, namely assembly line work and component and product standardization. Henceforth, it was to be the speed of the assembly line that determined individuals' work rates.

As it expanded from the 1960s onwards, Fordism faced certain difficulties that affected the productivity gains that could be generated. First, it gave rise to demotivation and apathy among workers overtaken by boredom and a feeling of dehumanization. Second, the division of tasks (and the time required to execute them) was subject to obvious technical limits. Third, any increase in the horizontal division of labour gave rise to an increase in the vertical division (which manifested itself in an increasingly top-heavy and hierarchical planning office), making the organization unwieldy and increasing organization costs. Finally, as Fordism expanded, the returns diminished. Some activities lend themselves fairly well to this production system, while others, such as certain service activities for example, are more refractory.

Thus fragmented work organization systems began to be called into question for a combination of technico-economic and psycho-social reasons. As a result, the Fordist fortress was gradually eroded by the introduction of autonomous production islands, worker participation and flexibility (considered as a source of productivity gains). From the mid-1980s onwards, the proliferation of incremental changes made to the

Fordist system reached a threshold that justified the change of name to neo-Fordism or post-Fordism.

Thus Toyotism is one of the emblematic management cultures and labour processes of the post-Fordist era. Whereas the Fordist system was based on the mass production of standardized goods that downstream marketing departments had to sell, the modern, post-Fordist system is governed by upstream demand. On the basis of the demand expressed by customers, small series of products are manufactured to meet that demand. These smaller production runs do not, however, lead to reduced productivity caused by a decline in the level of specialization. In fact, this lower level of specialization results in task enrichment and productivity gains generated by increased motivation and the devolvement of responsibility to individual workers and the consequent elimination of control functions. Furthermore, the costs engendered by a more flexible production system are offset by the greater flexibility of information technologies (CNC machines that can be quickly reprogrammed). These new production systems, which generate productivity gains, are better suited to the specificities of a greater number of service activities than Taylorist and Fordist systems.

In order to evaluate the consequences of these post-Fordist changes and organizational innovations for company performance (and in particular for productivity), some statistical institutes have developed annual surveys. One such is Statistics Canada, which in 1999 launched an '(annual) workplace and employee survey'. As Table 5.2 shows, this survey serves as a basis for measuring, first, the frequency of innovative work organization practices (in reality post-Fordist) and, second, the frequency of organizational changes in private companies.

Some recent statistical studies have attempted to establish the relationship between these 'post-Fordist organizational innovations' (focusing solely on one of them or on an undifferentiated group) and productivity in firms. Thus Bélanger (2001, see also Bouliane, 2005) has evaluated the surveys devoted to the influence on productivity of the introduction of work organization systems based on increased worker participation. This evaluation produced the following results.

1. These 'high worker participation' systems are increasingly common in firms.
2. These 'organizational innovations' (like the others) influence productivity in different ways: by increasing output per individual, reducing the number of workers, intermediate consumption and breakdowns and improving the level of knowledge within the organization.
3. It is difficult to measure the actual impact of these changes on productivity, since other factors are also at work (economic situation,

Table 5.2 The items in the Workplace and Employee Survey questionnaire (after Bouliane, 2005:3)

Innovative workplace organization practices	Organizational changes
Sharing information with employees	Re-engineering
Employee suggestion programmes	Increased use of job rotation
Problem-solving teams	Adoption of variable working hours
Flexible task design	Increased integration
Joint employer–trade union committees	Implementation of total quality management
Autonomous work groups	Increased use of part-time workers
	Reduction of manning levels
	Increased use of outside suppliers
	Increased centralization
	Increased use of overtime
	Increased collaboration with other firms on R&D
	Increased use of temporary workers
	Decentralization
	Reduction of the number of layers of management

technical change, competition, and so on), from which it has to be isolated. Furthermore, the various studies do not interpret organizational innovation in the same way.

4. All the studies in the survey suggest there is a positive link between 'high worker participation' systems and productivity. However, the extent of the productivity gains generated is said to differ considerably from sector to sector, depending on the types of technologies used. Thus these organizational changes seem to generate greater productivity gains when they take place in a capital-intensive environment.

A report published by the European Work Organization (EWON, 2001) also sought to take stock of the relationship between 'new forms of working organization and the impact on performance' in Europe. As before, this investigation highlights the methodological difficulties inherent in any attempt to measure that impact. Nevertheless, the report concludes that there is a positive correlation in all the numerous case studies examined. Table 5.3 summarizes the main European studies mentioned in the EWON report.

Table 5.3   New forms of work organization and their impact on performance: the conclusions of some European studies (Bouliane, 2005)

Authors/ organizations	Country	Year	Target populations	Results
TNO (Dutch applied scientific research organization)	Netherlands	1999	3600 firms and their employees	Socio-technical production systems perform better
NUTEK (Swedish economic and regional growth agency)	Sweden	1996	700 private companies	Training and delegation of power to employees increase productivity by between 29 per cent and 60 per cent
Lay *et al.* (1999)	Germany	1999	1300 manufacturing companies	Productivity in the few companies that have adopted new forms of work organization is 8 per cent to 30 per cent higher
European Foundation for the Improvement of Living and Working Conditions	10 EU countries	1999	5800 managers EPOC Surveys (Employee Direct Participation in Organizational Change)	65 per cent of managers believe that increased worker participation is beneficial to firms in terms of productivity
Cully *et al.* (1999)	Great Britain	1999	Managers surveyed as part of the UK Workplace Employee Relations Survey	Identification of 16 innovative forms of work organization that generate productivity gains, according to the managers

More generally, a very large number of empirical studies in economics and management studies have been devoted to examining the link between a number of HRM practices (for example, profit-sharing systems, employee share ownership, different forms of formal or informal participation in work-related decisions, task enrichment programmes and the introduction of training programmes) and corporate performance, which is often evaluated in terms of productivity (for a summary see Barraud-Didier, 1999).

The Types of External Relations

An organization's external relations can be regarded as a particular aspect of the organization of the production process, which we have already considered above. After all, the relations that an organization establishes with its external environment (whether it be with suppliers, consultants, customers, competitors or even the government) can be more or less effective (that is they can affect its productivity gains to a greater or lesser extent).

External relations can be organized in a number of different ways, which constitute a form of innovation that is often underestimated in the literature. They include, among others, the new forms of partnership and service contracts or charters.

The question of outsourcing occupies an important place here. As far as its relationship to performance is concerned, there are two different aspects to be considered: the efficiency of the act of outsourcing itself, and the efficiency effects produced by the actions of the external service provider (and possibly the innovation produced).

Transaction cost theory has been successfully applied in attempts to explain outsourcing processes. Like agency theory, it is a theory of the contracts concluded between agents who find it in their interests to cooperate or trade. The difference between the two theories relates essentially to first, the nature of the rationality (substantive in the case of agency theory, bounded in the case of transaction cost theory) and second, the contract's sphere of application (essentially between different organizations in transaction cost theory, broader in agency theory).

The main idea in this theory is that use of the market reveals the existence of certain costs, known as transaction costs, which increase a product's price. These costs are the consequence, on the one hand, of the bounded rationality and opportunism that characterize human actions and, on the other, certain common characteristics of market transactions (uncertainties, complexity, reduced number of exchanges). Thus it is the existence of transaction costs that justifies the establishment of firms (hierarchies) when they prove to be a way of economizing on costly market transactions.

This theory is then extended to situations in which a choice has to be made between making or buying, that is between outsourcing and producing goods or services internally. Thus depending on the level of transaction costs, it may be in a firm's interest to outsource some of its activities or to use its internal resources.

Incentive Systems (Contract and Incentive Theories)

Many organizational arrangements (whether they be inter- or intra-organizational) put in place with a view to improving performance can be interpreted through the application of agency theory (Halachmi and Boorsma, 1998). Agency theory, a pillar of the renewal of neoclassical orthodoxy, is concerned with the relationship that is established between two economic agents whose interests do not necessarily coincide.

The agency relationship is an (incomplete) contractual relationship, implicit or explicit, in which the principal uses the services of an agent, who may be inside or outside his own organization, in order to carry out a given assignment. The agents in question may be individuals (an employer and his/her employee, a service provider and his/her customer, and so on) or organizations (a supervisory body and one of its establishments, a principal and a subcontractor or a contractor and a project manager, and so on).

The key element in agency theory and the agency relationship is the existence of informational asymmetries between the agents. After all, each agent has a certain amount of personal information about himself (his characteristics and his environment) and about his own actions to which the other agent is not privy. The underlying hypothesis of agency theory is that agents will seek to take advantage of these informational asymmetries and flaws in contracts, in other words that they will behave opportunistically. Such opportunism is, according to Jensen and Meckling (1976), the cause of three types of agency costs:

- monitoring and management costs, which are incurred by the principal in an attempt to reduce an agent's opportunistic behaviour;
- bonding costs, which are incurred by the agent as he seeks to gain the principal's trust; and
- residual costs, which represent the losses suffered by the principal following decisions by the agent that do not coincide with the principal's interests.

Overall, in the light of these informational asymmetries (moral hazard and adverse selection), an agent may be less efficient than he could be in providing the service. Thus much of the effort expended on the development of agency theory has focused on the scope, first, for drawing up explicit contracts that stipulate as clearly as possible both parties' objectives and, second, putting in place monitoring arrangements designed to assure both parties that their objectives have been achieved, and incentive mechanisms, whose purpose is to encourage both parties to ensure that the stipulated objectives are indeed achieved.

The extensive literature in this area contains discussions of many other problems and many suggestions for ways in which the analysis might be refined. These refinements may be particularly valuable when it comes to improving performance in the public services. Some of them are outlined below (HM Treasury, 2003):

1. When the agent's work involves producing many different outputs, very strong incentives are required if the agent is to focus effectively on those that are strongly influenced by external factors outside the agent's control (Holmstrom and Milgrom, 1991). One might add that too many productivity ratios kill productivity. It is evident (and this will be verified in the Post Office performance tree in Chapter 7) that a proliferation of productivity ratios does not facilitate monitoring but instead produces perverse effects. After all, managers never succeed in improving all these indicators. In certain situations, the efforts put in to improving one indicator may even impact negatively on another. Consequently, managers will tend to disregard the objectives in order to focus on their preferred indicators (selected on the basis of personal inclinations or factors in the external environment).

2. Making several agents compete in the performance of the same task is conducive to benchmarking and improved performance (Holmstrom, 1982).

3. A situation in which several principals are pursuing the same objectives encourages opportunistic behaviour of the type known as 'free riding'. It has a negative effect on performance (Dixit, 1996).

4. So-called implicit incentives, which arise when the agent is sensitive to incentives other than that offered by the principal (for example, when the agent is considering working for another principal in the future), tend to enhance performance (Dewatripont *et al.*, 1999).

5. Principal–agent relations at several hierarchical levels can lead to collusion or conspiracy. Tirole (1986), for example, examines a three-way relationship that introduces an intermediate level between principal and agent. He concludes that the agent on the bottom level and agent on the intermediate level may collude with each other. The principal should bear this in mind in formulating his incentive strategies.

ECONOMIC FACTORS

The main factors influencing productivity in this group are: overall demand, the unemployment rate, the exchange rate and the degree of openness to trade and to international investment. These are, for the most part, macro- or meso-economic factors.

1. Global demand and productivity are generally reckoned to be linked in three ways (Harris, 1999):
    (a) Through the 'Verdoorn' effect, in which a growth in demand gives rise to a growth in production and hence in productivity because of learning effects and economies of scale. The converse of this is that firms whose output declines because of a lack of demand also see a decline in productivity because of the reduction in economies of scale and learning effects.
    (b) A reduction in overall demand may give rise to an increase in the unemployment rate, which in turn leads to a loss of competence among the working population and hence to a decline in productivity. The hypothesis, therefore, is that prolonged unemployment destroys competence and thus impacts negatively on productivity.
    (c) A third approach to the relationship between global demand and productivity growth is associated with the Austrian school. The hypothesis here is that economic crisis (that is a drop in demand) has positive effects on productivity, since it facilitates and accelerates the elimination of obsolete technologies and encourages a more appropriate allocation of resources. This is Schumpeter's notion of 'waves of creative destruction'.
2. As far as the causal link between the exchange rate and productivity is concerned, several arguments can be advanced here too (Harris, 1999). The simplest of these is that when a national currency loses value, national companies reduce their efforts to improve productivity in order to withstand international competition (after all, these firms retain the same level of earnings in national currency). In classical macroeconomics, however, the opposite effect is posited, namely that it is the decline in productivity growth in a given country's industries relative to its trading partners that causes the deterioration in the exchange rate.
3. Over and above the exchange rate issue, many studies in international economics have highlighted the fundamental role played by openness to trade and international investment in determining productivity growth. Many arguments have been advanced in order to explain this causal relationship (Harris, 1999):
    (a) traditional arguments based on the notion of competitive advantage, which leads to better use of the available resources;
    (b) certain levels of economy of scale that small countries could not achieve if they were not open to trade and investment;

    (c) the diffusion and assimilation of ideas and technologies from abroad, as a by-product of international trade and foreign direct investment;

    (d) the increased importance of exports, which encourage productivity growth, as is well known . . .

4. However, other economic factors also play a role. They include industrial structure, organization size, labour mobility, tax burden, inflation rate, and so on.

SOCIAL FACTORS

These determinants go beyond the traditional economic framework. It is only relatively recently that they have attracted attention from researchers. The hypothesis here is that the socio-political environment can fundamentally influence the productivity of firms and other organizations (Harris, 2002).

The following are the main factors that are taken into consideration:

- wealth inequalities;
- earnings inequalities;
- the degree of social cohesion;
- political stability; and
- the climate of trust between social groups and freedom of association.

The position and role of trade unions and their relations with employers' organizations can also be included among these social factors (they could also be included with the political and institutional factors). Trade union action can have an effect on productivity, whether it be positive or negative. Trade unions can contribute to a decline in productivity or play a part in programmes to improve it. They also play a role in the distribution of productivity gains.

As Gamache (2005) notes, there is virtual unanimity as to the influence exerted by the socio-political environment on productivity, and the debate is concerned more with the methods used to measure the effects. Public services also play a role here.

POLITICAL AND INSTITUTIONAL FACTORS

These factors are closely linked to the social and macroeconomic factors. Their effect on productivity frequently makes itself felt through their influence on microeconomic factors (technical, organizational and human).

According to Harris (2002), government policies (whether macro- or micro-policies or social policies), the structure of the financial market and the nature of the various institutions (education, legal and political systems) also exert a medium- and long-term influence on productivity growth, in particular by acting directly or indirectly on many of the other factors (economic, technological, socio-political, and so on). Public services also play a role here, since they influence productivity in the other sectors of the economy.

CONCLUSION

The literature on the levers of productivity is sufficiently extensive to serve as a basis for drawing up a typology of the main generic factors influencing productivity (which have been outlined in this chapter). However, the links between the various levers and productivity itself are far from being definitively established. They constitute a tangled web of causalities, which may complement or contradict each other. They also manifest themselves directly or indirectly and according to different timescales and have to be analysed at different levels, whether micro, meso or macro. Most of the factors influence variables other than productivity. Thus they may have more general effects on overall performance. This applies, for example, to human factors such as training. Similarly, technical factors, particularly when they are based on ICTs (such as electronic government) do not necessarily (or solely) lead to increased productivity through the substitution of capital for labour, as was frequently the case in the early phases of computerization, but rather to a complementarity between capital and labour and the production of new services.

It should also be remembered that one of the essential factors influencing productivity is quite simply the *measurement* itself, when it is used as an incentive and as a basis for benchmarking.

All the generic factors examined in this chapter concern services and public services (whatever they may be) and internal service functions (including steering functions). Nevertheless, it is hypothesized that these generic factors can take a specific form in certain service sectors. In the following chapters, therefore, which are given over to the levers of productivity in market services and then in public and government services, we will be emphasizing these specificities. For example, we might point out that public services not only constitute a training ground for implementing levers of productivity but are themselves also a lever that can generate productivity gains in the other sectors of the economy, particularly, as we have already stressed on several occasions, through the political, institutional and social factors.

6. Productivity factors in services

INTRODUCTION

As was noted in Chapter 2, the specific characteristics of service activities influence the definition and measurement of productivity. Those same characteristics also affect the nature of the levers of productivity and the productivity strategies that firms adopt.

The literature in this area is particularly extensive. We propose, therefore, to offer a simplified survey, focusing on the theoretical analyses and attempting to identify some general principles and results. We begin by examining, from an essentially theoretical perspective, some generic productivity levers in services (particularly technical and human levers). We then go on to identify some more general strategies (that is strategies based on a number of different levers) that are deployed in service activities. Thus three groups of generic strategies are identified, which differ in the levers used, the way in which the different levers are incorporated into the strategy and the place occupied by productivity in the strict sense. The first group is made up of productivity strategies that attempt to eliminate the specific characteristics of services (we will call them assimilation strategies), while the second consists of specific rationalization strategies that seek to take account of the specificities of services (we will call them particularist or differentiation strategies). The third group includes strategies that attempt, within the same company, to strike a balance between the two previous objectives (we will call them integration strategies).

SOME PRODUCTIVITY LEVERS IN SERVICES

In recent years, much consideration has been given by both theoreticians and policy-makers to efforts to strengthen performance in the service sector. Attempts have been made to shape the policy, economic and institutional environments by implementing liberalization strategies, tax cuts and agreements on the international trade in services. We shall not attempt to analyze these general factors here, preferring instead to concentrate on the technical and human levers, which are all the more interesting for having long been regarded as the principal weaknesses of service activities.

We will consider them separately, even though they are even more difficult to separate out from each other in services than in manufacturing. It is seldom that any of these productivity factors comes into play in isolation; equally, they are seldom effective by themselves. Thus there are many cases in which a technical lever is placed in jeopardy because of a failure to act on the human lever.

The Technical Levers

In view of the proliferation of theoretical and empirical studies on this topic, a synthetic approach to the technical levers of productivity is adopted here. In particular, we intend to focus on the most significant theoretical models and on the general lessons that can be drawn from them. Thus we will begin by describing Baumol's model, which uses this technical lever to distinguish service industries from manufacturing industries. We will then turn to a particularly prolific group of studies, which we will describe as information technology impact analyses. We will examine several typological and theoretical approaches to technological trajectories in services (Soete and Miozzo's typology, Lakshmanan's typology and Barras' model). Whereas the first following sections will be concerned with the capital accumulation and in particular innovation component of the technical lever, the last section will be given over to the relationship between R&D and productivity in services.

Baumol's model

Baumol's model takes as its starting point a general hypothesis in which services are regarded as having a (naturally) low level of capital and technological intensity. Naturally, therefore, the technical lever of productivity has little impact on this type of activity. In a short article published in 1967, William Baumol put forward a macroeconomic model that was particularly simple but rich in implications in order to explain the hegemony of service sector employment. Baumol's so-called unbalanced growth model divides the economy into two sectors:

1. a sector (described as non-progressive) in which labour productivity is constant because of its low level of technological intensity; and
2. a sector (described as progressive) in which labour productivity increases because of the introduction of technologies.

According to Baumol, most services are in the non-progressive sector. Productivity gains are difficult to achieve because there are only limited opportunities for mechanization, since the final product is often one and the same thing as the labour that produces it. Baumol's argument is illustrated by some examples that are particularly rich in their implications and are now well known, such as the concert by a wind quintet: it is difficult to imagine how the quintet's productivity might be increased, and in any event such an outcome could certainly not be achieved by increasing the musicians' work rate.

Baumol's model includes two other important hypotheses:

1. Wages are the same in both sectors of the economy and they increase at the same rate as productivity gains in the progressive sector.
2. Production costs can be reduced to wage costs.

Taking these hypotheses as his starting point, Baumol diagnozes what he calls 'cost disease'. Since there are no productivity gains to be made and wages continue to rise, the unit prices of goods in the non-progressive sector (services) increase exponentially, whereas those in the progressive sectors (manufacturing industry) are constant.

Baumol's model produces three other results:

1. The products of the non-progressive sectors (that is services) for which demand is not highly price-inelastic (theatre productions, for example) will tend to disappear unless subsidized by the state.
2. Employment should gradually shift from the progressive sectors to the non-progressive sectors. Thus employment in manufacturing should tend asymptotically towards zero.
3. The overall rate of growth in an economy should tend towards zero (if the working population remains constant), since the sector in which productivity is constant accounts for all economic activity.

Baumol's models have given rise to much criticism. In particular, nobody can deny that the technological lever also plays a fundamental role in the dynamic of contemporary service societies. It should be noted that, in response to some of this criticism, Baumol himself put forward an adapted model in 1986 that takes account of the sometimes invasive introduction of computer technology into services. This new model comprises three sectors:

1. a sector in which productivity is increasing (for example consumer durables);
2. a sector in which productivity is constant (for example theatre productions, concerts and so on);
3. an intermediate sector characterized by asymptotic stagnation, that is one in which productivity begins by rising before stagnating because of

its hybrid structure (this is the case, for example, with information technology, which comprises hardware and software).

Information technology impact approaches to productivity

A whole host of studies have been devoted to the consequences of ICTs for productivity in services, at the micro-, meso- and macreconomic levels. These investigations, which focused initially on large, mass-market preindustrial companies (in banking, insurance and so on), now embrace other activities as well. Thus many studies (Djellal, 2002a, b; Secrétariat d'État au Tourisme, 2000, 2001) have pointed to the 'invasive' nature of NICTs, observing that their use has spread to services traditionally described as non-informational (for example cleaning and transport services, hotels and catering). Researchers have investigated the reasons for this 'invasion' and its theoretical consequences. The main explanation put forward is that the output in activities that traditionally involve the processing of material mediums has become more complex. As a result, there has been a shift away from activities dominated by goods and material processing functions and technical systems towards more complex activities, in which the output is enhanced, to varying degrees, in space and in time, by information, knowledge and relation processing operations. The theoretical consequences envisaged included, for example, the emergence of a productivity paradox in activities that hitherto seemed to have been unaffected by this phenomenon.

Two results should be highlighted. First, the theoretical effect of ICTs on productivity differs according to their nature (that is their location in the organization or production process). Thus back-office ICTs (particularly centralized computer systems) are regarded as having a positive effect on productivity. On the other hand, the impact of front-office ICTs is regarded as negative or indeterminate. Moreover, ICTs may influence variables other than productivity, particularly quality, spatial location, tradability, and so on.

In order to review in a very simplified way the extensive literature dealing with the impacts of information technologies, we will construct a matrix that combines the possible areas of impact (employment, skills and work organization, productivity, tradability and quality) with two successive models of technological innovation: the introduction, first, of mainframe computer systems and then of personal computers and networks. Some or all of the analytical concerns of a large number of studies fall within the scope of this 'matrix' (Table 6.1).

The first model, which is based on standardization, the Taylorization of tasks (data capture/keyboarding) and the exploitation of economies of scale, equates to the computerization of back offices. The main impacts

Table 6.1 Matrix of the main analytical concerns of IT impact studies in services

	Mainframe systems	Personal computers, networks
Employment		
Skills, work organization		
Productivity		
Tradability		
Service product (quality)		

expected in theory are a growth in productivity, a reduction in employment and deskilling of the labour force.

In the second model, personal computers and networks affect a very wide range of different tasks, not just back-office ones. Furthermore, they tend to generate economies of scope and to reduce routine tasks in favour of sales and advisory activities, which generate more value added. Thus the main hypotheses tested are summarized by the following question: does the introduction of personal computers and networks not give rise to increased employment, workforce reskilling and a reduction in productivity?

However, ICTs should not be considered solely in terms of their impact on services, which merely reflects the substitution of capital for labour. Account must also be taken of their increasing endogenization in service economies, that is the complementarity between capital and labour that they make possible. Services are no longer considered simply in terms of their adoption of ICTs, since they are also playing an increasingly active role in the production and diffusion of such technologies. For this reason, innovation in services is often regarded as a hybrid category combining ICTs and organizational engineering, that is the design and development of organizational forms.

In the light of these links and multiple effects, it has become increasingly difficult to measure the impact of ICTs on services. Any attempt to do so comes up against Solow's famous productivity paradox, that is the observation that, as new information technology is introduced, worker productivity may go down, not up.

This now longstanding question of productivity and its links with ICTs is far from exhausted. It lies at the heart of many recent studies, whether their aim is to assess the potential dynamism of 'knowledge-based economies' or to re-examine the problems Solow's paradox poses for particular activities. Thus Pascal Petit (2002) has analysed the growth and productivity potential of contemporary developed economies, which are characterized by a high degree of tertiarization and growth regimes based on waves of ICTs. Petit notes that this potential is considerable but that it is subject to numerous constraints and that it is unequally distributed among the various sectors and social categories. In order to re-establish some degree of equilibrium, it is not sufficient to redistribute productivity gains and the associated earnings. Significant changes also have to be made within 'disadvantaged' activities and groups. Petit examines the way in which the principal OECD countries have gone about 'expanding the base of this new growth' and paving the way for the knowledge-based economy. Two factors related to the service sector play an important role in this comparison: the countries' capacities to transform social services and services to households and their ability to make the complex or knowledge-intensive business services sector a generator of innovation and a medium for change and innovation.

A second theoretical perspective: technological trajectory approaches
The question of the link between technology and productivity also lies at the heart of several theoretical models of the service economy. In these models, the analyses are based on taxonomic approaches that identify those trajectories in which the productivity gains are mediated essentially by mechanization and NICTs. The same question also lies at the heart of Barras' reverse cycle.

Lakshmanan (1987) identifies the following three main types of services: 'service-dispensing activities', 'task-interactive services' and 'personal-interactive services'. Their characteristics are summarized in Table 6.2.

According to Lakshmanan, service-dispensing activities follow a 'natural' technological trajectory (in Nelson and Winter's sense of the term) characterized by a tendency towards increasing mechanization and the exploitation of economies of scale. Taking standardization as their basic principle, these activities make use of technologies involving the processing of large volumes of information and materials, such as cash registers in supermarkets (which in some ways are similar to industrial assembly lines), the technologies used to process mail in sorting offices and the various aspects of mechanization in the fast-food industry (hot chain, cold chain and so on). The technological trajectory at work in some task-interactive and personal-interactive services is intended to reduce communication costs. The favoured technologies here are the various information and telecommunications technologies.

Soete and Miozzo (1990), for their part, attempted to adapt the taxonomy of sectoral technological trajectories developed by Pavitt (1984) to services. In doing so, they identified a number of technological trajectories at work in different service industries:

Table 6.2   Taxonomy of technological trajectories in services

Type of service	Main characteristics	Technical innovations
Service dispensers (retail and distribution, telecommunications, fast-food industry)	Minimum contact with consumer, established production technologies, exploitation of economies of scale	Automation of many processes, ATMs, high-volume processing machines
Task-interactive services (accounting, legal and financial services)	Intermediate to high level of customer contact, unique customer requirements, high information needs, information subject to interpretation, customer objectives known but outcomes uncertain	Telecommunications introduced to increase efficiency and service quality, direct-access information systems
Personal-interactive services (health, social security)	Dynamic and uncertain environments, imprecise customer objectives, link between solution and outcomes difficult to measure, adverse selection and moral hazard	Rapid increase in use of equipment (for example medicine) Direct-access information systems

Source: Lakshmanan, 1987.

- Firms dominated by suppliers of equipment and technical systems, which are not very innovative and are content merely to acquire their process technologies from industrial suppliers. This first category can be further divided into two groups: personal services (repair services, cleaning, hotel and catering, retailing, laundry services, and so on) and public and social services (education, health, public administration).
- Network firms, which follow a technological trajectory based on cost reduction and networking strategies. They can also be divided into two groups depending on the principal medium of service delivery. Thus the taxonomy makes a distinction between physical networks, which are made up of firms whose services are based on tangible mediums (transport, wholesale trade), and informational networks, in which codified information is the medium of service delivery (finance, insurance, communications). Here, the power relationship between these firms and their equipment suppliers has been reversed to such an extent that it is possible to speak of industrial 'suppliers of technologies dependent on services'.
- Specialized suppliers and science-based services, which are particularly active in terms of technological innovations (which may be

based on their R&D activities). In particular, this category includes knowledge-intensive business services firms (IT services, engineering, and so on).

For Barras (1986, 1990), the various waves of computerization (mainframe systems, mini-computers and then personal computers and networks) gave rise to an innovation life cycle in services in which a phase of incremental process innovation gave way to a phase of radical process innovation and then to a phase of product innovation. This innovation cycle is the reverse of the traditional cycle described, in the case of manufacturing industry, by Abernathy and Utterback (1978). The innovation lies not in these technical systems themselves but rather in the change they make possible across the whole range of learning processes (learning by doing, using, interacting, consulting, and so on).

The incremental process innovations that predominated during the first phase of the cycle were back-office innovations aimed at increasing productivity (efficiency). They involved, for example, the computerization of insurance policy records and of personnel and wage records. The radical process innovations that took place in the second phase mainly affected front-office functions. Their main aim was no longer to increase efficiency (productivity) but rather to enhance performance in the sense of effectiveness. Examples include the computerized management of housing waiting lists in town halls, the on-line registration of policies in the offices of some insurance companies and computerized book-keeping in accountancy firms. The installation of ATMs in banks also belongs in this category. Product innovations, for their part, are still relatively rare, for the moment at least. Home banking is the most obvious example. Some aspects of electronic administration are another. However, there are also new services, still at the experimental stage, such as interactive and completely computerized auditing and accounting procedures in auditing firms or the entirely on-line services being introduced by insurance companies. The growth of this type of innovation will depend on the existence of a public informational infrastructure able to harness the capabilities of the enabling technologies.

R&D in services and the new productivity paradox
The question of R&D in services and its relationship to productivity is also particularly interesting, even though it is seldom discussed in the literature. The few existing studies conclude that R&D is weak in services and that it therefore has little impact on productivity.

However, some recent methodological studies have revealed that R&D in services is underestimated (Djellal *et al.*, 2001, 2003). Official definitions (particularly those in the Frascati Manual) take account only of scientific and technical R&D. In services, however, the content of R&D may be different.

In order to reflect to some extent the specificity of services, a new definition of R&D should take account of the following facts.

1. As far as the 'R' component is concerned, empirical investigations have confirmed that traditional (basic or applied) research is indeed carried out in services. They also show that service firms carry out research in the social sciences and humanities (again both basic and applied). Furthermore, this research in the social sciences and humanities occupies an essential place in services. The current definition of R&D does not exclude this area of research; as it stands, however, it cannot be used to break the 'industrialist' habit of considering such research as a very marginal activity and one in which the economic and strategic issues at stake are of lesser importance.
2. Within the social sciences and humanities, one specific area occupies an extremely important place, particularly as far as services are concerned. This is research into productive organizations and the behaviour of economic agents (particularly customers). Such research deserves to be explicitly included in the general definition. After all, research in these areas (non-technological R&D) has given rise to many innovations in services: new modes of service provision and new services, as well as new types of relations (new ways of organizing relations) with other partners, such as suppliers, for example, and so on.
3. There is considerable activity in services in the D component of the R&D process. An enormous amount of experimental development is carried out, which it would perhaps be more accurate to call design and development (D&D), particularly since the D&D process can take place without any prior R. This is the sphere of service or organizational engineering, where the focus is on the production of scripts, plans, models and blueprints and the arrangement of animate and inanimate 'objects'. This engineering or D&D involves putting into practice, as it were, the findings of SSH research into organizations and the behaviour of agents.
4. R&D projects in services are seldom specialized projects, that is they do not often fall within the scope of a single type of discipline. They are frequently composite projects, in which several families of disciplines are inextricably linked (technological R&D relating to hardware or software and non-technological R&D in the social sciences and humanities and organizational engineering). Clearly, a set of analytical or survey tools that captures only technological R&D will underestimate the R&D effort in service firms.

All things considered, if, as we believe, R&D is underestimated in services (for lack of an adequate definition), a new productivity paradox can be formulated: R&D in the service sector is not (adequately) reflected in the productivity statistics. To paraphrase Solow, we can say that 'we can see R&D everywhere, including in services, except in the productivity statistics'.

The Human Levers

The argument that has long prevailed is that human resources in services are of low quality. The literature contains many studies that caution against such a mistaken notion. Again, we will not examine the analyses in detail, but will confine ourselves to citing a number of resonant phrases. Thus in terms of job creation, for example, the service society is said to be nothing other than a 'servant society', a 'hamburger society' and a 'bad jobs society' (Bluestone and Harrison, 1986; Cohen and Zysman, 1987; Gorz, 1988; Thurow, 1989; Mahar, 1992).

If it is accepted, this hypothesis means that improving competences in services is a significant potential lever for productivity. All that needs to be done is to raise individual competence levels (which would not present an insurmountable difficulty, given the service sector's backwardness in this area) and productivity will rise. In fact, this general observation has to be qualified and any forecasts of the size of this reservoir of productivity scaled down.

These negative views of employment in the service society are, after all, counterbalanced by recent analyses which, continuing the work of Porat and, particularly, Bell (see Box 6.1), define contemporary economies and societies as information and knowledge economies and societies, characterized by a sharp increase in intellectual work. Thus, for example, Drucker (1989: 202, cited by Bonneville, 2001) notes that 'it was in the 20th century that intellectual work began to spread, and very quickly. In one century, the American population tripled, increasing from 75 million in 1900 to 250 million today; but over the same period, the number of teachers in higher education rose from 10 000 (most of them working in small parish establishments) to 500 000. All the other categories of knowledge workers – accountants, doctors, paramedical professions, analysts of all sorts, managers and so on – have expanded at a similar rate. And other countries have followed the same trend as the United States.' As Bell also observes, it is in the constantly growing service sector that these 'knowledge workers' are concentrated. The expansion of the service sector has changed the nature of human work and brought about the advent of a knowledge economy. As Perret (1995) notes, 'this development has affected all sectors to varying extents, including manufacturing: we are witnessing a "tertiarization" of work, defined broadly as an intensific-ation of the symbolic activities and social interactions that productive processes entail.'

BOX 6.1 THE THEORY OF THE POST-INDUSTRIAL SOCIETY: DANIEL BELL (1973)

In his major work entitled *The Coming of Post-Industrial Society*, the American sociologist Daniel Bell (1973) combines economic and sociological arguments in order to interpret positively the advent and domination of the service society.

The main arguments advanced in support of this thesis can be summarized as follows.

1. Post-industrial society is a service society. Services will inevitably be the main employers in such a society because of two fundamental economic laws: the law of productivity and Engel's law. Since productivity increases more rapidly in manufacturing than in services, it is only logical that employ-ment will increase less rapidly in the former sector. Further-more, Engel's law states that demand gradually shifts towards services as incomes rise. As a result, demand shifts first away from agricultural products towards manufactured products and then towards 'higher goods', that is services.

2. As this service society develops, higher-level services will develop in which the mediums of service provision are human beings and knowledge (in particular, health, culture, leisure, research and public administration), to the detriment of so-called lower-level services characterized by the processing of tangible goods (transport, distribution, and so on).

3. It establishes the primacy of theoretical knowledge and science-based technologies. For Bell, research organizations (universities, research centres, and so on) constitute the heart of the post-industrial society.

4. It also establishes the pre-eminence of the professional and technical classes. The post-industrial society is characterized by an extraordinary increase in the number of 'white-collar' workers (that is professionals in possession of knowledge: teachers, health professionals, management specialists, lawyers, engineers, and so on). On the other hand, the working class will gradually disappear.

5. Finally, the post-industrial society is characterized by a change in value systems. The sociologistic value system, based on the general interest and social justice, will tend to replace the economistic system dominated by problems of cost.

Once again, examination of the statistics makes it easy to demythologize analyses that purport to show that service sector jobs are inherently low skill. While it is true that service societies create deskilled jobs, it is equally true that they now provide most of the openings for high-level managers and professionals (Noyelle, 1986; Gadrey, 1996b; Meisenheimer, 1998; Rubalcaba, 2007). Table 6.3 illustrates this to some extent in the case of France (for the period 1985–2002) by tracing the evolution of 'manual' jobs and of jobs for 'managers and the higher intellectual professions' in manufacturing and industry. The figures show that, while there was indeed a steady increase in the share of manual workers in services, the share of 'managers and higher intellectual professions' also rose constantly, and more rapidly than in manufacturing.

Overall, therefore, there are more managerial jobs in services than in manufacturing. Certain service activities that are particularly dynamic in contemporary economies have the highest competence levels: this applies, for example, to knowledge-intensive business services (consultancy, engineering, R&D). Their competence levels are defined by the very terms of their remit, which is to provide support for companies and organizations seeking to develop their own technological, managerial and strategic competences. It should be noted that the (internal) design, planning and steering functions that concern us here fall into these categories. This rise in competence levels also applies, at the opposite extreme, to operational services, which have not traditionally been knowledge-intensive. Thus in cleaning services (Djellal, 2002b), for example, which are sometimes regarded as the last refuge of the least skilled jobs, two different employment systems, associated with different innovation models, can be identified:

1. a neo-Taylorist system based on quantitative flexibility and characterized in particular by a workforce that is predominantly female, foreign and low skill, extensive use of part-time work and a low rate of managerial staff;
2. an (emerging) model based on organizational adaptability and characterized by the increased professionalization of cleaning services. In this model, the rates of feminization and part-time working are lower, there is a higher share of managerial staff and new functions are emerging.

Table 6.3 *Employment by sector and occupational category: evolution from 1995 to 2002 as a percentage of total employment in each sector. Numbers employed in thousands in brackets*

	1985		1990		1995		2002	
	MHIP	M	MHIP	M	MHIP	M	MHIP	M
Manufacturing and construction	6.7% (462)	58.3% (4038)	8.0% (521)	56.2% (3664)	8.8% (507)	53.8% (3061)	10.1% (581)	53.5% (3075)
Services	11.6% (1468)	16.5% (2084)	13.6% (1907)	17.1% (2411)	15.4% (2358)	16.7% (2552)	17.0% (2926)	16.6% (2862)

Key: MHIP = managers and higher intellectual professions. M = manual workers. Example: in 1995, the number of manual workers was 3 061 000, which represented 53.8 per cent of employment in manufacturing (including construction).

Source: Insee, annual employment surveys; Gadrey, 2003.

THREE PRODUCTIVITY STRATEGIES

Since our purpose here is to offer a general survey and not to itemize all the practices and strategies actually put in place, we can start by noting that the productivity strategies adopted in services can be based on three different principles. The first involves doing everything possible to ensure that services resemble (standardized) goods. This is the assimilation principle. The second involves taking advantage of the specificities of services (particularist or differentiation principle). The third and final one constitutes an attempt to strike a balance between the previous two principles; this can be done in various ways, for example by adopting assimilation strategies in certain areas of the activity and differentiation strategies in others, or by developing integrated systems.

Assimilation strategies

The aim of these strategies is to eliminate the specificities of services, to make them differ as little as possible from goods. Consequently, they have to be made less ill-defined, less (or not at all) interactive and less immediate. Diversity has to be reduced in order to develop a product that can be embodied in an explicit contract. When these aims are achieved, the determinants of productivity are absolutely the same as those used in manufacturing. It follows, therefore, that attempts can be made to improve productivity by drawing on any of the factors identified in the previous chapter.

Table 6.4   Industrial rationalization and professional rationalization (after Gadrey, 1996a)

	Industrial rationalization (industrialization)	Professional rationalization
Evolution of content of operational work	• drive for high level of process standardization • high degree of specialization • application of very detailed programmes developed by the 'technostructure'	• improvement of methods, procedures formalized in as much detail as possible • gradual development of individual and collective routines based on experience of service delivery • learning how to adapt to cases outside the norms, which are usually in the majority
Evolution of 'products' and outcomes of services provided	• services provided in the form of quasi-products or 'standard contracts' • possible nomenclature of cases ('range' of products offered) • low level of individualization	• dialectic between the standardization of cases ('typification') and their increasing complexity (integrated services) • dialectic between standardization of cases ('typification') and individualization of solutions
Performance evaluation criteria	• productivity (quantitative measurement by groups of standard cases) • emphasis on control of resources, monitoring of work and standard costs	• multi-criteria, multi-actor evaluation • emphasis on monitoring of outcomes • institutional quality standards for profession

Thus assimilation strategies are synonymous with industrialization strategies. Despite being frequently used, this notion is particularly vague and can mean several different things. It can be assumed, as Gadrey (1996a) suggests, that in general terms, 'the notion of industrialization denotes a process whereby an organizational category that is not part of the industrial world tends to move closer to that world, at least on certain levels that are regarded as significant'. An analysis of what characterizes the industrial world in terms of its operational principles (particularly work organization and performance assessment criteria) reveals various complementary facets of industrialization (see Table 6.4).

Thus according to Gadrey (1996a), if the industrial world is defined by its production of material or tangible goods, then industrialization denotes a process of evolution towards the production of tangible goods, to the detriment of the provision of intangible services. In other words, the industrialization of services involves replacing intangible services with tangible goods that provide (or are supposed to provide) the same utilities. The best-known theoretical model developed on this basis is probably the theory of the self-service society developed by Jonathan Gershuny (1978, 1983) and Gershuny and Miles (1983) (see Box 6.2).

BOX 6.2   THE SELF-SERVICE SOCIETY ACCORDING TO JONATHAN GERSHUNY (1978)

Gershuny's thesis belongs to the 'neo-industrialist' school of service economics. It stands in opposition to the so-called 'post-industrial society' theories generally associated with the American sociologist Daniel Bell (see Box 6.1). Drawing in particular on the 'new consumer theory' derived from the works of Lancaster and Becker, it affirms 'the pre-eminence of goods over services'. In other words, in contrast to Bell's prediction, the developed economies are not, it is argued, evolving towards a service society but rather towards a self-service society. Gershuny's main objective is to develop a theory (of the growth and relative decline) of services.

His analysis is constructed around the following three strands: the contrast between the formal and informal sectors, use of the notion of function (or service function) and the introduction of the notion of social innovation as a complement to Engel's law.

Gershuny examines the structure of final consumption (or needs) not through the traditional categories of goods and services but rather in terms of functions: food, housing, leisure, transport, education, health functions, and so on. For Gershuny, these functions can be satisfied in two different ways. Consumers can, in his own terminology, make use either of the formal sphere (that is obtain services from an external provider) or of the informal sphere. In the latter case, two factors are combined, namely a purchased good (item of equipment) and the domestic work required to operate it. There are many examples of this alternative. To mention only the most obvious ones, they include the transport function, which can be satisfied by using a private vehicle, public transport or a taxi, and the leisure function, which can be satisfied by going to the theatre, cinema or a concert or by purchasing audio-visual equipment (radio, television, video recorder, and so on).

On the theoretical level, Gershuny does not refute Engel's law, which is used in post-industrial society theory (that is, the shift in final demand from goods towards services), but considers it in terms of service functions. Thus the hierarchy of needs is itself shifted away from the dualism of goods (lower) and services (higher) towards a hierarchization of functions (the leisure function is higher than the food function, for example). This means that the share of goods in the composition of a household's final consumption can rise relative to that of services while remaining (paradoxically) consistent with Engel's hierarchy.

Within the same function, the transition from the formal to the informal satisfaction of needs is described as social innovation. In other words, a social innovation reflects the change in the way consumers satisfy a need (function); it has both a technological and a social component.

Analytical and statistical implementation of this theoretical apparatus leads Gershuny to conclude that social innovation produces a shift away from a service society towards a self-service society (preference for the 'informal' satisfaction of needs).[1] This is clearly a reversal of the main conclusions of post-industrial society theory. The self-service society would, after all, be characterized by the primacy of goods over services in final consumption and of the individual over the collective. The main analytical argument advanced in explanation of these developments is the tendency in services towards relative lower productivity and hence to higher prices relative to goods.

Can an approach of this kind be consistent with the observed increase in the number of service jobs? Do public services not constitute a counter-example to the prospect of widespread self-service? These are the two main questions that are generally levelled at the theory of the self-service society.

Gershuny advances two arguments to counter the paradox expressed in the first question. The first concerns the productivity gap between the sectors: productivity in manufacturing is rising more rapidly than in services, he argues, which means employment growth will be stronger in services. The second relates to the development of services linked to manufacturing: these are not services intended for final consumption by households ('final services'), which are the sole object of Gershuny's thesis, but 'intermediate services'.

In response to the second question, Gershuny advances an argument that looks to the future. In his view, public services (education, health, administration, and so on) will enter the informal sphere under pressure from social innovations that are currently emerging but have not yet reached maturity. Computer-assisted teaching and medical diagnosis and the Open University are harbingers of a general trend.

Of the two most fundamental criticisms levelled at the theory of the self-service society, one is empirical in nature, the other theoretical. The statistical analyses carried out by Gadrey (1985) and Delaunay and Gadrey (1987) in the case of France do not confirm the argument that goods are being substituted for services. The theoretical criticism concerns the notion of 'service function'. The economic (and economistic) argument Gershuny advances in order to explain why needs will be satisfied mainly in the informal sector does not take sufficient account of socio-cultural variables. The service function cannot be understood solely as a technical concept; rather, it must be broken down into a number of social functions (Gadrey, 1985; Delaunay and Gadrey, 1987). Thus in the transport function, for example, the 'formal solution' (that is, the use of public transport services) is very often the least expensive, as some studies have shown; nevertheless, this has not prevented the self-service option (that is the use of private vehicles) from being the predominant solution. As Gadrey (1985: 20) notes, this is because 'it is far from being obvious that these two solutions equate to the same "function", that is to the same type of travel need (for work or not, within urban areas or long distance, and so on)'. Similarly, in the catering function, the formal solution has gained from socio-cultural changes (such as the increase in women's employment, for example), even though it is more expensive.

If the industrial world is defined in terms of a certain mode of production (the type of work organization and technologies that predominated in the heavy industry of the post-war period), then industrialization will denote the tendency to transfer that mode of production to service firms and organizations. As Gadrey (1996a) rightly notes, given the extreme diversity of past and present manifestations of the industrial world, any reference to that world loses its meaning if the particular industrial world in question is not specified. The most practical and most frequently used reference point is probably the heavy industry of the post-war period. In this case, the industrial world (the model for the industrialization of

services) can be described in terms of the following characteristics
(Gadrey, 1996a):

- the work procedures in use in operational centres, which are responsible for producing or selling goods or services, are highly standardized and specialized (rigid division of labour);
- the job of the specialists in the technostructure is to design the organizations and standardize and monitor tasks;
- the organizations produce standardized services (quasi-products) on
  a large scale (mass production);
- these organizations prove to be fairly effective in a simple and stable
  environment. They enter into crisis when this environment becomes
  complex and uncertain.

In the first case, industrialization is regarded as the process leading to the
replacement of services by manufactured goods used in the home (self-
service), for example the substitution of domestic washing machines for
launderettes or watching a DVD at home rather than going out to the
cinema, and so on. In the second case, industrialization denotes the standardization of work procedures which, in the case of services, is synonymous with or leads to standardization of the service itself. The product, in
this case, is not a good but a quasi-product: for example a standard insurance policy or financial product, a standard holiday, a standard fixed menu
in a fast-food restaurant. In this case, industrialization means ceasing to
handle non-standard cases.

In the management literature, the assimilation strategy has sometimes
been established as a strategic rule. Levitt (1972) advocates the systematic
industrialization of services, particularly through the use of industrial production methods. Similarly, Shostack (1984) sees this industrialization
strategy as a solution to the 'divergence' (degree of freedom) and complexity of service provision; at the same time, she recommends (Shostack, 1984)
the development of flowcharts or blueprints of the service delivery process
(see Figure 6.1). These flowcharts are, indeed, similar to a service production 'manual'. It is undoubtedly Shostack (1981, 1984) who has made the
greatest contribution to our knowledge of these concepts and instruments,
whose usefulness she defends in normative terms. However, other authors
(Lovelock, 1992; Kingman-Brundage, 1992) have also contributed to the
development of this type of diagrammatic representation, on both the
empirical and the theoretical levels.

Kingman-Brundage (1992) identifies two types of blueprints representing the process of service provision: a 'concept blueprint', which gives an
overall view of the service, that is it shows the way in which each function

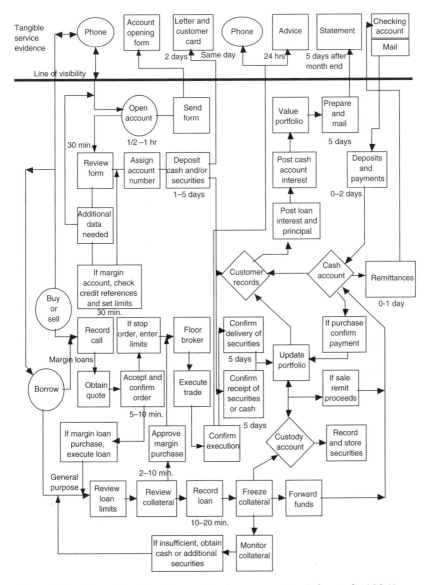

Figure 6.1   Blueprint of a discount brokerage service (Shostack, 1984)

or department fits into the overall service, and a 'detailed blueprint', which describes the service in detail.

A blueprint is task-oriented, that is it represents the basic actions performed by the various parties involved in the process of service provision.

However, it describes both a process, that is a set of actions or tasks performed in order to achieve an objective (service characteristics), and a structure, that is physical installations, an organizational structure, computer network, and so on. In a theoretical (general) blueprint, the structure is represented by a vertical axis along which are positioned the service firm's internal management functions, the support functions and the interaction with customers. Various 'demarcation' or interaction lines are drawn between the various elements in the structure (customer interaction line, line separating what are traditionally known as the front and back offices, internal interaction line, and so on). The process is represented by a horizontal axis, along which are positioned the various basic actions carried out in sequence by those involved in providing the service.

The blueprint can serve many functions and involve different departments in a service firm. It is a tool that enables customers to 'imagine' the service on offer, just as the future owner of a house under construction might examine the architect's plans. In its simplified versions, therefore, a blueprint can be used as a communications and marketing instrument. It also enables service providers themselves to gain a better understanding of the service they are providing and to monitor quality. Thus staff training can be based on the blueprint, particularly when a new service is being launched. In a way that is, paradoxically, both Taylorist and anti-Taylorist, a blueprint locates each individual's task within a process but also enables individuals to locate their own function within the system as a whole. Finally, it can help to improve the service being provided (incremental improvement innovation). In a vaguely defined service provided informally, an incremental improvement is not visible. In this sense, a blueprint provides those responsible for developing a service reference points for implementing improvements. The blueprint can also be regarded as a sort of prototype.

It should be noted that the application of Taylorism and Fordism (mass production of standardized goods to be sold by marketing departments) is ultimately limited to a small number of service activities, such as fast-food restaurants, large-scale retailing, mail sorting offices, and so on. It is post-Fordist systems (governed by upstream demand and producing small series of products designed to meet the needs of particular groups of customers) that will be applied to a greater number of services.

There is probably another mode of industrialization, which is located at the intersection between the previous two. It is associated with information and communication technologies, and in particular with their use in service delivery. After all, the provision of a wide and open range of electronic services, in a variety of different fields, also reflects a certain form of industrialization. However, it is true that computerization in its decentralized, networked form can also be seen as a fundamental factor in integrationist productivity strategies, serving as a basis both for 'servicization' processes assisted by decentralized computer systems and for more standard industrialization processes associated with back-office computer systems.

Rationalization can also be defined in terms of performance assessment criteria. Thus industrial rationalization emphasizes productivity, that is quantitative measurements based on groups of standard cases. This form of rationalization uses productivity indicators to evaluate performance. The hypothesis advanced here is that measurement of these indicators may indeed pose problems in services but that those problems can be resolved by methodological improvements and technical refinements. Above all, however, this form of rationalization leads to products being designed (both in their functional characteristics and the processes used to produce them) in such a way that they can be measured in terms of productivity indicators. In other words, assimilation strategies are not confined simply to application of a technical concept, which is valid by definition, but they also construct that validity. They influence both theoretical concepts and products.

Differentiation Strategies

The dominant hypothesis here is that services have certain specificities that have to be taken into account or that have to be maintained (that is prevented from disappearing). Consequently, industrialization in the sense of the term used in the previous section is neither practicable nor desirable. This does not mean, however, that all strategies for improving productivity or performance have to be abandoned. Indeed, there are certain strategies for rationalizing production processes and products at work (or waiting to be mobilized) that should not be confused with industrialization. Some service activities are better suited than others to these particular strategies, the main ones being services with a high cognitive and relational content (professional services).

Gadrey (1996a) uses the term 'professional rationalization' (see Table 6.4) to denote these strategies for improving the performance of professional services. According to Gadrey (1996a), this professional rationalization, which should not in any way be regarded as synonymous with industrial rationalization (or industrialization), manifests itself in two different ways:

1. Institutional rationalization (regulation), which involves establishing rules governing the entire profession. The most obvious of these rules are the barriers erected at the entry to certain professions. However,

there are also rules that fix or influence working methods and procedures (particularly good and bad working practices).

2. Cognitive rationalization, which can be embodied in three strategies:
(a) the standardization ('typification') of cases; (b) the formalization of
problem-solving procedures (methods); and (c) the use of individual or
organizational routines. As far as the process of standardization in
consultancy services is concerned, the aim will be, for example, to identify standard cases, standard contracts and standard solutions. Efforts
to formalize cognitive procedures will focus on the development of
problem-solving methods or methodologies. Routines, for their part,
are automatic response programmes to the problems encountered by
individuals or organizations. They are acquired through individual or
organizational learning processes. The standardization ('typification')
of cases, the formalization of methods and the use of routines are not,
of course, rationalization processes that exist independently of each
other. This is particularly evident in the last two cases, since methods
can be defined as the linking of routines in sequence.

It is this second type of rationalization that is of greatest significance for
our investigation of performance and productivity. After all, it is at this level
that a firm can really have a decisive effect on the levers of performance.
This cognitive rationalization has several effects or consequences. First, it
is a means of saving on resources, particularly time. Standardization
('typification'), formalization and routines make it possible to perform
the same tasks more quickly. They are sources of productivity gains.
Nevertheless, the dominant criterion for assessing performance is not productivity. In professional rationalization, multi-criteria and multi-actor
assessment indicators are favoured, with an emphasis on monitoring outcomes and adherence to the profession's quality standards. Cognitive rationalization emphasizes the accumulation of past experience and the
establishment of an organizational memory. Ultimately, it enables firms to
become the dominant partner in their relationships with customers by
exploiting the difference in expertise derived from past experience (memory)
and the competitive advantage conferred by improvements in methodology.

In earlier studies of consultancy activities (Gallouj, 1994), we identified
two generic modes of accumulating and circulating expertise and experience
in which the various aspects of this cognitive rationalization are reflected:
first, strategies whose aim is to accumulate knowledge within consultants'
memories or to optimize the accumulation process (recruitment and out-
placement strategies, training and socialization strategies, and so on);
second, modes of accumulation based on physical media, such as paper and
computer and audiovisual media. A variety of situations can be observed

here, ranging from the mechanical accumulation of output to strategic accumulation based on clearly defined procedures and mechanisms and objectives consistent with the consultancy company's overall strategy. The frequency of this latter mode of accumulation increases with size of firm.

Thus the knowledge accumulated in inanimate media by a consultancy company can be placed in one of three categories depending on the extent to which the initial material has been subject to 'formal' transformation (exploitation).

- Raw accumulation
  This denotes the systematic accumulation of knowledge and experience without any real transformation of the material. It falls within the scope of the standard documentation function. This category includes academic knowledge, scientific and technical information, legal opinions, which are the basic informational input in the case of legal consultancy, candidates' applications in the case of recruitment consultancy, market data and documentation stored in its 'raw' state: memos, notes, contracts, correspondence relating to a contract and so on.
- Selective accumulation
  Here it is the normative dimension that predominates in the management of experience. The provision of any service is followed by a process of sorting, selection and standardization, with only those 'experiences' that are genuinely new being retained in such a way that they can be reused in one way or another. Experience thus captured can be exploited in two different ways. Most of the time, this function is the responsibility of, or dependent on, the consultant or consultants who provided the service. However, it may also be entrusted to a 'specialist' consultant. Such a situation is fairly rare, but we have encountered it in large consultancy companies. The aim is to use this form of specialization in order to prevent 'withholding' behaviours and to optimize the process.
- Formalized accumulation
  This is a mode of accumulation that usually follows the previous one, with the aim of making an organization's expertise reproducible, both internally and externally. This category includes all the experience and know-how embodied in methods, tools, software, standard contracts and publications.

When professional rationalization is taken to extremes, it is impossible not to equate it with industrialization. Thus there are professional service activities that are concerned only with identified standard cases. In the area of medical services, for example, one example would be a private clinic that treats only inguinal hernias and has taken standardization to the point where obese people or patients with a history of heart disease suffering from hernias are refused treatment (Djellal and Gallouj, 2005). This clinic provides highly standardized treatment packages and makes use of surgeons who have achieved high levels of productivity in their work. In some areas there are also clear trends towards self-service. However, as Gadrey (1996a) notes, this industrialization of professional services has to be regarded as the exception rather than the rule.

According to Gadrey, several arguments can be advanced to explain why most professional services are unlikely to be industrialized and, consequently, why particularist strategies are likely to be favoured, at least in many professional services.

The first argument is that standardization, the development of 'quasi-products', cannot be reduced to a strategic decision taken by a service provider. It is not sufficient simply to decide that it will happen, since it depends crucially on the 'nature of the problems to be solved'. However, the nature of these problems, like the corresponding solution, often proves resistant to any attempt at standardization. Since the customers themselves have a high level of professionalism, implementing standardized solutions is often perceived as intellectual weakness on the service provider's part, when it is not seen as a swindle pure and simple. The second argument is that the service relationship is fundamental to this type of activity, whether in identifying the problem or jointly developing a solution. Standardization, however, simply serves to undermine that relationship or even destroy it altogether. The third argument concerns the information sources required for industrialization. In the industrial model, the technostructure holds the information required to develop and monitor procedures. In professional services, however, it is the professionals themselves (consultants, doctors, professors) who hold the information required for industrial rationalization of work procedures and not the technostructure or the management structure, where they exist.

Integration Strategies

Different arguments can be deployed to justify differentiation and assimilation strategies. They may be necessary, to some extent, because of the basic nature of the service in question: industrialization may seem either unlikely (this applies to most professional services, particularly consultancy services) or, conversely 'natural'.

Both types of strategy may result from a managerial decision taken in the light of the economic and technological environment (a different choice

Table 6.5 Different strategies in the same sectors

	Assimilation strategies	Differentiation strategies
Banking	ATMs, electronic banking	Account management, advice
Restaurant trade	Fast food	Gastronomic restaurant
Retail and distribution	Discount stores, automated warehouses, e-commerce	Local shops
Health	Automated diagnosis, highly specialized treatment centres	Intensive care units in a regional hospital centre
Travel agency	On-line agency	Traditional agency
Hotels	Budget hotel	Traditional luxury hotel

being conceivable). Thus at any given time, service firms operating in the same sector may make different strategic choices. Numerous examples can be cited, whether in catering, health, distribution, banking, and so on (see Table 6.5). Thus a firm in the restaurant business might adopt an assimilation strategy (that is industrialization) by developing the fast-food formula (Taylorist division of labour in a highly mechanized central kitchen, very limited customer contact), the most famous example being that of McDonald's, of course. Conversely, it might adopt a particularist (differentiation) strategy based on an artisanal (and artistic) form of work organization and extensive customer interaction.

However, firms can simultaneously adopt opposing differentiation and assimilation strategies. This is what we denote here by the term synthesis or integration strategies. Such strategies are particularly common in large companies in the banking, insurance, retail and distribution, tourism and transport sectors, for example.

Strategies which, at certain times (today in particular), have been described as integration strategies are in reality frequently part of an historical process that has unfolded in two successive phases, the first dominated by assimilation strategies (industrialization) and the second by differentiation strategies, reflecting the rise to prominence of the service dimension. In other words, in the service activities under consideration here, there was initially a tendency to replace the original artisanal mode of organization with an industrial mode based on productivity gains; this was followed by a second phase in which customized services, the service relationship and so on were reintroduced (Sundbo, 1994, 2002). The term synthesizing or integration strategy is used to reflect the fact that the new differentiation strategies did not replace the assimilation strategies.

This progression over time from industrialization to a renewed emphasis on the specificities of services (servicization), as well as the possible co-existence of these two approaches in certain firms, can be illustrated by examples drawn from a number of service activities.

The (long-term) development of large cleaning companies is our first, very interesting example. The industrialization phase, which seems particularly appropriate for a highly labour-intensive, low-skill activity, essentially involved increasing capital intensity by introducing various cleaning technologies (robotization of certain cleaning processes, installation of specific cleaning cradles, introduction of trolleys adapted to particular environments, and so on), putting in place standard cleaning protocols and monitoring work (for example through the use of quality control and job description software, and so on) in order to obtain a standardized output, namely 'surface cleanliness'. The subsequent differentiation phase (servicization) was characterized by an increase in the diversity and complexity of the 'outputs'. Thus these firms moved from providing a standard cleaning service that made intensive use of low-skill labour towards services requiring high skill levels and a certain degree of initiative: bio-cleaning in hospitals, cleaning integrated into the production and bacteriological monitoring processes in the agro-food industry, 'computer cleaning' and so on.

Examination of the long-term evolution of the retail and distribution sector shows that, from the 1940s and 1950s in the USA and from the 1970s in France, supermarkets followed a natural technological trajectory of increasing mechanization and economies of scale based on two fundamental innovations: self-service and the establishment of chains of stores. For a long time, the innovation model at work focused essentially on the materials logistics function (introduction of Fordist logistical systems) and on strengthening the self-service relationship and then, in a second phase, on the information logistics function. For some years in the USA, and more recently in France, change in the retail and distribution sector has taken two new directions, both of which fall within the scope of a relational trajectory (Gadrey, 1994):

1. The addition of 'new services' or new service relationships, which equate to new functions or sets of new service characteristics and reflect the adoption of two different strategies (which sometimes become merged): supply support strategies and strategies based on the conquest of new markets. The new services include, for example, information terminals for customers, bagging at the checkouts, crèches, home deliveries, the development of financial and insurance services, the opening of travel agencies and petrol stations and the introduction of individualized counter services.

2. The improvement of service relationships through the introduction of loyalty and credit cards and other benefits for loyal customers. In other words, the natural (material and informational) technological trajectory that is still at work has had another trajectory superimposed on to it, one that might be described as a contact or relational service trajectory.

Finally, the dialectic between industrialization (assimilation) and servicization (particularism or differentiation) is particularly evident in financial services. Large banks and insurance companies today combine standardized quasi-products and automated self-service, on the one hand, with 'high value-added' and tailor-made services, on the other; these latter developed in the context of highly interactive service relationships in which customers play an active role. The first alternative reflects a strategy based on industrial rationalization, the second one a strategy based on professional rationalization, in which standardization is rejected in favour of the development of problem-solving methods (in the style of consultants' methodologies).

CONCLUSION

The number and diversity of studies devoted to examining productivity levers and strategies in services, particularly in management sciences, make any attempt to investigate these questions a difficult exercise indeed. It is this difficulty that justifies the general and theoretical approach to these questions that we have adopted in this chapter.

Focusing on the theoretical analyses, therefore, we examined how economists and specialists in the management of services, each in their own way and with their own specific concerns, have investigated certain productivity levers or factors (particularly technical, organizational and human ones). We outlined and discussed several paradoxes about productivity in services: Solow's (now venerable) paradox, the (new) paradox of the link between R&D and productivity, and two myths, one that services are characterized by weak capital intensity, the other that low skill levels prevail in services (both of which have obvious implications for productivity and performance).

We then identified three generic productivity strategies. Assimilation strategies, first, involve transforming services into goods or quasi-goods. Such strategies transfer the traditional industrial processes of mechanization, division of labour and specialization to services. The aim is to achieve productivity gains by trying to make the services in question as tangible as possible, with the least possible degree of interaction. However, differentiation strategies are not synonymous with disorder and confusion. They do not ignore rationalization or the specificities of services. Rather, they attempt to implement rationalization techniques and methods that are adapted to services. Thus they eschew industrial rationalization (which predominates in assimilation strategies) in favour of professional rationalization based, according to Gadrey (1996b), on the standardization (typification) of cases, the formalization of procedures and the use of routines. This professional rationalization gives rise not only to productivity gains but also to improvements in quality and in indirect outputs, that is the outcomes for consumers of the services. Integration strategies, finally, involve combining the previous two opposing strategies in different ways.

Most of the findings presented in this chapter can be transferred without difficulty to public services. None of the theoretical studies we have drawn on in this chapter exclude public services from their analyses. Indeed, the contrary is the case. After all, it should not be forgotten that public services are, above all, services. This means that our aim in the next chapter will essentially be to highlight some possible strategies associated with the specificities of the public or non-market aspect of public services.

NOTE

1. This use of the term *self-service* is to be distinguished from self-service as a way of putting consumers themselves to work in service firms.

7. Productivity factors in public services

INTRODUCTION

As we noted in the general introduction, the relationship between public services and productivity can be considered at two different levels. The first is productivity in the public sector itself and the second is the influence that public services exert, particularly through the various public policies, on the other sectors of the economy. The importance of this second level in the case of the Department of the Economy and Finance is obvious. However, it is equally relevant in the case of the Department of Health Care or the Department of Education which, by improving individuals' health and knowledge, have a positive influence on the national economy. Although the focus here is on the first level, that is the question of productivity (and performance) within the public sector, it is clearly difficult to dissociate this question from that of productivity (and performance) influenced by the public sector.

This chapter is divided into three parts. In the first part, we briefly examine some of the real and assumed specificities of public services and their consequences for productivity levers and strategies. The second part is concerned with general strategies and policies for improving productivity in government services. The emphasis here is on general levers and recommendations; at this stage, actual applications to a particular government department are disregarded.

The third part is given over to an examination of the way in which these 'general policies' are applied to particular departments as a whole (organizational level) or in certain parts of those same departments (intra-organizational level). In contrast to the first part of this book, we have decided here not to tackle these two analytical levels in two separate chapters (organizational and intra-organizational). While it was possible, and indeed useful, to separate these two levels in investigating how to define and measure productivity, analysis of productivity levers, determinants and strategies is doomed to be largely redundant if such a distinction is made. After all, the productivity levers that organizations rely on are essentially 'intra-organizational' levers that impact on different parts of an organization.

The illustrations provided are drawn from the literature. By combining different angles of approach (macroeconomic, sectoral, microeconomic and case studies), we hope to take satisfactory account of a number of different aspects of productivity factors in public services.

THE SPECIFICITIES OF PUBLIC SERVICES AND THEIR CONSEQUENCES FOR PRODUCTIVITY LEVERS

Productivity gains in public services are regarded as low. Various reasons are generally adduced to explain this state of affairs. Some of these were for a long time regarded as 'natural'. In public services, even more than in market services, capital intensity and technical change are said to be weak, by the very nature of such services, and this, it is argued, explains the excessive employment levels. In Baumol's model, outlined in the previous chapter, the emblematic example of the non-progressive sectors is of course the public service.

Other reasons are specific to public services and are regarded as the (negative) consequences of the protected status and absence of competition characteristic not only of the organizations (often described as bureaucracies) but also their employees (civil servants). These organizations and the individuals that work in them are said to have no incentive to improve their performance because they operate in protected or monopolistic environments.

Another reason, specific to public services, concerns the nature of property rights. In contrast to private property, the public sector is characterized by debased property rights, which are neither exclusive nor transferable. It is the political market, rather than shareholders, that maintains control and it is the body of citizens as a whole that owns public services, provision of which is entrusted to the government. Thus the problems inherent in agency relationships (already described in Chapter 5) are even more acute in public services than in market services: the opportunities for the ultimate owners, that is citizens, to exert control and the incentives to improve performance are considerably reduced.

Another specific characteristic of public services (compared with market services) concerns the objectives pursued by managers. There is now an extensive literature devoted to the objectives of private sector managers, in which the goal of profit maximization occupies a central position. This goal is irrelevant to public services, but there is also a body of literature on the specific objectives pursued by public sector managers. Thus Rees (1984, cited by Knox Lovell, 2002) identifies four types of economic objectives for public services: allocative, distributive, financial and macroeconomic. The question of efficiency and productivity is included in the allocative objective. As far as this allocative objective is concerned (see Knox Lovell, 2002), it might reasonably be assumed that the goal of public service managers is to maximize the provision of services for a given volume of resources. However, consideration is also given in the literature to the view that public sector managers can have other objectives that do nothing to encourage productivity or efficiency; these might include, by way of example, extending the scope of their power by increasing the number of people in their charge, increasing their budgets and their spending capacity and focusing on the most visible and most spectacular outputs at the expense of more useful but less visible ones (Lindsay, 1976). Other characteristics of public sector managers relating not to their objectives but to their competences are also described in the literature (Greiner, 1996; Osborne and Gaebler, 1992) as likely to have a negative effect on the levers of productivity. These public sector managers (particularly in the USA, for example) tend to have 'non-quantitative' educational backgrounds (in law, for example). Consequently, their ability to handle quantitative indicators, and their inclination to do so, are limited.

Moreover, the organizations that provide public services are also regarded as rigid or lacking the flexibility required to improve productivity. A productive organization is said to be flexible when it is able to respond to a change in demand by varying its output without any significant increase in the unit cost (Le Duff and Papillon, 1992).

In the case of public service organizations, it is often difficult to increase output in order to respond in the short or even medium term to a variation in demand (see schools, day nurseries, and so on). There are many explanations for this inertia. First, public service managers are obliged to adhere to rigid procedures that exist in order to safeguard the principles of equality between citizens (in terms of the location of infrastructure, recruitment, and so on). Second, they have less freedom to substitute resources (Knox Lovell, 2002), particularly when it comes to changing the balance between labour and capital. Furthermore, they have only limited resources to spend on building or acquiring equipment. Finally, the stability of unit costs also plays a role here. Since they are unable to reduce expenditure when demand falls, public service managers will tend to minimize risks by limiting or staggering their investment in physical or human capital.

If we consider now the nature of the output rather than its volume, public service managers, as Fox (1999) notes, have no control over the mix of services provided, unlike their private sector counterparts. They have only limited freedom to influence the nature of the product provided. They cannot, on their own initiative, stop providing a service or offer a different one. Consequently, they have only limited control over resource allocation and thus limited influence over performance. Nevertheless, this freedom is, by definition, greater in design, planning and steering departments than in the others.

The second condition that has to be fulfilled if unit costs are not to rise is that inputs (factors of production) can be reduced, which is sometimes difficult or even impossible in public services. After all, some of these factors are long-term infrastructure, in other words assets that cannot be redeployed. The human resources are made up largely of civil servants who cannot be dismissed. Furthermore, controlling unit costs may require a reduction in the volume of output when demand falls. This seems all the more logical since services cannot be stored. However that may be, it is commonly the case in services that output volume is maintained (at least for a certain time) despite a decline in demand: mail delivery schedules remain unchanged, even though the number of letters may be reduced; the same applies to local transport services, which run according to the same timetable even when the number of passengers falls, and so on.

In reality, as we observed in the first part of the book, one important reason for the low productivity in public services is that it has been incorporated as an implicit hypothesis into the methods used to measure productivity in these services (output measured in terms of input).

However that may be, and in the light of the prejudices outlined above, it is not difficult to understand why the productivity levers for public services favoured in national and international policies tend, as we shall see below, to emphasize the introduction of tangible technologies and, in particular, of market forces, in human resource management and in organizational management in general. Thus in France, for example, the civil service also recruits employees for non-civil servant positions. This type of recruitment can be used as a means of flexibility (sometimes in a way that is regarded as improper), since such posts are not covered by the codified recruitment procedures for civil servants. Thus, as in the assimilation strategies described in the previous chapter in the case of market services, management effort is being directed towards eliminating the specificities of public services. Management techniques are being imported from the market sector in order to improve productivity in the public services. Thus it is mainly the technical, human and organizational levers that are being brought into play. Of course the political and institutional lever also plays a role here, in the sense that the public administration does not confine itself to creating the framework conditions that help to determine productivity in the other sectors of the economy but also creates them for itself.

The institutional context (factor) plays a very important role in the organizational factors that influence productivity in public services. Thus in Canada, for example, 'the law on bargaining units in the social affairs sector, which amends the law on the collective agreements negotiating regime in the public and parapublic sectors' is regarded by some as having had a positive effect on the organizational changes needed to produce productivity gains. This legislation, which decentralized the negotiating of collective agreements, has made it possible to implement organizational changes that take account of local needs and realities (Ministry of Labour, Quebec, 2005).

GENERAL POLICIES FOR IMPROVING PRODUCTIVITY IN PUBLIC SERVICES

Most countries in the world have adopted (or claim to have adopted) national strategies (policies) for improving productivity in government services. These strategies vary in their sophistication and the coherence of their integration into broader public policies (reforms). It is not our intention here to conduct a systematic examination of these strategies. Rather we will confine ourselves to a few cases. It is obvious that these strategies are nothing other than more or less original variations of the typology of productivity factors described in Chapter 5, amended to take account of local realities. We begin by setting out a list of recommendations for improving productivity drawn up by the government of Malaysia and sent to all its ministries. These recommendations were drawn up some time ago, and the country is not representative. Nevertheless, the list has a certain resonance, since it applies the typology of levers in an (elementary) academic way. We will then examine the way in which the European Union as a whole has for some time been tackling the broad principles of this issue, before turning our attention to the national policies (or certain aspects of those policies) adopted in three different countries: the UK, Canada and France.

An Example of a Basic List of Recommendations for Improving Productivity in Public Services

Management science provides a certain number of basic recommendations for strategies that might be adopted in order to exert a positive influence on the levers of productivity. These recommendations are sufficiently general to be applied to any manufacturing or service activity, regardless of the activity's cognitive level.

Table 7.1 provides a list of the instructions sent by the office of the prime minister of Malaysia to its senior officials (chief secretaries of ministries, heads of federal departments and local government authorities). Although they were issued some time ago in a country that is not representative, this list of recommendations, which focuses strictly on the notion of productivity, itemizes, with simplicity, the actions that are desirable in order to increase productivity in public services. In a way, it reflects (basic) managerial concepts. It is aimed at the public services at various levels (including the internal steering functions). However, it can be applied to any service (or manufacturing) activity.

The suggested actions naturally concern the three generic factors that were considered in Chapter 5. The human factor concerns employees, of course, while the technical factor covers the following levers: technology, raw materials and equipment. The organizational factor includes processes, organizational structure, management style and work environment.

A General European Perspective

Most European countries embarked several years ago on reforms explicitly aimed at improving productivity (or performance) in the public sector. The European Commission (2004, 'European competitiveness report'; Joumard *et al.*, 2004) identifies three types of reforms aimed at improving productivity in this sector: (a) 'management' reforms; (b) privatization and outsourcing; and (c) introduction of information technologies. Once again, these reforms bring into play the main levers already identified. One strategy that to a certain extent combines the previous ones is worth highlighting: this is the benchmarking strategy.

Management reforms

Human resource management is an essential factor in improving productivity in public services. Many authors consider it the key productivity factor in public services, since it is the factor that determines the others (Holzer and Lee, 2004). In particular, it encompasses recruitment, training, redundancy and promotion strategies, as well as the issue of pay differentiation. Public services in all countries have particular practices in all these various areas; they generally include recruitment by competitive examination, no possibility of redundancy, promotion by competitive examination and pay differentiation based on predetermined pay scales (and progression by seniority in certain segments). Another important characteristic of human resources in public services, which applies to all developed countries, is that pay (including that of senior officials) is lower than in the private sector. This characteristic may have consequences for the

Table 7.1   *A list of basic actions to improve productivity in the public service (Government of Malaysia, 1991)*

Factors	Management action
1. Manpower	(a) Train employees in areas related to their work
	(b) Determine and disseminate positive values
	(c) Motivate employees to produce excellent work
	(d) Encourage the involvement of employees in objective-setting for the organization and in the productivity problem-solving process
	(e) Create effective communications in the department/office
	(f) Set performance standards for employees
	(g) Place employees in jobs which are in line with their ability and skill
2. Systems and procedures	(a) Review system and work procedures in order to overcome weaknesses which restrict productivity
	(b) Streamline existing system and work procedures
	(c) Abolish rules and regulations which are not in line with the goals of the department/office
3. Organizational structure	(a) Coordinate the functions of divisions and units within the organization
	(b) Establish a flexible and dynamic organization structure
	(c) Ensure that staffing levels of divisions and units within the organization are appropriate to the responsibilities given
	(d) Clearly define areas of responsibility of each division and unit within the department/office
4. Management style	(a) Establish the vision and objectives of the department/office and disseminate them to all employees
	(b) Plan and establish the performance goals of the department/office and measure actual achievement
	(c) Create a work culture which emphasizes productivity
5. Work environment	(a) Create an office layout suitable to its work operation
	(b) Equip the office with basic facilities
	(c) Provide facilities for the staff
6. Technology	(a) Examine existing work process to identify areas suitable for automation and mechanization
7. Materials	(a) Carry out quality inspections at the preliminary stage on inputs received from the supplier
	(b) Provide training in quality for suppliers
	(c) Practise a good inventory system to avoid carrying excess stock of materials
8. Capital equipment	(a) Maintain capital equipment according to schedule
	(b) Ensure that equipment is located in a suitable area
	(c) Schedule utilization of equipment use to ensure optimal use

ability of government departments to attract high-performing human resources. Conversely, given the economic situation, the public service in some countries is overflowing with over-qualified personnel in deskilled jobs (Kopel, 2001), which may be a demotivating factor and further reinforces the wage differential with the private sector.

In most European countries (and, beyond Europe, in the English-speaking countries such as the USA, Canada, Australia and New Zealand), reforms have been introduced in the area of human resource management that are intended, essentially, to transfer to the public sector the management techniques used in the private sector (Rouillard *et al.*, 2004). Thus more traditional recruitment methods and incentive and motivation mechanisms, such as merit pay systems, have been introduced, at least on an experimental basis. Efforts are being made to improve initial and continuing training at all levels.

However, merit pay systems have obvious perverse effects on productivity. In public services, each individual's contribution to the common effort is sometimes difficult to determine. The evaluations that are carried out, usually by line management, may be subjective. Such an incentive system may undermine solidarity and contribution and damage the overall productivity of the group and organization as a whole. In some cases, merit pay, based on certain indicators (for example, the number of parking tickets issued by a police officer), may give rise to overzealousness that will harm the overall performance of the service provided.

Over and above human resource management, organizational management as a whole has followed the same principle of introducing private sector management principles into the non-market sphere. These practices are explicitly aimed at improving performance and at user satisfaction – users having become customers. The main examples of this new approach are probably what is known as 'new public management' (NPM) and 'total quality management' (TQM) applied to public services. As Rouillard *et al.* (2004) note in their analysis of the reform of the Canadian civil service (particularly in Quebec), this intrusion of economic rationalism and market values into the public sphere is reflected in the emergence of a new terminology in public services: 'business plans', 'value added', 'products', 'customer satisfaction', 're-engineering public services' and so on.

The general philosophy underlying the new public management is to implement strategies whose target or main concern is the customer or user and whose results can be evaluated. The NPM can be said to be a customer-focused, evaluation-based form of management. From this general point of view, the NPM is constructed on the following three principles: very precise formulation of the objectives to be attained, the introduction of 'management contracts' as incentives to improve performance and the establishment of independent 'cost centres' (decentralized budgetary control).

This last principle brings to mind a more general principle of longer standing, namely the decentralization of public administration. Decentralization is seen as a means of improving performance, since it brings service providers closer to users and their specific needs. However, it may also erode the benefits to be gained from economies of scale and scope and it is not always wholly consistent with national objectives.

Total quality management, for its part, can be defined as 'a management system focused on the individual, whose main aim is to achieve continuous increases in customer satisfaction at the lowest possible cost' (Lindsay and Petrick, 1997). Many public services have adopted TQM strategies. Gueret-Talon (2004) describes the case of the Nice Côte d'Azur Chamber of Commerce and Industry, which launched a total quality approach in 1998, for which it received the European Quality Prize by choosing the EFQM (European Foundation for Quality Management) Excellence Model.

Privatization and outsourcing

The second strand of the reforms aimed at improving productivity in public services identified by the European Commission (2004) is privatization and outsourcing. Such measures can take three different forms:

- privatization pure and simple of a public service, that is the state's complete withdrawal from provision of that service;
- outsourcing or subcontracting of certain parts of a service activity; and
- public–private partnerships (PPPs).

The hypotheses underlying such measures are that the link with the market economy (which may vary in strength from case to case) creates incentives to increase work effort and improve productivity. However, there is no real evidence that provides conclusive support, on the theoretical level, for the view that the private sector is superior to the public sector when it comes to productivity and performance. The studies that have been carried out in this area are contradictory: for example, outsourcing can give rise to transaction costs that may be harmful to performance. Several experiments conducted in developing countries seem to confirm this (Batley, 1999). Furthermore, there is a widespread view that, in the UK, it was bungled privatization (particularly of the railways) that encouraged the development of hybrid schemes such as public–private partnerships (HM Treasury, 2003).

PPPs are a (relatively) new organizational form in public management; they encompass a diverse set of realities, and are associated with the effort to improve productivity and performance (Dumez and Jeunemaitre, 2003). Although they are consistent with the principles of the new public management, which are neo-liberal in inspiration, they have been used by governments of both left and right. They can cover an extremely broad spectrum of public service activities. Thus there are examples in education, energy, car parks, ports, hospitals, tram systems, prisons, waste processing, defence, police, and so on. The amounts of money involved vary considerably, from several hundreds of thousands of euros to several billions. They can take a number of different forms. Sharle (2002) identifies three forms of PPP:

- BOO (build, own, operate). In this form, the private partner builds the infrastructure and owns and manages it. The government draws up the tender specifications and supervizes the building process.
- BOT (build, operate, transfer). Here, the private partner builds the infrastructure, manages it and then, after a certain number of years, transfers ownership to the public partner.
- BTO (build, transfer, operate). In this form, the private company constructs the infrastructure for the government, which will be the owner. The government then leases it back to the private partner, who manages it.

Information and communication technologies

The third strand of reform is the introduction of ICTs into public services. The introduction of ICTs seems to confirm Barras' model to a certain extent (Barras, 1990). As in other pre-industrial mass services, the introduction of the various generations of ICTs (mainframes, mini-computers and networked PCs) was followed by the emergence, first, of incremental process innovations (intended to increase productivity), then of radical process innovations (focusing on quality) and finally of product innovations, such as e-government.

E-government is expected to improve performance in public services in various ways: by increasing the availability of information, reducing the time required to access information, eliminating redundant information systems and establishing links and common standards between the various government agencies.

The European Commission has drawn up an action plan (eEurope 2005) to encourage the development of e-government throughout Europe. The American government, which seems to be furthest advanced in this regard (with European countries such as Denmark, the UK and Sweden hard on its heels) (UNPAN, 2004), also launched an extensive programme for developing e-government in 2002. In particular, it includes a disaster management system, a system for accessing federal or regional aid programmes, electronic education, electronic job search and electronic filing of tax returns.

Benchmarking strategies

There is a fourth reform strategy aimed at improving performance in public services. This is the 'comparison' or benchmarking strategy. A strategy of this kind falls within the scope of strategies 1 and 2 identified previously. After all, benchmarking can be used as an instrument of indirect competition in areas in which direct competition is not possible. Furthermore, it is a management technique that has long been in use in the private sector and which has been taken up recently by the public sector.

Lawrence *et al.* (1997), in a study, it is true, of Australia,[1] which focused on the distribution of electricity and gas, telecommunications, transport in its various forms and ports, relied heavily on the following performance indicators: price indicators, service quality, labour productivity, capital productivity, and so on. The Australia international benchmarking strategy is regarded as pioneering. The objective of comparing performance is to produce action tools, not only for government policies but also for service–providing organizations themselves.

It should not of course be inferred from this general outline that the strategies for reforming the state and improving productivity in government departments adopted by Western countries are all heading in the same direction. The principles of the new public management are being adapted to national specificities. Two different types of reform can be identified, depending on the extent to which these principles are applied: the first can be described as 'post-bureaucratic', while the second can be said to be based on 'economic rationalism' (Rouillard *et al.*, 2004). The English-speaking countries tend to fall into the second category, Continental European countries into the first.

The British Strategy

Within Europe, the UK has long been regarded as a pioneer of this strategy of improving public service performance through the introduction of market techniques and mechanisms (Jowett and Rothwell, 1988). The British government has recently developed a general framework for improving productivity in public services (HM Treasury, 2003). This framework, which draws on some of the general principles outlined previously, is based on the following three principles:

1. A focus on outcomes and not just on inputs or outputs. The aim is to evaluate (and improve) public service performance on the basis of results.
2. 'Constrained discretion' for providers of local public services. This constrained discretion involves the abandonment of traditional, standardizing centralization, which penalizes and undermines local initiative and ignores local needs and environments. However, this discretion must be monitored (by appropriate evaluation mechanisms) in order to avoid excessive disparity in service provision.
3. Improvement of public service governance.

The adaptation of governance structures is considered likely to improve productivity in public services. HM Treasury is drawing here on the lessons of agency theory (see Chapter 5) concerning the effectiveness of governance structures. Thus the Treasury particularly emphasizes the following three conditions:

1. Clear formulation of objectives (that is outputs). Public service providers that have a certain number of clear objectives to attain are known to be more efficient and effective than others in terms of both cost and service quality. This was very clearly established by the Audit Commission (2001) in the case of local public services. Furthermore, establishing an (appropriate) hierarchy of objectives (prioritization) also plays a key role in the level of performance achieved, as the Audit Commission has also established. These operational findings are echoed in the academic literature. Thus, for example, Dixit (2000) (see also Dolton, 2003) analyses the extent to which some of the objectives assigned to education (providing children with basic skills, preparing them for work, instilling ideals of citizenship and fostering emotional growth), even though they are not contradictory, compete for resources and the attention of teachers. Smith *et al.* (2003) pose the same question with regard to health services by drawing up a list of the many goals health services are required to attain. It is perhaps here that convention theory can best demonstrate its usefulness. The problem would not be to hierarchize an open list of priorities but rather to socially construct (through dialogue and comparison) a goal that would be valid for a given time, in a given society or community. It will be noted that this question of goals conceals another question, namely that of who the customers of public services really are.
2. The need for incentive mechanisms. The aim here is to put in place mechanisms that encourage public service providers to try to achieve the goals that have been set. In developing such mechanisms, the

motivations specific to public service employees (public service spirit) should not be ignored in favour of the traditional market mechanisms.

3. The need for clear and reliable information. After all, information is indispensable if goals are to be set, performance evaluated, each individual's contribution assessed, and incentive mechanisms built.

An Integrated Approach to Productivity in Ministerial Administrative Services in Canada

The Canadian government is currently implementing a strategy for transforming internal services in its ministries based on productivity and performance (Treasury Board of Canada Secretariat, 2005). This general strategy is described as an 'integrated approach to the transformation of internal services'. What does it involve?

The Treasury Board Secretariat was entrusted with development of this strategy. The starting point was the observation that, in carrying out similar administrative and technological functions, federal departments and agencies use a very great variety of different, compartmentalized and sometimes redundant practices. This diversity of practices damages the interoperability of (administrative and technical) systems. It has negative consequences for 'the operational efficiency and productivity for the government as a whole'. Furthermore, it makes it difficult to compare the performance of different internal services, since it makes it impossible to gather comparable data on costs, outputs and outcomes.

Thus implementation of this integrated approach, which is the responsibility of the Treasury Board Secretariat, is explicitly intended: first, 'to improve operational efficiency'; and second, to produce 'more complete and more reliable data on government operations and performance'. This integrated approach applies to all aspects of ministries' internal services, including finance, human resources, equipment and information technologies.

Thus the intention, in embarking on a re-engineering of processes in internal services and of information technologies and launching processes of standardization, rationalization and consolidation (and elimination of duplication), is to put in place 'shared service models'.

The aim is to create a 'corporate administration shared services organization' (CA-SSO) that will provide all ministries with (financial, material and HR) administrative services on a shared basis. This will be a new legal entity, headed by a deputy minister-level CEO, that will be a service provider for the other ministries.

This general strategy has a strong IT component. After all, the aim is to continue the reduction, initiated several years ago, in the number of different (financial, personnel, equipment) management systems used by ministries and to harmonize these systems by putting in place 'shared systems' which will perform better and reduce costs.

The French Strategy

The (current) French strategy for improving productivity in public services is part of the overall strategy for reform of the state. The four objectives of this reform (presented by the Minister for the Public Service, Reform of the State and Regional Development to the French National Assembly in November 2003) are as follows:

- to streamline and introduce greater transparency into the structures of the state and its working methods;
- to modernize administrative services and reduce operating costs;
- to obtain productivity gains; and
- to introduce into the public service the notions of performance targets and results.

Productivity is explicitly included as a priority in the third objective. In fact, however, it is present implicitly in the other three. After all, the first and second objectives can be regarded as factors that make it possible 'to obtain productivity gains', while the fourth objective broadens out the topic.

In order to fit into this overall strategy, each ministry is required to draw up its own reform strategy, which is updated annually.

These ministry reform strategies were introduced in 2003 (see Sénat, 2004). As part of the process of drawing up its strategy, each ministry was required systematically to re-examine the remit and organization of its various departments in order to propose reforms (that abandon, delegate, outsource, reinforce or modify some parts of these remits) that are consistent with decentralization and implementation of the Organic Law on the Finance Acts.

In 2004, each ministry had to review its reform strategy, update it and set more ambitious targets. Concrete action programmes for improving the productivity and effectiveness of its various departments, the quality of their 'output' and the rewards offered to officials in recognition of their efforts have to be proposed; in all cases, measurable commitments had to be made. Coordination of the ministry reform strategies was the responsibility of the Ministry for the Reform of the State, which organized the necessary process of consultation.

Once the consultations were completed, 225 actions out of the more than 500 proposed were adopted. Half of them were measures intended to increase the productivity of government departments, while the other half were designed to increase the effectiveness of government actions or the quality of the service provided (Sénat, 2004). For each of these actions, a quantified and dated commitment was drawn up, in accordance with the strategy of promoting a 'results-driven culture' in government departments. In total, the actions were to generate savings of the order of 1.5 billion euros per year.

BOX 7.1 EXAMPLES OF REFORM MEASURES TAKEN BY VARIOUS MINISTRIES (SOURCE: SÉNAT, 2004)

- Rationalization of public purchases (various ministries)
- Improvement in the efficiency of the use of supply teachers (Education Ministry)
- Reform of the administration of television tax (Finance Ministry)
- Transfer of administration of family benefits paid to civil servants to the family benefit offices (civil service)
- New system for life-time registration of vehicles (Ministry of the Interior)
- Introduction of electronic version of the Official Journal (Office of the Prime Minister)
- Outsourcing of the management and maintenance of vehicles in the commercial range (Ministry of Defence)
- Reduction in the number of central departments (Infrastructure, Finance)
- User help and support: Marianne Charter (all public services)
- Reduction in time taken to repay VAT credits to firms (Ministry of Finance)

This first review showed some ministries to be better learners than others. Thus among the ministries that were most active in proposing reforms, the Ministry of Finance put forward the following measures (among others): outsourcing of the hallmarking of precious metals, the merger of three central administrative departments, reduction in the time taken to pay back VAT credits to firms, a policy of disposing of the Ministry's property assets and moving to less expensive areas (example: the move of the customs department to the Paris suburb of Montreuil), the non-replacement of employees who retire, and so on.

Several new institutional arrangements are closely linked with this reform, in particular the Organic Law on the Finance Acts[2] (the so-called LOLF or *loi organique relative aux lois de finances* of August 2001) and the public–private partnership.

The LOLF is a reform of the ordinance of 2 January 1959, which governed the state's finances. The main changes introduced by this budgetary reform are as follows:

- It breaks with the traditional principle that the state budget is managed on an annual basis. It can now be managed over a period of several years.
- Expenditure can now be removed from the original budget headings. Funds allocated to a particular heading can be transferred to another heading (for example, funds allocated to personnel can be reallocated to infrastructure).[3] Funds are no longer categorized by the nature of the expenditure (personnel, IT and so on) but rather by overarching purpose (security, education, health, culture, and so on), the aim being to make public expenditure transparent and to strengthen parliamentary scrutiny. More precisely the new budget architecture has three levels: 47 overarching objectives (that may be the responsibility of several different ministries) that form the basis of the major public policies and are divided into 158 programmes, which are themselves broken down into an exhaustive set of specific actions (see www.moderfiefinances.gouv.fr; Lacaze, 2005). Table 7.2 illustrates the way in which the 'Solidarity and integration' objective is broken down into programmes and actions.
- It introduces greater ministerial responsibility. Ministers must commit themselves to targets and account for the results, in particular by drawing up first an annual performance plan for each programme and then an annual performance report, which reviews the actions implemented, the costs, the objectives set and the results obtained or expected in the short and medium term, as 'measured by precise and soundly based indicators'. The performance targets laid down in the performance plans are divided into three different categories: effectiveness (that is the final outcome of the public action), efficiency (that is economic use of resources) and the quality of the services provided to users.

The LOLF was piloted in 2005 and came into force on 1 January 2006. It can be anticipated that this reform will have certain consequences for

Table 7.2   The 'Solidarity and integration' objective, broken down into programmes and actions

Programmes	Actions
Policies promoting social inclusion	Prevention of exclusion
	Actions in support of the most vulnerable
	Management and leadership of fight against exclusion
	Repatriates
Reception and integration of foreigners	Population and involvement in the regulation of immigration
	Social care of asylum seekers
	Integration
	High Authority in the fight against discrimination and for equality
Actions in support of vulnerable families	Support for families in their role as parents
	Support for single-parent families
	Protection of children and families
Handicap and dependency	Personalized assessment and guidance for handicapped people
	Encouragement to enter labour market
	Means of existence
	Compensation for the consequences of handicap
	Elderly people
	Management of programme
Sickness protection	Access to supplementary sickness protection
	State medical aid
	Compensation fund for asbestos victims
Gender equality	Access for women to positions of responsibility and decision-making
	Equality at work
	Equality in law and in dignity
	Linking of life course phases
	Support for gender equality programme
Management and support of health and social policies	Central management of health and social services
	Statistics and research
	Management of social policies
	Management of health policies
	Steering of social security
	Support for health and social department

Source: www.moderfiefinances.gouv.fr

productivity. It will make it easier to substitute capital for labour, for example, and to outsource certain functions.

The public–private partnership is another institutional arrangement likely to influence productivity and performance in government departments. The ordinances introducing this arrangement were published in July 2004. However, PPPs had already been planned for hospitals, police stations and prisons. The purpose of these PPPs is to reduce the financial burden of public infrastructure projects on the state, since the design, financing, construction, maintenance and management of these projects are entrusted to the private partner, with the state paying rent only.

Of course the French strategy also has two other aspects that we will not investigate in detail here (and which are closely linked to the previous ones). One is the reform of human resource management. Enquiries are being conducted into civil servants' mobility and career development. The other is e-government, which is seen as a significant source of productivity. Thus the so-called ADELE plan (from *administration électronique*/e-government) is a central element in the reform of the state. It is aimed at users, who will be offered an increasing number of teleservices (on-line forms, a variety of information on line, and so on). It also concerns the various administrative departments, which are now networked. One example of an inter-departmental service is VIT@MIN, a tool developed in order to facilitate the exchange of information on the modernization of government between central departments and decentralized offices. The e-government programme is also planned in such a way as to make available on-line training tools for civil servants.

STRATEGIES FOR IMPROVING PRODUCTIVITY ON THE ORGANIZATIONAL AND INTRA-ORGANIZATIONAL LEVELS

In the last part of this chapter, we outline a number of strategies for improving productivity that have been implemented in various public services. Our focus has shifted away from general policies to the microeconomic level, at which the strategies of individual organizations are played out. Three instructive cases will be examined here. The first concerns a productivity improvement system put in place by the French Post Office (known as the performance tree). We will discuss the principles underlying its construction and its limitations as well as possible improvements. The second case is an examination of recent outsourcing strategies in French government departments. The third focuses on the productivity strategies adopted by the health and social affairs department in the wake of the recent reforms.

The Lessons to be Learnt from the Post Office's Performance Tree

The performance tree is an extremely important performance evaluation tool used in the French Post Office. Some years ago, we were commissioned by the Post Office to evaluate the tool, a project on which we report briefly here (Gallouj, 1999). Our aim is simply to outline the broad principles on which this tool is based and to examine certain perverse effects linked to these principles and to the way the tool is used. We will also suggest some ways in which it might be improved.

The Performance Tree: Underlying Principles and Purposes

The performance tree (the working of which in regional financial services centres is presented more concretely and in greater detail in Box 7.2) is based on a model of the work organization system in the organizational unit in question (financial centre, post office, sorting office or any other unit). This organizational unit is broken down in an extremely detailed way into *types* of activities, *groups* or *families* of activities and *basic activities* which, taken as a whole, constitute a virtual representation of the system of work organization. For each of these analytical levels, the volume of work (traffic) and/or time spent is quantified on the basis of data that are gathered periodically, whether automatically or manually.

These data are used as a basis for the calculation at local level of performance and quality ratios. In essence these are technical performance (and quality) ratios. These various local performance evaluations are then centralized. Comparisons are made and rankings drawn up, which are then returned to the local level. Thus the performance tree is a very detailed instrument for workload analysis and benchmarking between establishments or departments. It is a tool for measuring labour productivity by type of activity at a highly disaggregated level; it enables establishments or departments to rank themselves and be ranked in general terms as well as by a particular type of task, whether operational or functional.

The performance tree has several possible purposes or uses. For example, it can be used to improve performance (instrumental use) and to justify resource allocation decisions (objectification). These two uses usually converge on a final productivist goal, which is *to improve productivity by 'taking back' jobs*.

Figure 7.1 shows the various possible paths (whether straight or roundabout) converging on the performance tree's ultimate goal, which is to

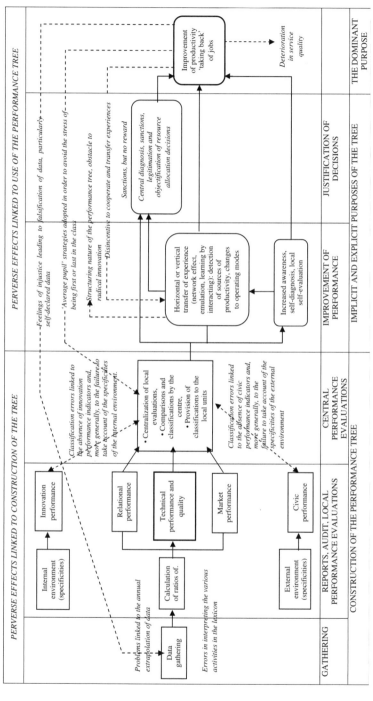

Note: This diagram depicts the various stages in the construction and use of the performance tree. The perverse effects and possible problems are shown in italics.

Figure 7.1 The performance tree: mechanisms and limitations

190

increase productivity by reducing the labour input. Productivity improvements can be achieved by the following routes:

1. Through awareness, self-diagnosis and self-assessment at the local level, which can impact on labour productivity either directly or by taking the following more roundabout routes.
2. Through the horizontal or vertical (that is centrally organized) transfer of experiences, which brings into play the network effect. Each establishment identifies potential sources of productivity gains and makes voluntary (learning through interaction) or enforced (see third route) changes to its operations.
3. Through the penalties imposed as a result of the ranking and diagnosis made by the central authority and leading to a reduction in jobs, that is a 'mechanical' increase in productivity. In this case, the ranking is used as an instrument to justify decisions on resource allocation.

BOX 7.2   THE PRINCIPLES UNDERLYING THE CONSTRUCTION AND USE OF THE PERFORMANCE TREE IN THE CASE OF REGIONAL FINANCIAL SERVICE CENTRES (RFSCs)

Breakdown of activities

The activities of the RFSCs are analysed and broken down exhaustively into three levels:

-   *Types of activity.* There are 18 in all (for example: modules, sight deposits and Cheops network operations, ordinary savings, house purchase plans, stock market investment plans, human resources and so on), divided into three broad groups: current and savings account production services, shared production services and functional services.
-   *Families of activities.* Each of these types of activity is itself broken down into a total of 93 families of activities. The type of activity termed 'Post Office bank account module', for example, comprises the following 15 families: verification procedures, account opening, changes, account closures, orders for cheque books, products, electronic banking services, legal department, complaints, outstanding payments,

irregular securities, commercial contracts, large accounts, relations with post masters and various.

- *Activities*. Each family of activities is broken down into basic activities, of which there are several hundreds in total. Thus the 'opening Post Office bank account' family comprises three basic activities: receipt of files, examination of files/ decisions and opening of accounts.

- The breakdown into a tree-like structure ends at this third level. In reality, the activities themselves are broken down into more or less clearly identified *tasks*, which do not appear in the index but have to be taken into account.

  In theory, this breakdown must obey several principles: it must be very detailed, precise and simple in order to avoid local interpretations and to make it transferable from one centre to another. It must be sufficiently detailed to be independent of the particular organization of the RFSC in question.

Quantification principles (based on internal documents)

Once the various levels of an activity have been identified, they have to be quantified. There are several possible sources of quantification:

- All the available statistics on volume and performance can be used, except for those based on standard times (such as statistics 538 and 539). The available statistics may be electronic (for example, the number of cheques keyed into terminals and the number of recycled cheques are provided directly by the computer system) or manual in origin (for example: counting number of telephone calls).

- In the absence of statistics, assessments are carried out over set periods (several days or weeks) and annual figures are extrapolated from the data thus gathered.

The overall objective is, for each activity in the national list, to estimate the volumes or the actual annual working times. Depending on the nature of the activity in question, working times can be estimated in two different ways, on the basis of volumes or frequency (daily, weekly, monthly, quarterly or annual):

- in the first case, the volumes are multiplied by the appropriate average unit processing times (average unit time estimated by employees themselves and not the national standard time given by statistic 538);

- in the second case, the frequency of activities is multiplied by the appropriate average times.

It should be noted that:

- Specific arrangements are made for quantifying managers' activities. In general terms, they are included in the supervision rates calculated both for the RFSC as a whole and for the five types of activities. However, when a manager intervenes directly and to a significant extent in an operational activity, his or her activity is estimated using the traditional procedure.
- For each family of activities, the 'various' heading is used to quantify the following elements: (a) tasks linked to the family of activities but not described as part of an activity (what might be called transfers of joint outputs); (b) time spent gathering information (reading), attending meetings and waiting times of various kinds (computer downtimes, for example); (c) time spent on filing, photocopying, archiving and compiling statistics gathered at department level.
- Quantification is supplemented by feedback exercises, which help to identify errors and to ensure that the figures obtained are credible. For each unit of analysis, feedback is provided by comparing the hours estimated using the performance tree and those worked by the available labour force.

The various ratios estimated are:

- productivity ratios (number of operations over time spent on operations);
- financial profitability ratios (for example: net banking income per employee);
- service quality ratios.

From performance tree results to proposals for improvements

Once the figures have been obtained, they have to be analysed. In each RFSC, about a hundred unit of analysis officers (UAOs) (one per family of activities) were appointed and trained. The analyses presented below are taken from an internal document produced for these unit UAOs. The sequential procedure suggested in the guide is as follows:

Examination of the ratios related to the general indicators
Referring to the document entitled 'families of activities', the UAO should examine the general indicator for the family under consideration and the various ratios derived from it (following the breakdown principle). The UAO should identify those over which he or she might be able to exert some influence (on the numerator, the denominator or both numbers simultaneously). Taking the 'cheques' family as an example, the document for that family is structured as follows:

List of RFSCs	General indicator for the family	Total value of cheques	No. of foreign cheques	Cheques > 20KF	Hours' downtime	No. of cheques with C/A on front	Cheques with C/A on front
	----------	----------	----------	----------	----------	---------	--------
	No. of cheques/ Total cheque hours	No. of cheques	Foreign cheque hours	No. of cheques	total cheque hours	Cheque with C/A hours	No. of cheques
	–						
	–						
	–						
Average Min. Max.							

No influence can be exerted on the ratio: Total value of cheques/No. of cheques. On the other hand, it is possible to influence the ratio: No. of foreign cheques/Foreign cheque hours.

Identifying the data and operations that can be influenced
In the previous example, the numerator cannot be influenced. On the other hand, it is possible to influence the denominator (foreign cheque hours). The operations in question are those connected with the processing of foreign cheques.

Selecting the operations that can be improved
UAOs can make use of a 'grid for identification of areas to be analyzed', which is structured as follows:

Name of operation: ....
Ratio linked to operation: .... Relevant general indicator............

Organization		Equipment			HR	
Is the organization appropriate?	Is the automation efficient?	Is the equipment efficient?	Is it properly distributed in terms of numbers?	Can staff operate the equipment properly?	Are the time slots appropriate?	Is the training provided appropriate?

Yes
No

Areas to be improved: ....
Reason for your decision: ....

Breakdown of operations into basic tasks and estimation of time taken
UAOs should begin by breaking down the current processing of the operation, that is list and arrange the tasks in order of execution and then estimate the time required to complete each one (see form for next stage below).

Analysis of each task in the operations
For each of the tasks listed during the previous phase, UAOs should answer the four questions in the following table.

Breakdown grid for the *current processing* of the operation

List of tasks in order of execution	Time required to complete tasks	Can the task be simplified?	What are the consequences at the level of the unit of analysis?	What are the consequences for subsequent tasks?	Conclusions of task analysis

Development of a new way of processing the operation and estimation of times required for the new tasks
This time, a new breakdown grid for the processing of the operation has to be filled in, taking account of the task analysis carried out previously.

Breakdown grid for the *proposed processing* of the operation	
List of tasks in order of execution	Time required to complete tasks
Write a report Write a report summarizing the recommended improvements and their advantages and disadvantages for the issuing unit of analysis and the others.	

The limitations of the performance tree

The limitations of the performance tree can also be examined by classifying them on the basis of whether they are linked to the principles underlying its construction or to its uses (see Figure 7.1).

Limitations linked to the principles underlying the tree's construction   These limitations can be divided into two broad categories depending on the stage of the construction process.

Thus in the data gathering phase, there are:

1. Possible errors in interpreting the content of the various basic activities and their aggregation into families and types, despite intensive and complex lexicographical work. For example, employees tend to confuse 'complaints' and 'information', whereas in reality these are two different activities that generally require different processing times.
2. Possible errors linked to the extrapolation of data to the annual level. They are, after all, gathered over a period of just a few days (usually two weeks), which can compromise their reliability.

In the performance evaluation phase at either local or central level, errors in the classification of establishments can occur. These errors can be attributed to the absence of indicators of internal and external environmental specificities, even though these specificities undeniably have consequences for performance evaluation and may distort some comparisons.

As far as indicators of *internal environmental specificities* are concerned, the performance tree takes no account, for example, of any possible specific characteristics of the labour force, which may be historically determined. Nor does it take into account the tasks certain units carry out on behalf of the others.

The *external environmental specificities* originate in the demographic and socio-economic variables that characterize the geographical and social milieu in which the establishment in question operates. The performance tree regards the various cases processed, whether customers or accounts, as homogeneous. No distinction is made between 'light' and 'heavy' cases, either in the customer structure or in the account structure. However, not all customers are the same, and the same applies to accounts. Since the performance tree does not take the share of 'social' or disadvantaged customers into account, it can be said to *disregard civic performance*. Thus civic performance is a 'repressed' aspect of performance. Consequently, it may be a cause of classification errors and of feelings of injustice, all the more so since the tree does not take account either of the (negative) relation between this type of performance and the others. For example, a relative weakness in technical and/or market performance may be due to (or offset by) a high level of civic performance.

Limitations linked to use of the performance tree The ultimate purpose of the performance tree is, we repeat, to increase labour productivity. Investigation of the various routes (see Figure 7.1) that can be taken in order to attain this goal reveals a number of perverse effects:

1. The goal of heightened awareness and local self-evaluation may become perverted, since it ultimately entails giving up a number of jobs. One of the consequences of self-evaluation may be self-sanctioning . . .
2. Similarly, since the ultimate aim of transferring experience and incremental innovation is also a form of self-sanctioning, there may in certain cases be a disincentive to cooperate and transfer.
3. While there are penalties for poor performance in certain areas of an activity, there is not, on the other hand, any reward for good performance in other areas. A unit will be 'punished' (by losing jobs) for the functions in which it performs poorly but will not be rewarded for those in which it performs well. In other words, it is better to be average in all areas in order not to suffer a reduction in employee numbers (whether externally imposed or self-administered).
4. If these limitations of the performance tree create feelings of injustice, they may give rise to fraud and data falsification strategies.
5. The performance tree does not take sufficient account of quality or of the productivity–quality dilemma (which is an issue in many service activities). Overemphasizing productivity (technical performance) may have negative consequences on service quality.

Reduction–simplification, addition–integration: the dialectic of improving the performance tree

The various possible improvements that are implicitly contained in this outline of the limitations and perverse effects of the methods can be linked to two opposing but complementary dynamics, one based on a process of reduction and simplification, the other on a process of addition and integration.

The aim of these two dynamics is to make the performance tree more operational. The first is intended to improve its effectiveness, that is its ability to attain the goal of reliably measuring and comparing performance. The second is intended to increase its efficiency, that is its ability to achieve its goal in an optimal way. In other words, improvements of the reduction–simplification type are intended essentially to generate support for the technical aspects of the performance tree by facilitating its practical implementation; improvements of the addition–integration type, on the other hand, are intended rather to generate 'moral support', in the sense that they help to reduce bias and the feelings of injustice that bias produces. Box 7.3 presents some examples of improvements based on these two dynamics.

BOX 7.3   SOME POSSIBLE IMPROVEMENTS (BASED ON THE INTERVIEWS WE CONDUCTED)

Reduction–simplification dynamic: technical reliability and feasibility

- reduce the volume of data and the number of ratios, retain only the most reliable family ratios and eliminate the ratios that are never used;
- restrict collection of self-declared data to a minimum (the SACSO tool is heading towards the automatic production of more reliable statistics in the current account modules);
- reduce extrapolations;
- measure and analyze changes in performance in the same centre;
- compare the performance of homogeneous groups of centres classified by size and types of technical systems used;
- allow a year for adaptation (without any data gathering) when innovative projects are introduced, so that the various

---

centres (and the various units within centres) are all at the same level;

- reduce the length of time between the various phases of the performance tree (data gathering, quantification, analysis, improvement), tend asymptotically towards just-in-time.

Addition–integration dynamic: reduce 'injustices' in the evaluation process, do not discourage quality

- integrate customer and account typologies and disadvantaged customers into the performance tree (the typology criteria will have to vary depending on the activity considered: for example by customers' age in the case of the inheritance activity and by the economic situation (volume of assets) of customers or accounts in the case of current and savings accounts);
- extend the data gathering periods or plan checks that take account of work cycles;
- combine the performance tree with risk data for the family codes;
- incorporate service quality ratios, particularly by seeking them out in qualipost, teleperformance and the general unit plan;
- incorporate certain organizational particularities (internal organization, services provided for others, use of service providers) when they are imposed on the centres;
- incorporate certain particular characteristics of the work force when they are 'enforced' (that is unavoidable or cannot be modified);
- incorporate certain particularities of the technical systems and the buildings when they cannot be modified.

Outsourcing in French Government Departments

There is an extensive literature on the reasons for and mechanisms of outsourcing (see Gadrey *et al.*, 1992). One important conclusion of these studies is that the arguments advanced to explain the outsourcing or delegation of functions cannot rely on transaction costs alone but must also take account of differences in expertise, which play a fundamental role. Such arguments are linked, both statically and dynamically, to the internal complexity of the processes involved in the production and distribution of goods and services, on the one hand, and, on the other, to the complexity of the external (physical, scientific and technical, economic, social and institutional) environment. They are also linked to the increasing prominence of uncertainty and risk. Here too, a distinction can be made between internal risk (that is risk linked to the internal environment) and external risk (risk linked to the external environment). This risk has to be evaluated, covered and prevented.

Danjou and Massa (2004) carried out an audit of outsourcing practices in French government ministries. Outsourcing, it should be noted, is defined restrictively as 'the (partial or total) delegation of functions on a multiannual basis'. Outsourcing is spreading (and is likely to spread still further) within central government departments, driven in particular by new legal arrangements, such as the Organic Law on the Finance Acts, public–private partnerships and the new public markets code.

This audit identifies a number of general causes of outsourcing in public services:

- the state of the public finances and economic criteria (lower costs, savings on the cost of civil service pensions, greater flexibility in managing the economic situation than if in-house employees are used);
- labour shortages caused by the introduction of the 35-hour week and job cutbacks in the civil service;
- qualitative restructuring of the labour force (reduction in the number of civil servants in category C, increase in the number of those in category A);
- lack of expertise in certain areas. This applies to 'technological' functions such as IT and reprographics as well as to buildings maintenance and even some caretaking and security functions.

The audit also identifies a number of factors specific to individual ministries. In the Ministry of Economics and Finance, for example, the outsourcing of photocopying services was intended to free up space: it was essentially a matter of estates management. In the Ministry for Social Affairs, Info Emploi, a job and careers information service which was set up by making permanent a help line established several years previously as a one-off, temporary exercise in communication with the public at large is now seen as a means of improving service quality. In the Ministry of Foreign Affairs, the recruitment of local staff can be problematic (because of national variations in the rigidity of dismissal protection legislation) and so outsourcing is frequently used.

However, there are of course certain factors that may be obstacles to outsourcing. These factors are no different from those encountered elsewhere.

Table 7.3   Ministry for Social Affairs: outsourcing of standard logistical support functions (after Danjou and Massa, 2004)

Logistical support function	Outsourcing
IT services	Yes
Photocopiers	No, machines purchased
Printing	Yes, but professional reprographics in-house
Caretaking	Yes, included in office rent
Security	Yes, included in office rent, but senior official appointed and staff designated
Cleaning	Yes
Reception	Yes, included in office rent
Building construction, estates management	No
Buildings maintenance	Yes in the case of rented offices; no in the case of state buildings (Hôtel du Chatelet, Minister's official residence)
Vehicle fleet	No
Catering	Yes
Mail	No

They may lie with the government (social risk, difficulty of assessing costs and so on) or they may be linked to providers (absence of same, risk of provider bankruptcy, risk of intrusion, risk of dependency on the provider and so on).

Among the functions that are often outsourced are logistical support functions such as cleaning, catering, caretaking, security, reception, telephone switchboard, estates management, buildings maintenance, IT services, photocopying, printing, vehicle fleets and mail sorting. Virtually all ministries outsource cleaning and catering. As far as the other functions are concerned (for example vehicle fleet management and IT services), there are significant differences between the ministries. Table 7.3 summarizes the ways in which these main general support functions are provided in the Ministry for Social Affairs.

Some outsourced functions are specific to particular ministries. In contrast to those listed above, they are closer to the heart of the 'core mission' of the ministry in question. As far as the Ministry of Social Affairs is concerned, the study reveals that the main areas of outsourcing (in the restricted sense described in the introduction to this section) are IT services and communications. IT has long been a target for outsourcing. Initially, the services were provided jointly by teams from the Ministry and external providers. IT services are now subcontracted in their entirety. Thus for its website, which is externally hosted, the Ministry calls on web editors. This subcontracting takes place on the basis of three-year, non-renewable public market contracts. Upgrade maintenance for both the Internet and the Ministry intranet and software development is carried out by external service providers. Communications are a relatively new target for outsourcing. The two main services mentioned are the 'Info Emploi' job and careers information service, which is subcontracted to external providers, who answer the public's questions either on the telephone or through the Internet, and the management of the Ministry's video library.

Productivity in the Ministry of Health and Social Affairs

One of the explicit aims of the recent reforms in the French Ministry of Health and Social Affairs (and this is true of all other government departments incidentally) was to improve productivity. These reforms have all helped, to varying degrees, to transform a bureaucracy engaged in a diversity of activities into an (increasingly specialized and narrowly based) organization engaged in *strategic steering and planning–design functions*. As the reforms have developed, the Ministry has, in various ways (delegation to various operators, decentralization, and so on) and to varying degrees, withdrawn from certain activities in order to concentrate on design–planning and steering functions. As a result of these developments, the concept of productivity has gradually lost if not its relevance then at least its effectiveness (in terms both of its definition and its implementation). As the Ministry proceeds along its new trajectory and is transformed into a planning and design organization, use of the concept increasingly comes up against the law of diminishing returns.

The recent development of the Ministry of Health and Social Affairs
Drawing once again, for heuristic purposes, on Mintzberg's canonic model (see Chapter 4), we can describe the recent development of the Ministry of Health and Social Affairs (MHSA) in terms of four guiding principles, which do not necessarily equate to chronological phases, since they can coexist in time.

- The first principle is delegation. It involves reducing the Ministry's scope by entrusting, in different ways and with varying degrees of autonomy, the management of its policies to various types of operator: social security organizations, hospitals, non-profit-making associations, health agencies and so on (see Figure 7.2). This principle may be reflected in the establishment of new agencies or in an

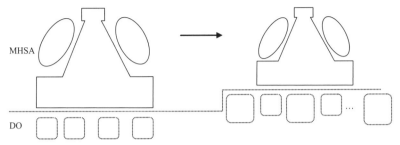

MHSA = Ministry of Health and Social Affairs, DO = delegated operators

Figure 7.2   Delegation and decentralization

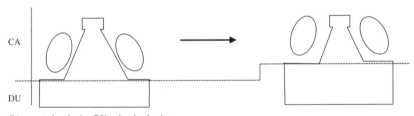

CA = central authority, DU = devolved units

Figure 7.3   Deconcentration

extension of the scope of the remit (that is the functions and prerog-
atives) of the existing agencies.

• The second principle is decentralization, which can be described in
the same terms as the previous development, that is it reduces the
scope of the MHSA. It involves the devolvement of a number of
health and social policies to the regional authorities. This applies, for
example, to the welfare of mothers-to-be and infants, child welfare
services and social services, all of which were transferred to the
departments (one of the 95 administrative divisions of France) in the
early 1980s.

• The third principle is deconcentration, which involves 'transferring
the taking of certain decisions from the central authority to authorities responsible for a district or area but still upwardly accountable
to the central authority' (Rochet, 2002). In Mintzberg's configuration
(see Figure 7.3), deconcentration will manifest itself in a shift in the
distribution of tasks between the central authority and the devolved
offices (operational centre). Thus for a department (ministry) as a
whole with a given scope, the central authority shrinks in favour of
the devolved offices.

Figure 7.4   A design, planning and steering authority

- The final principle consists in the (asymptotic, as it were) evolution towards design, planning and steering functions, in other words, towards a narrow focus on the technostructure component of the model (see Figure 7.4).

A general overview of the possible performance strategies

The principles outlined above (deconcentration, delegation to operators and decentralization) equate to structural performance levers, since they change the scope of the organization under consideration. If, for the purposes of simplification, structural reforms are set aside, a given structural configuration (that is one whose scope is relatively stable) can be investigated by identifying the possible performance levers that might be mobilized by the central authority (see Figure 7.5). We are dealing here with a set of possible generic strategies and levers that have not necessarily been activated at a given moment. It would be interesting to examine how the various ministerial reform strategies (MRS), in their various concrete manifestations, fit into this overall model. We will attempt to formulate a number of hypotheses on pp. 206–15. However that may be, the strategies adopted cannot be investigated properly without being located in the structural context (see pp. 202–204).

If we take as a reference point the MHSA's central departments (the technostructure and intellectual support services), three interrelated groups of performance strategies can be identified.

- The first group consists of internal performance strategies. It includes all those strategies that seek to improve the performance of the central authority itself (except for structural strategies, which are disregarded here for simplicity's sake). The levers on which these strategies are based may be human (human resource strategies, such as training, promotion and pay), organizational (re-engineering of internal processes, subcontracting, contractualization, standardization, and so on) or technological, whether tangible (computerization,

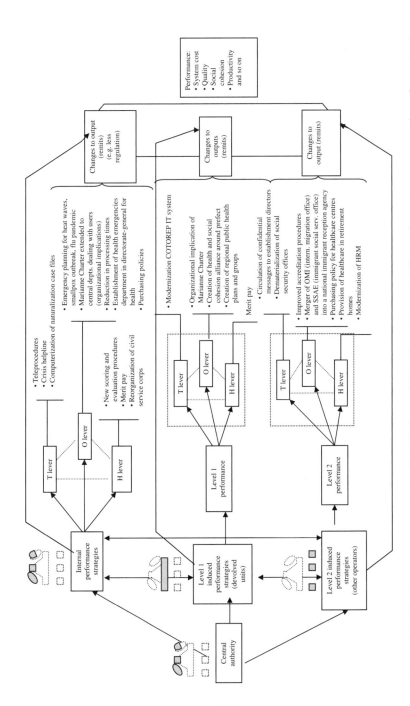

Figure 7.5   Performance strategies in the Ministry of Health and Social Affairs (for a given structural configuration)

205

automation) or intangible (methods). It should be noted that, in reality, tangible technologies are often located at the intersection between the technical and organizational levers. These strategies also rely on changes to the 'outputs' provided (that is the remits fulfilled), either directly or through implementation of the various levers already mentioned.

- The second and third groups comprise all the strategies for inducing improved performance in other units. It should not be forgotten, after all, that the primary purpose of the central authority, as a technostructure, is to 'coach' all the other units so that they perform better. We shall make a distinction here between level 1 induced performance strategies, which are applied to the devolved units, and level 2 induced performance strategies, which are applied to the other operators.

This distinction between these two groups of strategies (internal and induced) is the same as that made in the case of external consultancy and support service providers between their own internal performance and the performance they induce in their clients. In consultancy as in a central government department, the two terms of this distinction are, self-evidently, not independent of each other.

The aim of the induced performance strategies, whether applied to devolved units (level 1) or to other operators (level 2), is to induce improved performance from these two types of 'intermediate clients', not only by making use, once again, of human, technical or organizational levers but also by changing the nature of the remits. As in the case of outside consultants (whose induced performance level depends on the client's quality and competence), we can say that the level of induced performance achieved in the MHSA depends on the quality of the devolved unit or delegated operator under consideration.

Overall, these strategies are targeted at different aspects of performance: quality, social cohesion, productivity and, now in particular, reduction of the cost of the health and welfare systems (this is the purpose of the reform of the health insurance system, for example).

Reforms of the Ministry of Health and Social Affairs and diminishing returns for the concept of productivity

The various developments described above are (also) intended to produce productivity gains. However, the potential sources of productivity gradually dry up as the changes are introduced, leading to the adoption of strategies designed to exploit other aspects of performance (sometimes ambiguously).

The gradual depletion of potential sources of productivity If we take the central design, planning and steering authority as a reference unit, then the recent reforms described above encompass two general types of productivity strategy, one that could be described as *extensive* and another that could be described as *intensive*. This is a deliberate pedagogical simplification, since the dynamic nature of the organization means that the boundary between the two types of strategy is not always easy to mark out.

Extensive productivity strategies Extensive productivity strategies are designed to achieve overall productivity gains, outside the central authority, by reducing the scope of the central authority (through delegation, decentralization and deconcentration). The hypothesis here is that most of the productivity gains can be achieved in the delegated, decentralized or deconcentrated structures. It is here that there are relatively large numbers of employees, a very diverse range of professions and specializations, larger fields of standardization and opportunities to use technologies on a large scale. Thus it is hardly surprising that most of the studies of productivity in government services focus on these levels of analysis.

A traditionally important source of productivity, namely logistical support functions (their operational component only), can also be included in this group. After all, given the particular relationship between these activities and 'material process', productivity gains can be achieved through work organization, use of technologies, outsourcing and so on. These sources of productivity have been extensively exploited in government departments (see pp. 199–202), as they have in all large manufacturing and service companies.

A third potential source of productivity that can be exploited is located at the intersection between extensive and intensive strategies. We are referring here to the various entities or areas of responsibility at the intersection between a number of different ministries, or to those entrusted to the Ministry of Social Affairs but that could also be allocated to other departments. These are, for the most part, areas of activity that fall within the scope of the technostructure but in which performance levels are likely to be decreased by the fuzzy sharing of responsibilities between a number of different ministries or which would be more effective if they were allocated to other ministries. As already noted, the French Ministry of Health and Social Affairs combines two ministries (health and social ministries) that are sometimes separated in other countries. It is closely linked to the national employment ministry. More generally, one of its fundamental characteristics is that its main areas of responsibility (social policies in particular) are, to a significant degree, cross-cutting (inter-ministerial). One of the important consequences of this is that its own performance can be influenced by the strategies and performance of other ministries. This question of the sharing of work and responsibilities between ministries can of course be extended to include the question of how efficient and effective a single ministry dealing with both health and social issues is likely to be. In other words, would it not be more efficient to have two separate ministries?

Intensive productivity strategies   These intensive strategies are designed to exploit sources of productivity within a central authority reduced schematically to its technostructure (design/planning function). They involve a reduced central authority that has taken on a contracting owner or client role, actually 'doing' less and less but commissioning more and more; it is no longer an operational actor but functions as a strategist, planner and evaluator.

These intensive strategies are also characterized by a tendency, within the general design–planning functions, to prioritize strategic steering and control functions over regulatory functions, which are regarded as too burdensome because of the excessive number of regulations.

The notion of strategic management encompasses the following three functions:

1. a planning function, in which the strategic goals to be achieved are defined in the light of the dynamic of the internal and/or external environment;
2. an operational strategy development function, in which the strategic goals are translated into concrete action plans;
3. a control function, in which the results are monitored, measured or evaluated.

The management sciences literature provides a number of normative principles governing what constitutes good strategic management. These various principles can be justified theoretically, to varying degrees, by economic theories of contract. Although this is by no means an exhaustive list, these rules generally include the following:

● a clear formulation of goals (that is, an explicit contract whose terms are clearly specified). These goals must be consistent with each other (non-contradictory) and allocated to the relevant decision-making and action levels;
● a clear formulation of the operational strategies that is consistent with the strategic goals;

- a selection of suitable performance indicators that is varied (that is able to take account of different aspects of the activity in question) but limited in number;
- the need to prioritize management over the gathering of indicators; and
- the establishment of a reward system (and, conversely, of a system of penalties).

It is not our intention here to pass judgement on the validity of such principles. However, it is immediately clear that they have certain limitations. In particular, excessive contractualization (interlocking of goals and action plans) is damaging to innovation and to efforts to adapt to particular (local) environments or to change. The introduction of procedural rationality may prove to be more effective than that of substantive rationality. As the management of consultancy services seems to show, 'good' strategic management can be co-management, in other words a rich service relationship based on cooperation, trust and equivalent levels (if not types) of expertise among the protagonists in the relationship ('peer' relations without fear of sanctions).

These strategies focused on steering functions can bring into play all the productivity factors set out in the preceding chapters. Thus productivity in planning and steering departments can be increased by improving the tangible or intangible technologies deployed (computer systems as well as methods and other toolkits, such as indicators, score boards and so on), by improving the work organization system, by introducing a better division of labour between the various departments in the central authority (particularly one that resolves any problems related to the boundaries between them), by more effective external relations or even a better division of labour between the ministries.

The ministerial reform strategies adopted in this ministry furnish a number of examples of possible improvements, which do not have to be listed here. Some of them are mentioned in Figure 7.5, while a number of illustrations from other ministries are listed in Box 7.4.

BOX 7.4   EXAMPLES OF INTENSIVE PRODUCTIVITY STRATEGIES IN THE REFORM STRATEGIES OF VARIOUS MINISTRIES

- Establishment of general secretariat and groups in order to reduce the number of central departments (Ministry of Infrastructure)

- Reorganization of the civil aviation authority (Ministry of Infrastructure)
- Support and motivation measures (training, career enhancement and so on) for staff in central departments where jobs are being cut (Ministry of Infrastructure)
- Creation of a general secretariat to coordinate the actions of various departments (various ministries, incl. Ministries of Employment, Justice, Agriculture and so on)
- Development of a balanced scorecard for the minister and the committee of directors (Ministry of the Interior)
- Appointment of 'management control' officers in some sub-departments (Ministry of the Interior)
- Reorganization of central authority in order to incorporate three spheres of competence: sport, youth, voluntary sector (Ministry of Youth and Sports)
- Establishment in every department of a relevant system of indicators and scoreboard (Ministry of Justice)
- Introduction of merit pay for heads of department in the central authority (Ministry of Justice, Ministry of Agriculture and so on)
- Creation of a human resources information system shared by all units in the Ministry of Justice (Ministry of Justice)
- New sub-department of human resources in the central office of the department for the judicial protection of young people (Ministry of Justice)
- Reorganization of the department of prison administration (Ministry of Justice)
- Creation of a central information and communication department (Ministry of Justice)
- Relocation to a single site of departments spread over 11 different sites in Paris (Ministry of Foreign Affairs)
- Rationalization strategy for purchasing (Ministry of Economics and Finance)
- Organization of staff mobility between the various central departments (Ministry of Economics and Finance)
- Introduction of a collective performance bonus (Ministry of Economics and Finance)

Ultimately, the functional decomposition of output or 'product' that was mentioned in Chapter 2 may be useful here too in analyzing the potential sources of productivity, since steering functions may also in reality be broken down into material, information, knowledge and contact processing functions, even though most of the activities concern the second and, above all, third functions (knowledge processing). Thus productivity gains can be achieved in M type operations that involve the processing of tangible objects. These gains can be achieved in various ways: by mechanizing certain activities, changing work organization or using subcontractors.

Productivity gains can also be obtained in informational operations (I type) by introducing efficient information systems (hardware and software) and attempting to give the lie to manifestations of Solow's paradox, particularly through organizational integration programmes.

The knowledge processing component (K) of a service can also be a source of productivity gains. As in external consultancy activities, these gains are mediated through investment in internal and/or external training and the development of more or less formalized methodologies (intangible technologies). Thus just as outside consultants implement professional rationalization strategies based on the development of numerous structuring mechanisms (methodologies, models, blueprints, plans, scoreboards, toolboxes and so on), some of which are well known (BCG matrices and the Hay method, for example), internal consultants in the Ministry of Health and Social Affairs are developing procedures, structuring methodologies or, in Michel Berry's words (Berry, 1983), 'invisible technologies' for their own technostructure or for use in the devolved offices or by the delegated operators. We can include in this category the drafting of various contingency plans (heat wave plan, smallpox plan and so on), the development of accreditation procedures and the construction of new quality indicators, as well as, more generally and irrespective of the ministry in question, the simplification of administrative procedures.

Finally, productivity strategies may also be concerned with relational operations or functions (R). As far as planning/design public departments are concerned, these 'contact' relations concern internal 'customers' (the devolved offices, delegated operators and so on) rather than external (or final) customers. These relations have often been planned and interpreted within the framework of agency theories. They suffer from the limitations inherent in this type of relationship, as already outlined in Chapter 5. Agency theories seek to improve productivity by contractualizing and monitoring targets and performance, as well as by putting in place incentive mechanisms. In so doing, they tend to impoverish the social content of the service relationship. However, it is possible, as certain management and socio-economic theories of services recommend, to improve performance, if not productivity, by enriching this service relationship. Thus as in external consultancy relationships (Gadrey and Gallouj, 1998), a 'sparring' type interface (coproduction), in which service providers and customers cooperate closely and jointly manage the process, can prove to be more effective than a 'jobbing' type interface, that is simple subcontracting and monitoring. In other words, the effectiveness of the interface activity between the Ministry of Health and Social Affairs and its clients is a crucial issue. It should be viewed not from a strictly informational perspective but rather in cognitive, social and relational terms.

However, these intensive productivity strategies come up against certain mechanical limitations. The most important one concerns the human factor in productivity, whether it is a question of its quality or its quantity. The numbers employed in this planning/design department cannot be reduced below a certain level, since an imbalance between the numbers employed in the central administration and those in the various operators may reduce the effectiveness of the steering functions. At a certain point, the strategy of increasing the number of clients (deconcentrated departments and agencies) and reducing the number of service providers comes up against a threshold effect.

This is a qualitative as well as a quantitative problem. After all, given the diversity of activities and occupations that are being 'steered', it is by no means certain that the whole range of competences required for effective strategic steering can continue to be covered beyond a certain staffing threshold. As is clear from the economics and management of external consultancy activities, the whole justification for these activities is the gap in expertise and competence. In other words, the planning/design department, like external consultants, must not be structurally less 'competent' than its 'clients'. The same reasons (limitations of strategies based on replacing internal providers with external providers and the need for complementarity between these two types of providers) explain why the number of in-house consultants has been rising continuously since the 1970s, despite the explosion in outsourcing.

However, even though they cannot be eliminated altogether, there are various strategies that can be adopted to push these thresholds back somewhat:

- inter-ministerial strategies for sharing productivity gains (see shared services in Canada);
- use of the specific competences of the experts employed by the various operators (in hospital accounting departments or social security organizations, for example);
- use of outside consultants to provide very specific forms of expertise, when they exist and when outsourcing does not pose a strategic problem (risk of intrusion).

Another mechanical limitation liked to the human factor is competence (and perhaps also motivation). In general terms, central administrations have always been characterized by high levels of competence (and qualifications). It can reasonably be assumed that this level of competence will increase mechanically as activities become more tightly focused on design–planning and steering functions. Although it is always possible to improve competences (by strengthening in-house training even further, for example), it is unlikely that this is a particularly rich source of productivity gains. As for motivation or, more precisely, demotivation, it is frequently said to be a characteristic of employees in government administrative services. However, even if this is true, it seems reasonable to assume, in view of their level of responsibility and the nature of their work, that it is unlikely to be a fundamental characteristic of the experts in the technostructure, with whom we are concerned here.

A shift towards exploiting other performance goals As the traditional sources of productivity gains dry up, central government departments (and in particular the Ministry of Health and Social Affairs) facing demands to improve productivity have naturally and, in many cases, legitimately, turned to other performance goals.

The first goal: cost reduction and saving on resources This is not, of course, an illegitimate goal. It could even be extended beyond savings on 'costs borne' to an increase in 'costs avoided'. This distinction may prove to be particularly important in the sphere of health and social services. However, productivity gains should not be confused with cost savings. Such confusion is, nevertheless, a common occurrence.

It should be noted, incidentally, that in the traditional typologies of 'centres of responsibility' drawn up by specialists in management sciences, these entities (administrative departments) are generally regarded as 'discretionary expenditure centres'. They are entities with a diverse range of non-repetitive tasks whose efficiency and effectiveness are difficult to measure because there is no easy way to determine the link between the costs allowed and the results obtained (Le Maître, 1993). Their goal is to 'provide the best possible service within the budgetary constraints' and cost is the lever they can use to fulfil this objective.

However, while the organization's objective may be to reduce its costs, it is quite clear that cost reduction is not synonymous with productivity gains. A few illustrations will suffice to make the point convincingly. Reducing employees' salaries, for example, does not mean increasing their productivity. They will not be any more efficient in their work (and may even be less so). Failure to acknowledge this drains the concept of productivity of any analytical value.

The second goal: policy reform   Examination of this Department's ministerial reform strategy seems to suggest (and the same applies to all the other ministries) that policy reforms are currently being prioritized over structural or internal process reforms. Clearly, however, it is difficult to change these various policies or areas of responsibility (remit) without at the same time changing structures and internal processes.

There are two justifications for this order of priorities. The first is that many structural reforms have been introduced and the marginal productivity of new structural improvements is diminishing. The second is that these policy reforms have considerable financial implications, relative to their low management costs.

These policy reforms are reforms of the Ministry's remit, that is reforms of its 'products', both direct and indirect; in other words of both its outputs and its outcomes. Thus in a way we are dealing here with product innovations that are also institutional innovations. Reform of these remits can be considered from different points of view: the introduction of new remits, the improvement or reorientation of existing remits, the abandonment of existing remits that have become obsolete or their transfer to other entities.

In healthcare, the various 'products' or remits that are undergoing change (or reform) include, among other things, public health policy, the health security system, particularly warnings about and reactions to crisis situations, and the health insurance system. As far as social affairs are concerned, the main areas for reform are disability policy and asylum policy.

Internal performance and induced performance   The policy reforms are not, for the most part, aimed at internal performance. Their target is in fact performance as measured by the outcomes (that is the long-term results) of the Ministry's activities rather than by output. This being so, they seek to influence the induced performance of the various delegated operators, devolved offices, and so on (see pp. 204–206). The steering and planning-design services are acting here as a technostructure in Mintzberg's sense of the term. This induced performance has two important dimensions: first, a cost-saving dimension – the aim here is to economize on the resources managed by the operators, particularly in the area of health expenditure (see reform of health insurance and modernization of hospital management); and second, a service quality dimension, focusing on the quality of service provided to the end user (public health policy). These two dimensions are not independent of each other. They can be reconciled: effective policies for preventing cancer or hospital-acquired infections or for fighting drugs and drug addiction improve the quality of the service provided while at the same time economizing on resources. However, they can also prove to be contradictory.

Some new problems   These general developments pose other problems that impinge on the question of productivity.

As we have just noted, the Ministry of Health and Social Affairs has introduced numerous reforms relating to its remits (that is to its outputs) and to its structures (that is to its general organization). The scope of the organization has changed so much that any analysis of the evolution of its productivity over time is meaningless. After all, the nature of its output is no longer the same and the organizational reference unit is different. A similar difficulty is posed by some international comparisons of productivity in services. Thus a comparison of large-scale food retailing in France and the USA found that France was clearly superior in terms of productivity. In reality, however, this is merely a 'statistical illusion', since different outputs are being compared: large-scale food retailing in the USA is characterized by far greater service and relational intensity (Gadrey, 1996a).

It might also be asked whether, paradoxically, the Ministry's metamorphosis into a design, planning and steering centre might not ultimately mean it is locked into the 'technocratic ivory tower' that has been so decried in recent years. There is indeed a risk, inherent in the establishment of multiple agency relationships (of the contractor/project manager type), that these planning/design departments will become detached from the realities on the ground (which make themselves felt at the level of the devolved, delegated and decentralized offices). Decentralization and deconcentration bring the (decentralized or deconcentrated) departments closer to users, but do they not make the central functions more remote? This risk of remoteness from users, from the end customers may be combined with increasing difficulties in performance management associated with the proliferation of agency relationships.

CONCLUSION

In attempting to summarize productive strategies in services, we made a distinction in the previous chapter between assimilation strategies, which seek to improve productivity by industrializing services, and particularist strategies, which are based on forms of rationalization adapted to the specificities of service activities. This same distinction can also be used here, with a shift of focus away from the contrast between goods and services to that between market and non-market services. As far as productivity in public services is concerned, it is also possible to identify assimilation strategies, which ultimately involve the introduction into non-market services of the productivity strategies adopted in market services, and particularist strategies, which attempt to introduce practices adapted to the non-market aspect of these activities. The reforms being implemented in many countries, which draw in particular on the ideas of new public management, tend to have more in common with these assimilation strategies.

When one enters the black box of public organizations, as we have attempted to do in this chapter, the question of the productivity of internal functions (and in particular of the intellectual design, planning and steering functions) raises different problems. Presumptively, it combines several levels of difficulties. First, of course, there are those associated with the nature of the organizations in which they are located, namely government departments; second, the difficulties associated with the level of analysis adopted, that is the intra-organizational level, and, finally, the difficulties arising out of the nature of the functions carried out: these are intellectual functions analogous to (external) consultancy services.

In the preceding chapters, we considered at length the difficulties (in defining, measuring or attempting to increase productivity) associated with each of the levels. Our hypothesis is that, in view of their specificities, the problems posed by these functions fall within the sphere of performance rather than productivity. This does not mean that some productivity gains cannot be achieved but rather that it is difficult to envisage considerable gains being made in this area, particularly since such gains may, in some cases, have a negative effect on other, much more fundamental aspects of performance, particularly the short- or long-term effects, that is outcomes.

NOTES

1. More generally, however, the OECD emphasizes these benchmarking strategies as instruments for improving performance in public and private services (OECD, 2005).
2. Organic laws are types of laws whose purpose is to clarify the application of the Constitution. They carry less weight than the Constitution itself but more than ordinary laws.
3. It should be noted, however, that 'funds are not wholly interchangeable', since unused investment or operating funds cannot be used for recruiting personnel.

General conclusion

The concept of productivity, which was developed initially for use in industrial and agricultural economies, is a 'Fordist' concept that poses few difficulties when applied to standardized products, whether goods or services. After all, it describes the technical efficiency of a process in terms of the ratio between a volume of clearly identified output and a factor of production. Calculating such a ratio is a simple task when we are dealing with tangible outputs. The advent of the service economy and, more generally, of the intangible economy (beyond the service sector itself) has called into question if not the relevance of the concept then at least the methods used to measure it. The question of productivity in services raises important conceptual, methodological and strategic problems for economists, national accountants, corporate managers and government officials (whose task is to ensure that public resources are used efficiently).

We have tried, in reviewing the literature, to take stock of the theoretical, methodological and strategic debates on the problem of productivity in services. We have tried to make this survey as comprehensive as possible, mindful of the need to take into account the many different approaches adopted in terms of definitions, measurement and strategies (that is mobilization of the factors of productivity).

One of the findings of our study is that 'groups of levels' of difficulty can be identified when it comes to applying the concept of productivity (whether it is a question of defining the concept and measuring it or planning and implementing strategies to improve productivity). These groups differ depending on the level of analysis adopted.

The first group is located at the inter-sectoral level and pits the manufacturing sector against the service sector. After all, the notion of productivity is much more difficult to define, measure and implement in services than in manufacturing, where it originated. However, the two elements in this first group are clearly very far from being homogeneous. They can themselves be divided into various groups of levels, which makes it necessary to reconsider and qualify this initial general observation.

Adopting an intra-sectoral perspective this time, it is also possible to identify groups or clusters of levels of difficulty within each of the previous sectors. Thus the productivity question is more easily dealt with in traditional manufacturing industries than in the information and knowledge industries characterized by permanent innovation. It is relatively less problematic in market services than in non-market services. In market services, the concept of productivity comes up against difficulties as the cognitive content of the activities under investigation increases. Thus it is better suited to operational services than to knowledge-intensive business services. Within the non-market sector, the problem seems more acute in government services than in others.

The groups of difficulty levels are also present at the level of organizations themselves, regardless of the sector in question. Thus the difficulty is less severe in internal operational services than in intellectual design, planning and steering services.

If it is accepted, as a general hypothesis, that contemporary economies are increasingly service, knowledge and innovation economies, then taking account of the various 'order relations' described above implies that the notion of productivity will see a gradual shrinking of its scope of application. The rise to prominence of services, of information, of knowledge, of quality and of innovation within organizations and sectors of the economy increases the challenges facing the notion of productivity and its application.

If, for the various reasons we have just outlined, contemporary economies seem to be less and less *productivity* economies, they are increasingly becoming *performance* economies, in which *evaluation* is taking precedence over *measurement*. Multi-criteria analyses based on a concept of the product as a 'social construction' provide interesting ways of carrying out pluralist evaluations of this kind. Productivity (short-term technical performance) has not been abandoned. It still has a relatively important place, but other aspects of labour performance are also being considered: 'economic' performance of course, but also civic, relational, innovation and even reputational performance. These various kinds of performance may manifest themselves in the short term (output) or in the long term (outcome).

The fundamental advantage of such approaches is their flexibility and their ability to take account of the diversity of economic and social situations. Thus it is possible simply to abandon the concept of productivity when it appears to be inappropriate or of lesser importance than other aspects of performance. Moreover, these approaches make it possible to take account, in a systemic and non-distorting way, of the relationships between the various types of performance. They are not, after all, independent of each other. There may be positive or negative relationships between them that absolutely have to be taken into account, not only in any measurement of performance but also, and above all, in the planning of each particular performance strategy.

Bibliography

Abernathy, W. and Utterback, J. (1978), Patterns of industrial innovation, *Technology Review*, **80** (June–July), 41–7.

Adjerad, S. (1997), *L'évaluation des organismes de service public à vocation sociale: une approche par le produit*, PhD Thesis, University of Lille 1, October.

Adjerad, S. (1999), *Les mondes de production des services sociaux: le cas des caisses d'allocation familiales*, 6th IFRESI Conference, Lille, 21–22 April.

Afonso, A. and St Aubyn, M. (2005), Non-parametric approaches to education and health efficiency in OECD countries, *Journal of Applied Economics*, **8** (2), 227–46.

Afonso, A., Schknecht, L. and Tanzi, V. (2005), Public sector efficiency: an international comparison, *Public Choice*, **123** (3–4), 321–47.

Aigner, D. J. and Chu, S.F. (1968), On estimating the industry production function, *American Economic Review*, **58**, 826–39.

Aigner, D. J., Lovell, C. A. K. and Schmidt, P. (1977), Formulation and estimation of stochastic frontier production function models, *Journal of Econometrics*, **6**, 21–37.

Anderson, R. I., Fish, M., Xia, Y. and Michello, F. (1999), Measuring efficiency in the hotel industry: a stochastic frontier approach, *International Journal of Hospitality Management*, **18** (1), 45–7.

Arrow, K. (1962), The economic implication of learning by doing, *Review of Economic Studies*, **29** (80), 155–73.

Ashaye, T. (2001), Recent developments in the measurement of general government output, *Economic Trends*, **76** (November), 41–4.

Audit Commission (2001), *Managing to Improve Local Services*, London.

Barras, R. (1986), Towards a theory of innovation in services, *Research Policy*, **15**, 161–73.

Barras, R. (1990), Interactive innovation in financial and business services: the vanguard of the service revolution, *Research Policy*, **19**, 215–37.

Barraud-Didier, V. (1999), *Contribution à l'étude du lien entre les pratiques de GRH et la performance financière de l'entreprise: le cas des pratiques de mobilisation*, PhD Thesis, University of Toulouse I.

Barro, R. J. and Sala-i-Martin, X. (1995), *Economic Growth*, New-York: McGraw-Hill.

Barros, C. P. (2004), A stochastic cost frontier in the Portuguese hotel industry, *Tourism Economics*, **10** (2), 177–92.

Barros, C. P. (2005), Performance measurement in tax offices with a stochastic frontier model, *Journal of Economic Studies*, **32** (6), 497–510.

Barros, C. P. and Matias, A. (2006), Assessing the efficiency of travel agencies with a stochastic cost frontier: a Portuguese case study, *International Journal of Tourism Research*, **8** (5), 367–79.

Barros, C. P. and Santos, C. A. (2006), The measurement of efficiency in Portuguese hotels using data envelopment analysis, *Journal of Hospitality and Tourism Research*, **30** (3), 378–400.

Bartelsman, E., Van Leeuwen, G., Nieuwenhuijsen, H. and Zeelenburg, K. (1996), *R-D and Productivity Growth: Evidence from Firm-Level Data in the Netherlands*, Conference of the European Economic Association, Istanbul.

Bassanini, A., Scarpetta, S. and Visco, I. (2000), *Knowledge, Technology and Economic Growth: Recent Evidence from OECD Countries*, OECD Working Paper, May.

Batley, R. (1999), *The Role of Government in Adjusting Economies: an Overview of Findings*, International Development Department, University of Birmingham, Birmingham, AL.

Battese, G. E. and Cora, G. S. (1977), Estimation of a production frontier model: with application to the pastoral zone of eastern Australia, *Australian Journal of Agricultural Economics*, **21**, 169–79.

Bauer, P. W. (1990), Recent developments in the econometric estimation of frontiers, *Journal of Econometrics*, **46** (1/2), 39–56.

Baumol, W. (1967), Macroeconomics of unbalanced growth: the anatomy of urban crisis, *American Economic Review*, **3** (June), 415–26.

Baumol, W. J. and Bowen, W. G. (1968), *Performing Arts – The Economic Dilemma*, Boston, MA: The MIT Press.

Baxter, M. (2000), Developments in the measurement of general government output, *Economic Trends*, **562** (September), 3–5.

Bélanger, J. (2001), L'influence de la participation des employés sur la productivité: état de la recherche, *Gazette du travail*, **4** (4), 72–88.

Bell, D. (1973), *The Coming of Post-Industrial Society*, New York: Basic Books.

Bernatchez, J. C. (2003), *L'appréciation des performances au travail: de l'individu à l'équipe*, Sainte-Foy: Presses de l'Université du Québec.

Berry, M. (1983), *Une technologie invisible: l'impact des instruments de gestion sur l'évolution des systèmes humains*, Paris: CRG, mimeo.

Billaudot, B. (2001), *Régulation et croissance*, Paris: L'Harmattan.

Bluestone, B. and Harrison, B. (1986), *The Great American Job Machine*, Report for the Joint Economic Committee, December.

Boltanski, L. and Thévenot, L. (1991), *De la justification. Les économies de la grandeur*, Paris: Gallimard.

Bonneville, L. (2001), Un regard sociologique sur la notion de productivité dans le passage à la nouvelle économie, *Hermès: revue critique*, **8**, 1–16.

Boskin, M. J. (1996), *Towards a More Accurate Measure of the Cost of Living*, Report for the Senate Committee by the Advisory Commission to Study the Consumer Price Index, December, 5.

Boulianne, N. (2005), *Résumés d'études statistiques sur l'impact des innovations organisationnelles*, Direction de la Recherche et de l'Evaluation, Ministère du Travail, Québec, January.

Boyer, R. (2004), *Théorie de la regulation, les fondamentaux*, Paris: La Découverte.

Broussolle, D. (1997), *Un réexamen de deux problèmes de mesure de la production dans les services marchands: l'unité de production et la prise en compte du résultat*, Colloque de l'AFSE, September.

Burchell, B. (2002), The prevalence and redistribution of job insecurity and work intensification, in Burchell, B., Lapido, D. and Wilkinson, F. (eds), *Job Insecurity and Work Intensification*, London: Routledge, pp. 8–38.

Cameron, G. (1998), *Innovation and Growth: a Survey of the Empirical Evidence*, Nuffield College Oxford, mimeo.

Caplan, D. (1998), Measuring the output of non-market services, *Economic Trends*, **359** (October), 45–9.

Castagnos, J. C. (1987), Performance et gestion publique: un pari impossible, *Economies et Sociétés*, **12**, 141–73.

Caves, D. W., Christensen, L. R. and Diewert, W. E. (1982), The economic theory of index numbers and the measurement of input, output and productivity, *Econometrica*, **50**, 1393–414.

CBO (Congressional budget office) (1981), *The Productivity Problem: Alternatives for Actions*, Congressional budget office US Congress, Washington, January.

Centre APST (1992), *L'évaluation économique à l'épreuve des services*, report for Ministère de la Recherche et de la technologie, Centre APST University Aix-en-Provence.

CENV (Centre d'Etude sur le Niveau de Vie) (1998), *La productivité: secret de la réussite économique*, March, rapport pour L'Agence de promotion économique du Canada Atlantique.

Chaffai, M. (1997), Estimation de frontières d'efficience: un survol des développements récents de la littérature, *Revue d'économie du développement*, **3**, 33–67.

Charnes, A., Cooper, W. W. and Rhoades, E. (1978), Measuring the efficiency of decision making units, *European Journal of Operational Research*, **2**, 429–44.

Charnes, A., Cooper, W. W., Lewin, A. Y. and Seiford, L. M. (eds) (1995), *Data Envelopment Analysis: Theory, Methodology and Applications*, Dordrecht: Kluwer.

Chen, A., Hwang, Y. and Shao, B. (2005), Measurements and sources of overall and input inefficiencies: evidences and implications in hospital services, *European Journal of Operational Research*, **161**, 447–68.

Clark, C. (1940), *The Conditions of Progress and Security*, London: Macmillan.

Coe, D. and Helpman, E. (1995), International R-D spillovers, *European Economic Review*, **39**, 859–87.

Coelli, T. (2002), A comparison of alternative productivity growth mesaures: with application to electricity generation, in Fox, K. (ed.), *Efficiency in the Public Sector*, Dordrecht: Kluwer Academic Publishers, pp. 169–200.

Cohen, M. and Levinthal, D. (1989), Innovation and learning: the two faces of R-D, *Economic Journal*, **99** (397), 569–96.

Cohen, S. and Zysman, J. (1987), *Manufacturing Matters*, New York: Basic Books.

Cully, M., Woodland, W., O'Reilly, A. and Dix, G. (eds) (1999), *Britain at Work*, London, New York: Routledge.

Cunéo, P. (1984), L'impact de la Recherche-Développement sur la productivité industrielle, *Economie et Statistique*, **164** (March), 3–18.

Cunéo, P. and Mairesse, J. (1984), Productivity and R&D at the firm level in French manufacturing, in Griliches, Z. (ed.), *R&D, Patents and Productivity*, Chicago, IL: University of Chicago Press, pp. 375–93.

DAGPB (Direction de l'administration générale, du personnel et du budget) (2003), *Ministères de l'emploi, de la santé, de la famille, de la parité et de l'égalité professionnelle: Missions et Structures*, Paris: DAGPB.

Danjou, B. and Massa, E. (2004), *Services publics et externalisation: réalités, actualités et perspectives*, Rapport de stage, Ecole des Mines de Paris.

Debreu, G. (1951), The coefficient of resource utilization, *Econometrica*, **19** (3), 273–92.

Delaunay, J.-C. and Gadrey, J. (1987), *Les enjeux de la société de service*, Paris: Presses de la Fondation Nationale des Sciences Politiques.

Delfini, C. (1999), *Quelques éléments d'évaluation des services et de la performance à l'ANPE*, Services Group Seminar, University of Lille 1, mimeo.

Denison, E. (1962), *The Sources of Economic Growth in the United States*, Washington, DC: Committee for Economic Development.

Dewatripont, M., Jewitt, I. and Tirole, J. (1999), The economics of career concerns, *Review of Economic Studies*, **66** (1), 189–217.

Dixit, A. (1996), *The Making of Economic Policy: a Transaction Cost Politics Perspective*, Cambridge, MA: MIT Press.

Dixit, A. (2000), *Incentives and Organizations in the Public Sector: an Interpretative Review*, mimeo, Princeton University.

Djellal, F. (2002a), Technologies de l'information et services 'non informationnels', *Économies et Sociétés*, série EGS, **2** (June), 62–78.

Djellal, F. (2002b), Les services de nettoyage face aux nouvelles technologies, *Formation et Emploi*, **77**, 37–49.

Djellal, F. and Gallouj, F. (1999), Services and the search for relevant innovation indicators: a review of national and international surveys, *Science and Public Policy*, **26** (4), 218–32.

Djellal, F. and Gallouj, F. (2005), Mapping innovation dynamics in hospitals, *Research Policy*, **34**, 817–35.

Djellal, F., Gallouj, C. and Gallouj, F. (2001), *La R-D dans les services: à la recherche d'indicateurs utilisables*, Ministry of Higher Education, Research and Technology, December.

Djellal, F., Francoz, D., Gallouj, C., Gallouj, F. and Jacquin, Y. (2003), Revising the definition of research and development in the light of the specificities of services, *Science and Public Policy*, **30** (6), 415–29.

Dolton, P. (2003), Performance related pay for teachers, *Public Services Productivity Seminar Papers*, HM Treasury, London.

Donthu, N. and Yoo, B. (1998), Retail productivity assessment using data envelopment analysis, *Journal of Retailing*, **74** (1), 89–105.

Dopuch, N., Gupta, M., Simunic, D. A. and Stein, M. T. (2003), Production efficiency and the pricing of audit services, *Contemporary Accounting Research*, **20** (1), 47–77.

Drake, L. and Simper, R. (2003), The measurement of English and Welsh police force efficiency: a comparison of distance function models, *European Journal of Operational Research*, **147**, 165–86.

Drake, L. and Hall, M. J. B. (2003), Efficiency in Japanese banking: an empirical analysis, *Journal of Banking & Finance*, **27** (5), 891–917.

Drucker, P. (1989), *Les nouvelles réalités: de l'État-providence à la société du savoir*, Paris: InterÉditions.

Du Tertre, C. and Blandin, O. (1998), *Productivité et performance des activités de service: éléments de repères théoriques*, Intermediary research report, Direction de la stratégie et de la planification, La Poste, January.

Dumez, H. and Jeunemaître, A. (2003), Combinaison harmonieuse du public et du privé, ou mélanges des genres? Les partenariats public/privé nouveaux venus du management public, *Politiques et Management public*, **21** (4), 1–14.

Englander, A. S. and Mittelstädt, A. (1988), Total productivity: macroeconomic and structural aspects of the slowdown, *OECD Economic Studies*, **10**, Summer.

European Commission (2004), *Competitiveness and Benchmarking*, European competitiveness report, Enterprise and Industry publication.

Eurostat (2001), *Handbook of Price and Volume Measures in National Accounts*, Brussels: European Commission.

EWON (European Work Organisation) (2001), *New Forms of Work Organisation: the Benefits and Impact on Performance*.

Färe, R., Grosskop, S. and Lovell, C. A. K. (1985), *The Measurement of Efficiency of Production*, Boston, MA: Kluwer-Nijhoff.

Färe, R., Grosskop, S., Norris, M. and Zhang, Z. (1994), Productivity growth, technical progress, and efficiency changes in industrialised countries, *American Economic Review*, **84**, 66–83.

Farrell, M. J. (1957), The measurement of productive efficiency, *Journal of the Royal Statistical Society (series A)*, **120** (3), 253–81.

Farsi, M., Filippini, M. and Kuenzle, M. (2006), Cost efficiency of regional bus companies: an application of alternative stochastic frontier models, *Journal of Transport Economics and Policy*, **40** (1), 105–18.

Fernandez, C., Koop, G. and Steel, M. F. J. (2005), Alternative efficiency measures for multiple-output production, *Journal of Econometrics*, **126** (2), 411–44.

Fisk, D. and Forte, D. (1997), The federal productivity measurement program: final results, *Monthly Labour Review*, May, 19–28.

Fleck, J. (1994), Learning by trying: the implementation of configurational technology, *Research Policy*, **23**, 637–52.

Fourastié, J. (1949), *Grand Espoir du XXème siècle* [The Great Hope of the 20th Century], Paris: PUF.

Fox, K. J. (1999), Efficiency at different levels of aggregation: public vs. private sector firms, *Economic Letters*, **65** (2), 173–6.

Freeman, C. and Soete, L. (eds) (1987), *Technical Change and Full Employment*, Oxford: Basil Blackwell.

Fuchs, V. (ed.) (1969), *Production and Productivity in the Service Industries*, New York and London: Columbia University Press.

Fuentes, H. J., Grifell-Tatje, E. and Perelman, E. (2001), A parametric distance function approach for Malmquist productivity index estimation, *Journal of Productivity Analysis*, **15** (2), 79–94.

Gadrey, J. (1985), *Société de service ou de self-service: examen du cas français*, Johns Hopkins European Center for Regional Planning and Research, Working Paper No 14.

Gadrey, J. (1991), Le service n'est pas un produit: quelques implications pour l'analyse économique et pour la gestion, *Politiques et Management Public*, **9** (1), 1–24.

Gadrey, J. (1994), Les relations de services dans le secteur marchand, in De Bandt, J. and Gadrey, J. (eds), *Relations de service, marchés des services*, Paris: CNRS Editions, pp. 23–42.

Gadrey, J. (1996a), *Services: la productivité en question*, Paris: Desclée de Brouwer.

Gadrey, J. (1996b), *L'économie des services*, Paris: La Découverte (2nd edition).

Gadrey, J. (2002a), La théorie de la régulation à l'épreuve de l'économie de la qualité et du service, *Economies et Sociétés*, série EGS, No 4, 7/2002, 1095–117.

Gadrey, J. (2002b), Croissance et productivité: des indicateurs en crise larvée, *Travail et Emploi*, **91** (July), 9–17.

Gadrey, J. (2003), *Socio-économie des services*, Paris: Repère, La Découverte.

Gadrey, J. and Gallouj, F. (1998), The provider–customer interface in business and professional services, *Service Industries Journal*, **18** (2), 1–15.

Gadrey, J., Gallouj, C., Gallouj, F., Martinelli, F., Moulaert, F. and Tordoir, P. (1992), *Manager le Conseil*, Paris: Edisciences International.

Gadrey, J. and Jany-Catrice, F. (2007), *Les nouveaux indicateurs de croissance*, Paris: Repère, La Découverte.

Gallouj, C. (1997), Asymmetry of information and the service relationship, *International Journal of Services Industry Management*, **8** (5), 377–97.

Gallouj, F. (1994), *Economie de l'innovation dans les services*, Paris: Editions L'Harmattan.

Gallouj, F. (1999), *Evaluer et comparer les performances des établissements postaux: la méthode de l'arbre de performance en question*, Clersé, University of Lille I, Rapport de recherche pour la mission de la recherche de La Poste, November, 70 pp.

Gallouj, F. (2002a), Knowledge intensive business services: processing knowledge and producing innovation, in Gadrey, J. and Gallouj, F. (eds), *Productivity, Innovation and Knowledge in Services*, Cheltenham, Northampton, MA: Edward Elgar, pp. 256–84.

Gallouj, F. (2002b), Interactional innovation: a neo-Schumpeterian model, in Sundbo, J. and Fuglsang, L. (eds), *Innovation as Strategic Reflexivity*, London and New York: Routledge, pp. 29–56.

Gamache, R. (2005), *La productivité: définition et enjeux*, Travail Québec, February, mimeo.

Gershuny, J. (1978), *After Industrial Society? The Emerging Self-Service Economy*, London: Macmillan.

Gershuny, J. (1983), *Social Innovation and the Division of Labour*, Oxford: Oxford University Press.

Gershuny, J. and, Miles, I. (1983), *The New Service Economy*, London: Frances Pinter.

Gilbert, R. A., Whelelock, D. C. and Wilson, P. W. (2004), New evidence on the Fed's productivity in providing payments services, *Journal of Banking and Finance*, **28**, 2175–90.

Giles, A. (2005), *La productivité et l'emploi: un drôle de couple*, Forum sur la productivité et l'emploi, Québec, 14–15 March.

Goffman, E. (1968), *Asiles*, Paris: Editions de Minuit.

Gollac, M. and Volkoff, S. (1996), Citius, altius, fortius, l'intensification du travail, *Actes de la Recherche en Sciences Sociales*, **114** (September), 54–67.

Gordon, R. (2000), Does the 'New Economy' measure up to the great inventions of the past?, *Journal of Economic Perspectives*, **14** (4), 49–74.

Gordon, R. (2002), *Technology and Economic Performance in the American Economy*, CEPR, Discussion Paper Series, No 3213, February.

Gorz, A. (1988), *Métamorphoses du travail et quête de sens*, Paris: Galilée.

Government of Malaysia (1991), *Guidelines on Productivity Improvement in the Public Service*, Development administration circular No 6 OF 1991, July.

Green, F. (2001), *Why Has Work Effort Become More Intense? Effort Biased Technical Change and Other Stories*, Canterbury, Department of Economics, University of Kent.

Greene, W. and Segal, D. (2004), Profitability and efficiency in US life insurance industry, *Journal of Productivity Analysis*, **21**, 229–47.

Greiner, J. M. (1996), Positioning performance measurement for the twenty-first century, in Halachmi, A. and Bouckaert, G. (eds), *Organizational Performance and Measurement in the Public Sector*, London: Quorum Books, pp. 11–50.

Griliches, Z. (1964), Research expenditures, education, and the aggregate agricultural production function, *American Economic Review*, **54**, 961–74.

Griliches, Z. (1980a), Returns to R&D expenditures in the private sector, in Kendrick, K. W. and Vaccara, B. (eds), *New Developments in Productivity Measurement*, Chicago, IL: Chicago University Press.

Griliches, Z. (1980b), R&D and the productivity slowdown, *American Economic Review*, **70**, 343–8.

Griliches, Z. (ed.) (1984), *Output Measurement in the Service Sectors*, Chicago, IL: University of Chicago Press.

Griliches, Z. (1986), Productivity, R&D and basic research at the firm level in the 1970s, *American Economic Review*, **76**, 141–54.

Gueret-Talon, L. (2004), Management par la qualité: et si le service public devenait une référence sur le marché, *Politiques et Management public*, **22** (2), 39–54.

Halachmi, A. and Boorsma, P. (eds) (1998), *Inter and Intra Government Arrangements for Productivity: an Agency Approach*, Dordrecht: Kluwer Academic Publishers.

Hammond, C. (2002), Efficiency in the provision of public services: a data envelopment analysis of UK public library systems, *Applied Economics*, **34** (5), 649–57.

Handler, H., Koebel, B., Reiss, P. and Schratzenstaller, M. (2005), *The Size and Performance of Public Sector Activities in Europe*, WIFO (Osterreichisches Institut Für Wirstschaftsforschung), Working Paper No 246.

Harris, G. R. (1999), *Les déterminants de la croissance de la productivité canadienne: enjeux et perspectives*, Working Document, No 8.

He, Y. Q., Chan, L. K. and Wu, M. L. (2007), Balancing productivity and consumer satisfaction for profitability: statistical and fuzzy regression analysis, *European Journal of Operational Research*, **176** (1), 252–63.

Hempell, T. (2005), What's spurious, what's real? Measuring productivity impacts of ICT at the firm level, *Empirical Economics*, **30**, 427–64.

Hill, P. (1977), On goods and services, *Review of Income and Wealth*, **4** (23), 315–38.

HM Treasury (2003), *Public Services: Meeting the Productivity Challenge*, Discussion document, April.

Hollingsworth, B., Dawson, P. J. and Maniadakis, N. (1999), Efficiency measurement of health care: a review of non-parametric methods and applications, *Health Care Management Science*, **2**, 161–72.

Holmstrom, B. (1982), Moral hazard in teams, *Bell Journal of Economics and Management Science*, **13** (2), 324–40.

Holmstrom, B. and Milgrom, P. (1991), Multi-task principal agent analyses, *Journal of Law, Economics and Organization*, **7** (1), 24–52.

Holzer, M. and Lee, S.-H. (2004), Mastering public productivity and performance improvement from a productive management perspective, in Holzer, M., Lee, S.-H. (eds), *Public Productivity Handbook*, New York: Marcel Dekker, pp. 1–16.

Hulten, C. R. (1985), Comment: measurement of output and productivity in the service sector, in Inman, R. (ed.), *Managing the Service Economy*, Cambridge: Cambridge University Press, pp. 127–30.

Jaldell, H. (2005), Output specification and performance measurement in fire services: an ordinal output variable approach, *European Journal of Operational Research*, **161**, 525–35.

Jensen, M. C. and Meckling, W. H. (1976), Theory of the firm: managerial behavior, agency costs and ownership structure, *Journal of Financial Economy*, **3**, 305–60.

Jex, S. M. (1998), *Stress and Job Performance: Theory, Research and Implications for Managerial Practice*, Thousand Oaks, CA: Sage Publications.

Johnes, G. and Johnes, J. (1993), Measuring the research performance of UK economics departments: an application of data envelopment, *Oxford Economic Papers*, **45**, 332–47.

Jorgensen, D. W. (ed.) (1995), *Productivity: International Comparisons of Economic Growth*, Cambridge, MA: MIT Press.

Joumard, I., Kongsrud, M., Nam, Y. S. and Price, R. (2004), *Enhancing the Cost Effectiveness of Spending: Experiences in OECD Countries*, OCDE, Working Paper, 380.

Jowett, P. and Rothwell, M. (1988), *Performance Indicators in the Public Sector*, London, Macmillan.

Karasek, R. and Theorell, T. (1990), *Healthy Work: Stress, Productivity and the Reconstruction of Working Life*, New York: Basic Books.

Karlaftis, M. and Maccarthy, P. (1999), The effects of privatization on public transit costs, *Journal of Regulatory Economics*, **16**, 27–43.

Karpik, L. (1989), L'économie de la qualité, *Revue française de sociologie*, **XXX** (2), 187–210.

Keh, H. T. and Chu, S. (2003), Retail productivity and scale economies at the firm level: a DEA approach, *International Journal of Management Science*, **31**, 75–82.

Keh, H. T. and Chu, S. (2003), Retail productivity and scale economies at the firm level: a DEA approach, *OMEGA-International Journal of Management Science*, **31** (2), 75–82.

Kingman-Brundage, J. (1992), The ABCs of service system blueprinting, in Lovelock, C. (ed.), *Managing Services*, Englewood Cliffs, NJ: Prentice-Hall International Editions, pp. 96–102.

Knight, F. (1921), *Risk, Uncertainty and Profit*, Boston, MA and New York: Houghton Mifflin.

Knox Lovell, C. A. (2002), Performance assessment in the public sector, in Fox, K. (ed.), *Efficiency in the Public Sector*, Dordrecht: Kluwer Academic Publishers, pp. 11–35.

Koopmans, T. C. (1951), Efficient allocation of resources, *Econometrica*, **19**, 455–65.

Kopel, S. (2001), Le déroulement de carrières des 'surdiplômés de la fonction publique: propositions pour une gestion différenciée', *Politiques et Management public*, **19** (2), 25–43.

Kubr, M. (1988), *Management Consulting: a Guide to the Profession*, Geneva: BIT.

Lacaze, A. (2005), La Lolf: simple outil de management ou dogme écrasant? *Gérer et Comprendre*, September (81), 5–13.

Lakshmanan, T. R. (1987), *Technological and Institutional Innovation in the Service Sector*, Colloque 'echerche et développement, changement industriel et politique économique', University of Karlstad, Sweden, June.

Lawler, E. E. (1986), *High-Involvement Management: Participative Strategies for Improving Organizational Performance*, San Francisco, CA: Jossey Bass.

Lawrence, D., Houghton, J. and George, A. (1997), International comparisons of Australia's infrastructure performance, *Journal of Productivity Analysis*, **8**, 361–78.

Lay, G., Shapira, P. and Wegel, J. (eds) (1999), Innovation in production, *Technology, Innovation and Policy*, **8** (6).

Le Duff, R. and Papillon, J. P. (1992), La productivité des services publics, in Helfer, J. P. and Orsoni, J. P. (eds), *Encyclopédie du Management*, Paris: Vuibert, pp. 558–67.

Le Maître, D. (1993), *Evaluation de la performance et comportements opportunistes dans les centres de responsabilité*, PhD Thesis, University of Rennes 1.

Le Pen, C. (1986), La productivité des services publics non-marchands: quelques réflexions méthodologiques, *Revue d'Economie Politique*, **5**, 476–89.

Leibenstein, H. (1966), Allocative efficiency vs. X-efficiency, *American Economic Review*, **56** (June), 392–415.

Levitt, T. (1972), Production line approach to service, *Harvard Business Review*, **50**, 41–52.

Lewin, A., Morey, R. and Cook, T. (1982), Evaluating the administrative efficiency of courts, *Omega*, **10** (4), 401–11.

Lichtenberg, F. (1992), *R-D Investment and International Productivity Differences*, NBER Working Paper, No 4161.

Lindsay, C. M. (1976), A theory of government enterprise, *Journal of Political Economy*, **84** (5), 1061–77.

Lindsay, W. M. and Petrick, J. A. (1997), *Total Quality and Organisation Development*, Delray Beach, FL: St. Lucie Press.

Lovelock, C. (1992), A basic toolkit for service managers, in Lovelock, C. (ed.), *Managing Services*, Englewood Cliffs, NJ: Prentice-Hall International Editions, pp. 17–30.

Lowe, G. S. (2003), *Milieux de travail sain et productivité: un document de travail*, Division de l'analyse et de l'évaluation économiques, Santé Canada, April.

Lucas, R. (1988), On the mechanisms of economic growth, *Journal of Monetary Economics*, **22** (1), 3–42.

Lundvall, B. (1988), Innovation as an interactive process: from user–producer interaction to the nation system of innovation, in Dosi, G., Freeman, C., Nelson, R., Silverburg, G. and Soete, L. (eds), *Technical Change and Economic Theory*, London: Frances Pinter, pp. 349–69.

Mahar, M. (1992), Blue collar, white collar: good jobs are vanishing throughout the economy, *Barron's*, 11 May, 8–24.

Mahlberg, B. and Url, T. (2003), Effects of the single market on the Austrian insurance industry, *Empirical Economics*, **28**, 813–38.

Mairesse, J. and Cunéo, P. (1985), Recherche-développement et performances des entreprises: une étude économetrique sur données individuelles, *Revue Economique*, **36**, 1001–42.

Mairesse, J. and Hall, B. (1996), Estimating the productivity of research and development in French and United States manufacturing firms: an exploration of simultaneity issues with GMM methods, in Wagner, K. and Van Ark, B. (eds), *International Productivity Differences: Measurement and Explanations*, North Holland Amsterdam: Elsevier, pp. 285–315.

Mairesse, J. and Mohnen, P. (1990), Recherche-développement et productivité: un survol de la littérature économétrique, *Economie et Statistique*, No 237–8, November–December, 99–108.

Malerba, F. (1992), Learning by firms and incremental technical change, *Economic Journal*, **102**, 845–59.

Malleret, V. (1993), *Une approche de la performance des services fonctionnels: l'évaluation des centres de coûts discrétionnaires*, PhD Thesis, University of Paris IX-Dauphine.

Malleret, V. (1998), L'évaluation des performances des services fonctionnels: une étude empirique, *Finance, Contrôle, Stratégie*, **1** (1), 145–68.

Malmquist, S. (1953), Index numbers and indifference surfaces, *Trabajos de Estatistics*, **4**, 209–42.

Maniadakis, N., Hollingsworth, B. and Thanassoulis, E. (1999), The impact of the internal market on hospital efficiency, productivity and service quality, *Health Care Management Science*, **2**, 75–85.

Mansfield, E. (1961), Technical change and the rate of imitation, *Econometrica*, **29**, No 4, 741–66.

Mansfield, E. (1988), Industrial R&D in Japan and the United States: a comparative study, *American Economic Review*, **78**, 223–8.

Mayère, A. (1994), *Relations de service et enjeux d'industrialisation*, in De Bandt, J. and Gadrey, J. (eds), *Relations de service, marchés des services*, Paris: CNRS Editions, pp. 101–17.

Meeusen, W. and van den Broeck, J. (1977), Efficiency estimation from Cobb-Douglas production functions with composed error, *International Economic Review*, **18**, 435–44.

Meisenheimer, J. R. (1998), The service industries in the 'good' versus 'bad' jobs debate, *Monthly Labor Review*, February, 22–47.

Menon, N. M. and Lee, B. (2000), Cost control and production performance enhancement by IT investment and regulation changes: evidence from the healthcare industry, *Decision Support Systems*, **30**, 153–69.

Ministry of Labour (2005), *Changements organisationnels pour améliorer la productivité et l'emploi: recueil de cas vécus*, Québec (www.travail.gouv.qc.ca).

Mintzberg, H. (1979), *The Structuring of Organizations*, Englewood Cliffs, NJ: Prentice-Hall International Editions.

Murillo-Zamorano, L. R. (2004), Economic efficiency and frontier techniques, *Journal of Economic Survey*, **18** (1), 33–77.

Nachum, L. (1999), Measurement of productivity of professional services: an illustration on Swedish management consulting firms, *International Journal of Operations and Production Management*, **19** (9), 922–49.

Nadiri, M. (1980a), Sectoral productivity slowdown, *American Economic Review*, **70**, 349–55.

Nadiri, M. (1980b), Contributions and determinants of research and development expenditures in the US manufacturing industries, in von Furstenberg, G. (ed.), *Capital, Efficiency and Growth*, Cambridge, MA: Ballinger, pp. 361–92.

Nadiri, M. and Bitros, G. (1980), Research and development expenditures and labor productivity at the firm level, in Kendrick, J. and Vaccara, B. (eds), *Conference on New Developments in Productivity Measurement, Studies in Income and Wealth*, Vol. 44, Chicago, IL: University of Chicago Press, pp. 387–417.

Nadiri, M. and Prucha, I. (1990), Comparison and analysis of productivity growth and R&D investment in the electrical machinery industries of the United States and Japan, in Hulten, C. and Norsworthy, R. (eds), *Productivity Growth in Japan and the United States*, Chicago, IL: University of Chicago Press, pp. 109–33.

Nemoto, J. and Asai, S. (2002), Scale economies, technical change and productivity growth in Japanese local telecommunications services, *Japan and the World Economy*, **14**, 305–20.

Nonaka, S. (1994), A dynamic theory of organizational knowledge creation, *Organization Science*, **5** (1), 14–37.

Northwood, K., Hinchcliffe, C., Henderson, L. and Rawnsley, T. (2001), *Experimental Output Measures for the Australian Justice Sector*, Discussion paper No 1, Australian Bureau of Statistics.

Noyelle, T. (1986), *New Technologies and Services: Impact on Cities and Jobs*, College Park, MD: University of Maryland.

Odeck, J. (2000), Assessing the relative efficiency and productivity growth of vehicle inspection services: an application of DEA and Malmquist, *European Journal of Operational Research*, **126**, 501–14.

OECD (1995), *Services: Measuring Real Annual Value Added*, Paris.

OECD (1999), *Productivity Measurement in the General Government Sector*, Expert meeting, 18–19 March, Paris, PUMA/HRM/M(99)1.

OECD (2001), *Mesurer la productivité: mesurer la croissance de la productivité par secteur et pour l'ensemble de l'économie*, Paris (www.sourceOECD.org).

OECD (2003), *The E-government Imperative*, Paris.

OECD (2005), *Micro-policies for Growth and Productivity*, final report.

Oï, W. (1992), Productivity in the distributive trades: the shopper and the economies of massed reserves, in Griliches, Z. (ed.), *Output Measurement in the Service Sectors*, Chicago, IL: University of Chicago Press, pp. 161–91.

Olson, M. (1972), Evaluating performance in the service sector, in Moss, M. (ed.), *The Measurement of Economic and Social Performances*, New York: NBER, Columbia University Press.

Osborne, D. and Gaebler, T. (1992), *Reinviting Government*, Reading, MA: Addison Wesley Publishing Company.

Ouellette, P. and Vierstraete, V. (2004), Technological change and efficiency in the presence of quasi-fixed inputs: a DEA application of the hospital sector, *European Journal of Operational Research*, **154**, 755–63.

Oum, T. H., Yu, C. and Fu, X. (2003), A comparative analysis of productivity performance of the world's major airports: summary report of the ATRS global airport benchmarking research report, 2002, *Journal of Air Transport Management*, **9**, 285–97.

Parienty, A. (2005), *Productivité, croissance, emploi: la France dans la compétitivité mondiale*, Paris: Armand Colin.

Patel, P. and Soete, L. (1988), L'Evaluation des effets économiques de la technologie, *STI Review*, **4**, 133–83.

Pavitt, K. (1984), Sectoral patterns of technical change: towards a taxonomy and a theory, *Research Policy*, **13**, 343–73.

Perret, B. (1995), L'industrialisation des services, in Blanc, G. (ed.), *Le travail au XXIe siècle: mutations de l'économie et de la société à l'ère des autoroutes de l'information*, Paris: Dunod, pp. 37–8.

Petit, P. (1995), Employment and technological change, in Stoneman, P. (ed.), *Handbook of the Economics of Innovation and Technological Change*, Amsterdam: North Holland, pp. 366–408.

Petit, P. (1998), Formes structurelles et régimes de croissance de l'après-fordisme, les cahiers de CEPREMAP, No 9818.

Petit, P. (2002), Growth and productivity in a knowledge based service economy, in Gadrey, J. and Gallouj, F. (eds), *Productivity, Innovation and Knowledge in Services*, Cheltenham and Northampton, MA: Edward Elgar, pp. 102–23.

Porat, M. (1976), *The information economy*, PhD. Dissertation, Stanford.

Pritchard, A. (2002), *Measuring productivity change in the provision of public services*, NIESR Conference on Productivity and Performances in the Provision of Public Services, 19 November, London.

Pritchard, A. (2003), Understanding government output and productivity, *Economic Trends*, **596** (July), 27–40.

Pritchard, A. (2004), *Etude Atkinson sur la mesure de la production des administrations publiques au Royaume-Uni*, Office for National Statistics, Conference of European Statisticians, 8–10 June, Paris.

Ratchford, B. (2003), Has the productivity of retail food stores really declined?, *Journal of Retailing*, **79**, 171–82.

Rees, R. (1984), *Public Enterprise Economics*, 2nd edition, London: Weidenfeld and Nicholson.

Reynolds, D. and Thompson, G. M. (2007), Multiunit restaurant productivity assessment using three-phase data envelopment analysis, *International Journal of Hospitality Management*, **26** (1), 20–32.

Rochet, C. (2002), *Les établisssements publics nationaux: un chantier pilote pour la réforme de l'Etat*, Paris: La Documentation Française.

Romer, P. (1986), Increasing returns and long term growth, *Journal of Political Economy*, **94**, 1002–37.

Rosenberg, N. (1982), *Inside the Black Box: Technology and Economics*, Cambridge, MA: Cambridge University Press.

Rosko, M. D. and Mutter, R. L. (2008), Stochastic frontier analysis of hospital inefficiency, *Medical Care Research and Review*, **65** (2), 131–66.

Rouillard, L., Bourgault, J., Charih, M. and Maltais, D. (2004), Les ressources humaines: clé de voûte de la réforme du secteur public au Québec, *Politiques et Management public*, **22** (3), September, 91–6.

Rouse, P., Putterill, M. and Ryan, D. (2002), Integrated performance measurement design: insights from an application in aircraft maintenance, *Management Accounting Research*, **13**, 229–48.

Roy, W. and Yvrande-Billon, A. (2007), Ownership, contractual practices and technical efficiency: the case of urban public transport in France, *Journal of Transport Economics and Policy*, **41** (2), 257–82.

Rubalcaba, L. (2007), *The New Service Economy: Challenges and Policy Implications for Europe*, Cheltenham and Northampton, MA: Edward Elgar.

Salais, R. and Storper, M. (1993), *Les mondes de production Enquête sur l'identité économique de la France*, Paris: Ecole des hautes études en sciences sociales.

Sarkis, J. (2000), An analysis of the operational efficiency major airports in the United States, *Journal of Operation Management*, **18**, 335–51.

Sassenou, M. (1988), *Recherche-Développement et Productivité dans les Entreprises Japonaises: une Etude Econométrique sur Données de Panel*, PhD Thesis, Paris.

Schreyer, P. (2000), *The Contribution of Information and Communication Technology to Output Growth: a Study of the G7 Countries*, OECD, Directorate for Science, Technology and Industry, DSTI/DOC (2000) 2, 23 March.

Schreyer, P. and Pilat, D. (2001), Mesurer la productivité, *Revue Economique de l'OCDE*, **33**, 137–84.

Schwartz, Y. (1992), *Analyse des activités de travail et pertinence des ratios économiques*, in Centre, APST (rapport de recherche), pp. 67–107.

Scicluna, E., Foot, R. M. and Bird, R. (1980), *Productivity measurement in the public sector: the case of the police services*, 36th conference of IIFP, Jerusalem.

Secrétariat d'État au Tourisme (2000), *Tourisme et technologies de l'information et de la communication*, Paris: La documentation française.

Secrétariat d'État au Tourisme (2001), *Le tourisme des années 2010*, Paris: La documentation française.

Sénat (2004), *Projet de loi de finances pour 2005: fonction publique et réforme de l'Etat*, Rapport général No 74 (2004–2005), déposé le 25 novembre 2004 (http://www.senat.fr/rap/l04-074-321/l04-074-321.html).

Sharle, P. (2002), Public–Private Partnership (PPP) as a social game, *Innovation*, **15** (3), 227–52.

Shostack, G. L. (1981), How to design a service, in Donelly, J. H. and George, W. R. (eds), *Marketing of Services*, Chicago, IL: American Marketing Association.

Shostack, G. L. (1984), Service design in the operating environment, in George, W. and Marshall, C. (eds), *Developing New Services*, Chicago, IL: American Marketing Association, Proceedings Series, pp. 27–43.

Shu, W. and Strassmann, P. A. (2005), Does information technology provide banks with profit? *Information and Management*, **42**, 781–7.

Smith, A. (1960) (1st edition, 1776), *The Wealth of Nations*, New York: The Modern Library.

Smith, P., Mannion, R. and Goddard, M. (2003), Performance management in health care: information, incentives and culture, *Public Services Productivity Seminar Papers*, London: HM Treasury.

Soete, L. and Miozzo, M. (1990), *Trade and Development in Services: a Technological Perspective*, mimeo, MERIT.

Solow, R. (1956), A contribution to the theory of economic growth, *Quarterly Journal of Economics*, **70**, 65–94.

Solow, R. (1957), Technical change and the aggregate production function, *Review of Economics and Statistics*, **39**, 312–20.

Srinivasan, S. (1996), *Estimation of own R&D, R&D spillovers and exogenous technical change effects in some US high-technology industries*, University of Southampton, Discussion paper in Economics No 9607, February.

Stankiewicz, F. (2002), Productivité ou 'valorité' du salarié? Contribution au débat sur le travail, *Travail et Emploi*, **91** (July), 19–29.

Stevens, P. A. (2005a), A stochastic frontier analysis of English and Welsh universities, *Education Economics*, **13** (4), 355–74.

Stevens, P. (2005b), Assessing the performance of local services, *National Institute Economic Review*, **193**, 90–101.

Sundbo, J. (1994), Modulization of service production and a thesis of convergence between service and manufacturing organizations, *Scandinavian Journal of Management*, **10** (3), 245–66.

Sundbo, J. (2002), The service economy: standardisation or customisation?, *Service Industries Journal*, **22** (4), 93–116.

Thurow, L. (1989), *Towards a High-Wage, High-Productivity Service Sector*, Washington DC: Economic Policy Institute.

Tirole, J. (1986), Hierarchies and bureaucracies: on the role of collusion in organizations, *Journal of Law, Economics and Organization*, **2**, 181–214.

Toivonen, M. (2004), *Expertise as business: Long-term development and future prospects of knowledge-intensive business services*, Doctoral dissertation, Helsinki University of Technology.

Treasury Board of Canada Secretariat (2005), Lead an integrated approach to internal service transformation (http://www.tbs-sct.gc.ca/cio-dpi/intern_eng.asp).

Tulkens, H. (1986), La performance productive d'un service public: définitions, méthodes de mesure et application à la régie des Postes en Belgique, *L'Actualité Economique, Revue d'Analyse Economique*, **62** (2), 306–35.

UNPAN (2004), *UN global e-government readiness report 2004: towards access for opportunity*, United Nations Online Network in Public Administration and Finance (UNPAN), New York.

Valeyre, A. (2002), *Les formes d'intensification du travail industriel et leurs déterminants*, Conference 'organisation, intensité du travail, qualité du travail', 21, 22 November, Paris.

Verspagen, B. (1995), R&D and productivity: a broad cross-section cross-country look, *Journal of Productivity Analysis*, **6**, 117–35.

Vivarelli, M. (1995), *The Economics of Technology and Employment: Theory and Empirical Evidence*, Aldershot: Edward Elgar.

Von Hippel, E. (1976), The dominant role of users in the scientific instruments innovation process, *Research Policy*, July (5), 212–39.

Von Hippel, E. (1988), *The Sources of Innovation*, New York: Oxford University Press.

Williams, J. and Gardener, E. (2003), The efficiency of European regional banking, *Regional Studies*, **37** (4), 321–30.

Wölfl, A. (2005), La productivité des services est-elle sous-estimée?, *Problèmes Economiques*, **2870**, 32–7.

Worthington, A. and Lee, B. (2004), *Efficiency, technology and productivity change in Australian Universities, 1998–2003*, Working Paper 05/01, University of Wollongong.

Worthington, C. A. (1999), Malmquist indices of productivity change in Australian financial services, *Journal of International Financial markets, Institutions and Money*, **9**, 303–20.

Yaisawarng, S. (2002), Performance measurement and resource allocation, in Fox, K. (ed.), *Efficiency in the Public Sector*, Dordrecht: Kluwer Academic Publishers, pp. 61–81.

Young-Yong, L., Yong-Tae, P. and Hyung-Sik, O. (2000), The impact of competition on the efficiency of public enterprise: the case of Korea Telecom, *Asia Pacific Journal of Management*, **17**, 423–42.

Yu, K. (2003), *Measurement of Government Output: a Review*, Working Document, Ontario.

Index